INDIVIDUALLY MANA
accounts

Fō
pu
Aı
to
seı
aı

fo
ca
ra
fiı
aı

w

Individually Managed accounts

An Investor's Guide

ROBERT B. JORGENSEN, CIMA

John Wiley & Sons, Inc.

Published by John Wiley & Sons, Inc., Hoboken, New Jersey
Published simultaneously in Canada

For general information on our other products and services, or technical support, please contact our Customer Care Department within the United States at 800-762-2974, outside the United States at 317-572-3993 or fax 317-572-4002.

Wiley also publishes its books in a variety of electronic formats. Some content that appears in print may not be available in electronic books.

Library of Congress Cataloging-in-Publication Data:

Jorgensen, Robert B.
    Individually managed accounts : an investor's guide / Robert B.
    Jorgensen.
        p. cm.
    Includes index.
    ISBN 0-471-23863-5 (cloth : alk. paper)
    1. Portfolio management. 2. Investment analysis. 3. Investments. I. Title.
    HG4529.5 .J67 2003
    332.6--dc21

                                                            2002013610

Printed in the United States of America

10 9 8 7 6 5 4 3 2 1

Contents

Preface   xi

Introduction   1

PART ONE
Mutual Funds vs. Individually Managed Accounts: The Great Debate

CHAPTER 1
Know Your Investments   7

Individually Managed Accounts   13
The Goal of this Book   17
In the Next Chapter   18

CHAPTER 2
The Struggle for Tax Efficiency   19

Disadvantages of Mutual Funds   20
An SEC Mandate   23
Two Distinct Taxes   24
Variable Annuities Aren't the Answer   27
The IMA Approach   28
What A Professional Money Manager Can Do for You   30
In the Next Chapter   31

CHAPTER 3
The Impact of Expenses   33

All Kinds of Fees   34
The Supermarket Question   38

The "Chutzpah" Fee   39
"Soft-Dollar" Fees   39
The Real Impact of Fees   40
The Real Issue on Fees   41
In the Next Chapter   42

CHAPTER 4
The Feeling Isn't Mutual   **43**

What's Happening with *Your* Money?   44
Index Mutual Funds: the Real Story   51
Closed-End Funds and Exchange Traded Funds   55
Conclusion   57
In the Next Chapter   58

PART TWO

The Key Ingredients to Building a Professionally Managed Portfolio

CHAPTER 5
The Business of Investment Management   **61**

Stock Investment Styles   62
Fixed-Income Investment Styles   67
How Professional Money Managers
    Earn Their Money   70
In the Next Chapter   73

CHAPTER 6
The Reality of Managing Risk   **75**

Types of Investment Risk   77
Connecting with Investors   79
Operational Risk   81
Measuring Investment Risk   83
Time Out for Some Math Review   85
Derivatives   88
In the Next Chapter   90
Notes   90

CHAPTER 7
The Challenge of Asset Allocation

91

Different Strokes 93
The Asset Allocation Dialogue Among
　Professional Money Managers 95
In the Next Chapter 100
Notes 100

CHAPTER 8
The Folly of Self-Investing

101

Essential Qualities to Look for in an Investment Professional 102
What You Think You Know *Can* Hurt You 106
Three Investment Traps 106
Conclusion 114
In the Next Chapter 116

CHAPTER 9
Managing Your Investment Managers: The Process of Investment Management Consulting

117

First Things First: The Investment Policy Statement 118
The Next Step: Developing an Investment Philosophy 123
Why Work with an Investment Advisor? 125
How Do You Find a Competent Investment Advisor? 127
Referrals as Your Ultimate Solution to Finding
　a Financial Advisor 130
In the Next Chapter 132

PART THREE
The Secrets of Success: Money Managers and Clients Revealed— Interviews with Some of America's Best Money Management Firms

CHAPTER 10
Real Life Stories from the Field

135

The Reluctant Business Owner 135
The Divorcee 137

Mutual Fund Man   139
The Doctor Who Knew Too Much   141
The Margin Trader   144
Newsletter Man   147
In the Next Chapter   149

CHAPTER 11
Meeting Top-Tier Money Managers: Tax-Efficient and Growth Managers   151

Tax Efficient Discipline: John Springrose,
    of 1838 Investment Advisors   152
The Big Picture on Growth: Jack Sullivan,
    of Harris Bretall, Sullivan & Smith   160
Growth By the Numbers: Louis Navellier,
    of Navellier and Asso.   169
A Twelve-Point Focus: Jim Huguet, of Great Companies   176
In the Next Chapter   181

CHAPTER 12
Meeting Top-Tier Money Managers: Value and Core Managers   183

Thoroughly Modern Value: James Hesser,
    of Rorer Asset Management   184
Core Strategies: John Waterman, of Rittenhouse Nuveen   190
In the Next Chapter   202

CHAPTER 13
Meeting Top-Tier Money Managers: International and Fixed Income Managers   203

Value with a Global Touch: Robert Gallagher,
    of Brandes Investment Partners   203
The World of Bonds: Steve Wlodarski,
    of McDonnell Investment Management   209
In the Last Chapter   219

CHAPTER 14
IMAs Today and Tomorrow   221

Four Industry Perspectives   222
An Industry Poised For Growth   224
Advice And Guidance   224

Finding Success is in the Math 225
Managed Accounts for $50,000 227
Multidiscipline Accounts: the IMA of the Future? 228
Financial Technology for the Managed Account Industry 229
Conclusion 230

APPENDIX A
Investment Professional Certified Designations **233**

APPENDIX B
Industry Associations **237**

Regulating Agencies 238
Investment Licenses 239
IMA Platform Providers 240
Investor Resources 243

APPENDIX C
Sample Investment Policy Statement **245**

For: Individual or Family Trust 245
The Portfolio 246
Investment Objective 246
Time Horizon 247
Risk Tolerances and Performance Expectations 247
Asset Allocation 247
Rebalancing Procedures 249
Duties and Responsibilities 249
Adoption of the Investment Policy Statement 250

Investment Glossary **251**

Index **269**

Preface

This book was written to further educate investors and their financial advisors about the customized investment services generally known as Individually Managed Accounts. Throughout this book, I refer to this investment as Individually Managed Accounts, or IMAs, although they are also known within the financial services industry as Separately Managed Accounts. The acronym IMA best conveys the features that distinguish this form of asset management from other forms of investing.

Recent investment industry statistics confirm the increasing interest in IMAs by high-net-worth individuals and their advisors. According to the Boston-based research firm Cerulli Associates, IMA programs have expanded at a thirty percent annual rate since 1994. When this book went to press, total assets invested in IMAs were approximately $450 billion. Financial industry professionals expect total IMA assets to exceed $2.5 trillion by 2010. This represents tremendous double-digit growth for the balance of the decade.

This book is composed of three parts. Part I highlights those issues relevant to the challenge of achieving a real return from all types of investments including IMAs, net of fees, and taxes. Chapter 4 comprises an extensive study of IMAs versus mutual funds. The focus is primarily on embedded capital gains features of mutual funds that prevent individual investors from having any control over the money they invest in mutual funds. I believe mutual funds are excellent investment vehicles for the average investor. But after the careful perusal of this chapter, I think any reader with over $100,000 of investable assets will conclude that IMAs may be a better alternative.

Part II introduces fundamental issues related to investment management and investor behavior, drawing directly from my own experience of over twenty years, and on the empirical research conducted by academics and investment professionals over the past thirty-five years.

Part III was the most fun for me to write. It is intended to impart the real-life advantages of implementing IMAs as the key tactic of wealth management strategies.

I take full responsibility for the content, focus, and theme of this book. Some opinions expressed may be open to debate, although the recommendations are submitted in the spirit of a reasoned, prudent, and conscientious approach to advising investors.

I am very grateful to those who took a sustained interest in this book. I could not have written the book without the guidance, counsel, encouragement, and critique of the following people: James Malcolm for his assistance with the interviews, Stuart Rockett and Ralph Rieves for editing, and Tim Fitzpatrick for graphic assistance. Thanks go to my wife, Tara, for her patience with my chosen profession. I also thank my children, Lynn, Blaise, and Pierece for their love, and my Mom for her laugh.

introduction

Money is better than poverty, if only for financial reasons.
—Woody Allen

If you're reading this book, chances are you're one of more than 90 million people in this country who invests one way or another in the stock and bond market. And, thanks to the explosive growth of 401(k) plans, individual retirement accounts, and on-line investing and financial advice over the past decade, there's also a pretty strong chance your exposure to financial markets has increased over the past ten years.

Like many individual investors or business owners, you probably have a tidy sum tied up in stocks, bonds, annuities, and mutual funds. These easy-to-buy, consumer-friendly investment packages, along with the phenomenon of on-line trading, have contributed to the tremendous growth we have seen in financial services over the past twenty-five years. However, if you take a close look at your net returns after taxes, after commissions, and fees for some of these investments, you may be somewhat disillusioned to discover that your net returns are substantially lower than you expected.

After all is said and done, successful investing isn't about how much money you make. It's about how much you keep.

This book is about a method of investing that more than likely is somewhat new to you. It is for most investors. It's estimated that approximately only about 800,000 of the over 90 mil-

1

lion investors I mentioned earlier currently own Individually Managed Accounts (IMAs). This is about to change. According to Forrester Research (global research consulting firm based outside of Boston), the number of IMA investors is expected to explode to more than 5 million by the year 2010. As Jamie Punishill of Forrester comments in his ground-breaking report, *The End of Mutual Fund Dominance,* "Individually managed accounts are hot! Unlike mutual funds, which are prepackaged, opaque and standardized, IMAs let investors customize their money management."

In this book, I discuss not only how IMAs work and how you can hire your own professional money managers, I take you behind the scenes at some of the top money management firms in the world and reveal what it takes for these firms to successfully manage a forty- to sixty-stock portfolio day-in, day-out, year-in, year-out, bull market, bear market, or choppy market. We will explore hidden charges, hidden commissions, lower-than-predicted performance, and unexpected tax liabilities found in popular investments such as funds and annuities that you may have encountered while trying to reap the much-heralded windfall of stock and bond market investing. And I'll show you how to get past these hurdles.

If, like many investors whose portfolios have matured, and you are now willing to invest anywhere between $50,000 and $10 million, you're ready for the most effective, personalized form of investing available today: IMAs. Rather than pooling your money with other investors in a fund over which you have virtually no control, you may learn that you're better off hiring a professional money manager to work just for you, tailoring your finances to your specific goals and helping you increase your net returns through maximum net after-tax efficiency.

With this book, you'll gain first-hand insight from some of the most respected authorities in the professional money management industry. These are money managers who have achieved truly remarkable results for their institutional and high-net-worth clients over long market cycles. They will share with you how their successful strategies can be applied toward attaining your overall personal investment objectives. These are professional money managers, with specific financial portfolio management experience, not simply accredited sales people. Herein, we will examine and discuss the merits of an innovative alternative for the vast numbers of investors who, up to now, have invested their assets in traditional packaged investment products, traded equities with the help of a broker, or made decisions on their own via an on-line trading account fueled by ideas inspired by newsletters, magazines, television, or their hair stylists. Herein, I discuss the merits of IMAs, an innovative alternative for vast numbers of investors who, up to now, have invested in conventional stock and bond products. Most investment books and magazines seek to gratify readers by presenting a seemingly clear and simple road map to investment prosperity. Just trying to find the correct investment book, newsletter, magazine, or financial television show today is hard enough. There are more than 5,400 titles listed for *money* and *investing* found on one popular on-line bookstore. In addition, there are over 2,000 investment newsletters and magazines and at least 200 hours of television aired each week devoted exclusively to investing and finance covered on multiple channels. This doesn't even begin to cover the investment advisory industry, with over 500,000 stockbrokers, financial planners, trust officers, and insurance agents eager to advise and offer you more than 9,000 mutual funds and 40,000 individual equity securities that are currently publicly traded!

Generalized, simple financial approaches seldom serve the needs and wants of individuals. This book is not about investment gimmicks, nor does it contain specific investment advice per se. With this discernment, you will see why IMAs have become the number one new investment of choice for business owners and high-net-worth investors over almost all other investment strategies in just a few short years and is projected to expand dramatically over the next ten years. As a professional who has worked with professional money managers for over twenty years, I have attained tremendous first-hand awareness of the benefits IMAs can bestow upon investors. I'm confident this awareness will bring you liberation and profit for many years to come.

Mutual Funds vs. Individually Managed Accounts: The Great Debate

CHAPTER 1

Know Your Investments

The highest use of capital is not to make more money, but to make money do more for the betterment of life.
—Henry Ford

Do you ever get the feeling that just about everyone you meet these days has a sure-fire way to help you get rich in the stock market? You can't listen to the radio in your car for more than fifteen minutes without hearing a stock market report, or you can flip your dial and listen to dozens of syndicated investment programs broadcast from all parts of the country pitching all kinds of investment products and get-rich-quick strategies. A little more than a decade ago, there wasn't a single TV channel covering market news exclusively. Today, there are three nationally (CNBC, CNN, and Bloomberg) and many more regionally that run 24 hours a day. There has been an explosion of financial Internet sites as well, which comprises the number one e-commerce industry in America today with literally hundreds of thousands of information and product websites devoted exclusively to the investment industry. There are literally thousands of newsletters, journals, and magazines devoted to telling you how to get rich. Each seems to offer confident advice and promotes a different strategy.

Should you follow one specific strategy or listen to one financial expert or your neighbor who got a tip from his gardener? What about the licensed investment advisor you have worked with for many years? Can he or she help? The answer is usually yes, but how is that advisor compensated? Does that advisor work for fees, commissions, or a combination of the two? Does that advisor work for a big Wall Street firm or is the advisor independent? What kind of licenses does your advisor hold and what about experience? Should your advisor make buy-and-sell decisions for you, with you, or should he or she help you find a fund, an annuity or a money manager? Maybe the advisor wants to help you with your finances, but they failed to help you generate the type of returns or service you expected to receive for the annual fees and commissions you have been paying. Maybe you really like the advisor but wonder if they have been trained to manage your portfolio of stocks, bonds, and mutual funds to maximize your tax efficiency and build your wealth. What most investors don't know is that the NASD (National Association of Securities Dealers, the regulating body for the brokerage industry) Series 6 and 7 licenses that most brokers hold (myself included) is a license to *sell* stocks, bonds, and other investment products such as funds or unit trusts. This license does not indicate that the broker is trained to manage portfolios of stocks, bonds, or other securities.

So how do you decide where your core information should come from? Which newsletter should you read, which radio show should you listen to, which hour of CNBC should you watch every day, or what evening will the Nightly Business Report give you the investment edge you are looking for? Is there a simple published list of the best brokers or investment advisors and their track records of advice you can review or buy? Which of the 9,000 mutual funds currently available should you buy now? Can a subscription to Morningstar or *Smart Money* answer your questions? The answer, of course, is that there is no simple answer. If you are reading this book, you probably have used one or a combination of the aforementioned strategies to try to attain financial independence, and if you are like the average investor, unfortunately you have attained only average or, more likely, below average success, particularly during down market years.

Dalbar Inc. conducted a study on the investment success of all stock mutual fund investors from 1984 to 2000. The Standard & Poor's (S&P) 500 stock index during those 16 years had an annualized return of 16.29 percent per year. However, the average investor in these stock funds earned only 5.32 percent per year during the same time period.

How can this be? Did most of the funds perform that poorly? No. In fact, equity mutual funds performed very well during this period. The reason the average investor experienced such poor results compared with the index or the funds they were invested in is because he or she lacked the discipline to stay invested and stick with an investment plan. In other words, since the average holding period for the average mutual fund is down to only 2.8 years, it is clear investors are moving in and out of funds and equities too frequently and it is hurting their results (see Figure 1.1).

In my 20 years of investment experience in working with pension funds, 401(k)s, municipalities, and high–net worth investors, I have learned that having an investment plan (or Investment Policy Statement, see Appendix C) is extremely valuable as a road map for successful investing, but it is not enough. Investors need discipline to stick with the plan they have developed, hire good competent professional money managers to make the day-to-day investment decisions, and secure competent objective fee-based advisors to help implement the plan and keep the investor focused on long-term results.

One of my goals in these pages is to expose the misleading

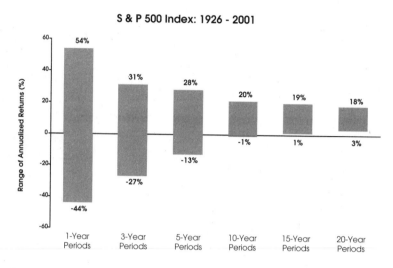

Source: Harris Bretall Sullivan and Smith, L.L.C.

Figure 1.1   Historical perspectives: investment performance range.

notion that investment knowledge is common knowledge and that investing in a portfolio that consists of thirty-plus individual equities or bonds is a part-time job and anyone can do it. Some of the smartest people, including CPAs, doctors, lawyers, professors, and engineers make basic mistakes when it comes to planning their financial futures, either because they don't have the time, the expertise, or the disciplined objectivity they need to manage their assets on their own. So what should you do? Should you talk to a friend, buy a magazine at the airport, or make some life-changing financial decisions based on what one single Wall Street analyst said at 4:00 P.M. when they happened to be home early from work one day. Don't assume your mutual funds or variable annuities or stocks you have owned for five years will continue to give you your fair share of market returns. Owning large positions in a Worldcom or Enron has shown the world that you need to diversify. You see, an investment plan is like a flight plan. It works great when there is no bad weather or you know exactly which path to take when you are flying through the same mountain range every time. But the one thing we know for certain is that financial markets are unpredictable, just like the weather. So like the pilot who needs to alter his course through the mountain pass when there is bad weather, we need to monitor our investments and make adjustments whern markets become volatile.

This book won't make you a financial expert, although it will help you focus on the real net return (after taxes and fees) of your investments and encourage you to take a new look at an old strategy for creating wealth: individualized account management guided by professionals.

Purchasing investment products for your family, retirement, or business is one of the most important decisions you'll ever make. This is simply because what you ultimately invest, how much, and when and how often you change your strategy will be critical to your quality of life—not only today, but for the rest of your life. Your investment decisions may affect the home you buy, your children's college education, your mother's health care, or whether you retire at age fifty-eight or sixty-eight.

Unlike many other things you buy, there is very little useful information for comparing the strengths and weaknesses of a given investment option. There is no simple subscription to the consumer's digest of the overall best investment or investment plan. Each investment product or service has different return characteristics and different risk characteristics, and when combined with other investments, may enhance or inhibit your probability of achieving your goals.

Consumer-friendly investment products, such as mutual funds and variable annuities, have experienced unprecedented growth recently. More than $7 trillion is invested in mutual funds alone. They have really become the "investment of choice" for investors seeking a simple solution for diversification and professional money management, and to that end they do an excellent job. It is interesting to consider, however, how most mutual funds are sold or what makes a fund popular. It invariably comes down to "recent and past performance," or a star rating with very little thought given to important information such as whether the original fund managers still oversee the operation of the fund; (is the portfolio trading at a premium or a discount compared to the market in general?), what are the annual expenses, and what is the best type of fund to buy based on market conditions.

Past performance drives lots of investment decisions not only with funds, annuities, or stocks, but sometimes with money managers also (Table 1.1). However, with Individually Managed Accounts (IMAs), you will know directly from the money manager or your advisor all the pertinent information about the portfolio in terms of who is managing the portfolio, what the current price-to-earnings ratio of the stocks, what sectors are invested in, and so forth. The main point I want to emphasize draws on a quote from Stephen Covey: "Begin with the end in mind." In other words, determine what you will need in the future to manage your children's college education, purchase your home, save for vacations, or plan for your retirement. I recommend you work with an investment advisor to develop an investment plan. Take time to build the correct investment strategy for your family and future. Unfortunately, the average individual investor spends

Table 1.1   Seventy years of bull and bear markets.

Decade	Average annual total return S&P 500 (%)	U.S. T-bills (%)	Inflation (%)
1930s	−0.06	0.55	−2.05
1940s	9.17	0.41	5.41
1950s	19.35	1.87	2.20
1960s	7.81	3.88	2.52
1970s	5.86	6.31	7.37
1980s	17.55	8.89	5.09
1990s	18.2	4.93	2.93
2000s	?	?	?

more time shopping for new cars in their lifetime than planning for their financial future, and this often shows when reviewing long-term results. Another important fact about performance of your overall investments is that it doesn't matter what your investments earn. What matters is your *return after taxes, after fees, after commissions, and after missed opportunities.* Unintended tax liabilities, high transaction costs, and lost time are the disadvantages associated with the most common methods of investing, such as buying pooled mutual funds or buying annuities or individual equities or bonds either on-line or through a broker.

Having started this book raising questions about what may not be working for the average investor, I'll now start to focus on IMAs. If you have purchased this book, you either have an IMA or you are ready to hire a professional money manager to oversee a portfolio designed specifically to help you meet your overall financial objectives. This method of investing offers you the most efficient, effective, and customizable investment available in the marketplace today. The IMA is the most likely means for you to achieve *absolute* return on your investments, given your overall investment objectives and personal level of risk tolerance.

INDIVIDUALLY MANAGED ACCOUNTS

An IMA is a portfolio of stocks and bonds that an investment professional manages for you in return for an annual fee, based on the market value of the portfolio. There are many advantages to this method, the most significant being that you get professional investment management designed specifically for your financial needs and goals. Unlike mutual funds, which are pools of assets over which you actually own shares in a mutual company, an IMA lets you directly own the stocks and bonds in your portfolio.

Institutional pension plans and wealthy families have used

professional money managers for decades, and until recently, the idea of having your own professional private money manager seemed out of reach for the average investor. In the 1920s and 1930s wealthy families like the Carnegies, the Mellons, and the Roosevelts employed professional money managers to manage their family's portfolios of stocks, bonds and real estate. Later, in the 1950s and 1960s, large state and corporate pension plans. The reason that these high end professional money management firms were unavailable to the average investor until recently is because of the high minimums. The minimum account sizes that the top money managment firms were willing to accept until recently was often as high as $10 to $20 million per account! Recent advances in technology and lowered minimum investment requirements and have now brought IMAs within the reach of millions of new investors. IMAs offer you the opportunity to increase your net returns with effective tax management strategies developed by professional money managers working to meet your specific personal goals.

Major Benefits of IMAs

Many people believe that because they work with a stockbroker, financial planner, or bank trust officer, that they already have a professional money manager dedicated to working for their best interests. That's not necessarily so. Investment consultants or financial advisors help investors choose among the literally thousands of investment options to design and implement a long-term plan for attaining overall financial objectives. As a general rule they do not have the infrastructure, research, or discipline to manage a stock and bond portfolio with 50 positions in this volatile environment.

I want to distinguish clearly between these financial professionals and professional money managers who possess the extensive experience and specialized education necessary to oversee investment programs designed to garner maximum return while minimizing tax liability. Professional money managers base their strategies and decisions on the expertise of the highest caliber research analysts, portfolio managers, and traders to maximize overall net return while attempting to reduce your risk and the taxes you pay. As you'll learn, the individuals involved with managing these investments are professionals. But do they meet your needs? Will they help you retire on time with the lifestyle you desire? Will they help you determine how much money to place with each firm. The answer is no. This is what your financial advisor is for.

The best (enduring) deals in any business activity are those that align the interests of all parties, in this case you, your advisor, and your money manager(s), to assure the probability of a positive outcome. Commissions on stock transactions, limited menus of investment options, and restrictive disclosure practices aren't generally conducive to the mutual satisfaction of everybody, although each of these conditions is characteristic of most standard forms of financial services.

With respect to commissions, manager compensation is generally not determined by the amount of money your investments have earned or lost. With respect to a bank trust department, who wants to experience the frustration of being told that "policy" doesn't permit investing in a particular security, regardless of your informed opinion? And with respect to mutual funds, why would you grant someone the absolute right to buy and sell securities if it causes you to pay more in taxes than you might need to?

And, why would anyone take action with your money without considering your tax-avoidance strategies? If not carefully managed for maximum efficiency, taxes could erode as much as forty percent of your investment gains.

IMAs offer an arrangement that benefits your advisor only when your investments increase in value. Here is a system that motivates your advisor to maximize the returns on your portfolio. And since it's your money, shouldn't you have the opportunity to discuss the stocks you want to own? With an IMA, you entrust your money to a professional money manager who will work with you and your financial advisor to build and manage your portfolio based on your objectives, goals, and expectations.

You Are in Control

Even though you entrust discretionary control of your portfolio, your professional money manager is attuned to your concerns, questions, and suggestions for attaining your financial goals. Your investment in an IMA is not pooled with other people's money in the way it would be in mutual funds. You can request that your money manager not invest in specific securities, for example, tobacco companies, or you can curtail investing in a sector such as computer stocks if you already have large holdings of computer and technology companies. You can keep daily track of your purchases on-line and review your performance on a time-weighted basis against relative benchmarks, such as the S&P 500, and can receive monthly statements about your specific account's activity and the market value of the securities.

You Monitor the Activity in Your Account

In addition to the information provided in your monthly statements, you have unlimited access to view all the individual positions in your portfolio at any time. If you own a mutual fund, you don't have the opportunity for frequent and detailed monitoring because specific positions in popular mutual funds are sometimes not disclosed until the end of a quarter. You can't follow daily purchases and sales within the funds if that information isn't released until the end of a quarter.

You Can Implement Tax-Efficient Investing

Your investment manager understands the erosive nature of taxes and is aware of the methods for maximizing tax efficiency in managing portfolios. A sharp professional money manager considers the tax implications of every investment decision and attempts to keep capital gains to a minimum with appropriate and effective buy-and-sell decisions.

You Could Lower Your Expenses

The services of a professional money manager range from as low as 0.50 percent to 2.25 percent annually, all-inclusive. This fee typically covers your professional money manager, the custodian, your investment advisor, and all trading costs. The range of fees is proportional to how much you invest in either one or a series of IMAs. While this cost appears on the surface as being higher than what some actively managed mutual funds charge, it isn't. If you invest the time to decipher fees and expense disclosures found in mutual fund prospectuses, you will discover a vast array of operating expenses, distribution fees, sales charges, and deferred sales charges. Some of these expenses are expressed as a percentage, and some are expressed in dollars. Mutual fund trading expenses are typically not reported, even though they are drawn from your principal. Chapter 3 is devoted to an extensive examination of investment costs.

THE GOAL OF THIS BOOK

My goal is to provide you with an authoritative reference covering all the things you need to consider when investing your money: options and alternatives, costs, risks, and the myths and the realities. I, along with the professional money managers I have worked with over the years, want you to have the benefit of our collective educations and experience in explaining the professional money management industry in as simple and straightforward a manner as possible. I want you to know how to select, retain, and work with an investment manager, and I believe the IMA is the most effective means available in the marketplace for investing your money today.

Why shouldn't your personal investment strategies for your family or your company's retirement plan be tailored specifically to your long-term investment goals? You can have the built-in flexibility to exclude specific securities from your portfolio if you don't like the way a certain company conducts its business. And, you can limit your exposure if you already have large holdings of a particular industry. Why wouldn't you want the ability to occasionally check your investments on-line and thereby better understand your portfolio's performance relative to the market? And who wouldn't make the most of what they earn by using a professional money manager to help manage assets in the most tax-efficient manner?

Remember, no investment manager, whether for a mutual fund, a variable annuity, or an IMA , is infallible, regardless of their past performance or experience. It's impossible to pick a manager who won't, on occasion, make some mistakes while working to enhance your wealth. With that in mind, don't waste your time searching for infallibility. Instead, focus on identifying the best manager(s) for helping you attain your overall long-term goals.

IN THE NEXT CHAPTER

Taxes are the most important factor in determining what you actually keep in investment returns. Chapter 2 describes and explains what you need to know about tax planning and "tax efficiencies." Several pages are devoted to discussing the disadvantages of mutual fund investments with regard to your personal tax-planning strategies.

The Struggle for Tax Efficiency

The hardest thing in the world to understand is the income tax.
—Albert Einstein (1879–1955)

Absolute return on your investments is your gain *after all fees and taxes.* Those who have most of their investments in tax-deferred accounts, such as 401(k) plans, individual retirement accounts, and annuities might think that a discussion on tax efficiency is irrelevant to their circumstances. They are partly right, but only partly. This discussion might be irrelevant to their present circumstances. But what I have to say here will be relevant as soon as they are required to take title to that tax-advantaged money, and reinvest in taxable vehicles. This begins at age 59¹/₂ for retirement plans and becomes mandatory at age 70¹/₂.

Today's accepted investment strategies and tactics evolved from those used in managing large pools of defined-benefit pension plans during the 1970s and 1980s. Those funds were not subject to taxes, and investment managers who learned their trade during that era were not conditioned to think in terms of after-tax returns. In turn, most present-day managers in many large investment companies learned the business from those managers who came to the investment world thirty years ago. Their focus hasn't been on after-tax returns either.

Over the past ten years, there has been an enormous increase of individuals and families possessing large pools of assets that are subject to taxes on the returns and income generated from those pools. Perhaps you find yourself in this situation. These people have been, and are increasingly frustrated by the advice of financial advisors who seem unaware of or unconcerned about the tax consequences of investing in a mutual fund or a variable annuity.

Professional money managers who oversee IMAs know that tax-efficient strategies are of paramount importance when it comes to helping you make the most or your money and keep what you make.

DISADVANTAGES OF MUTUAL FUNDS

Investing in mutual funds is like swimming in a community pool. You have no individual rights of ownership. You have no say about the pool's hours of availability, the temperature of the water, the cost of admission, the level of chlorination, or whether the pool is being used for a swim party when you want to get in your fifty laps. In other words, you're in the water, but you have no say or control over the conditions in which you are immersed. You have as much, and as little, claim on the pool's conditions as any of the other people in the pool. Your preferences are not distinguishable from those of anyone else. You own communal shares in the pool, and that type of ownership has defined limits on what you can control.

When you buy shares in a mutual fund, you own shares of the mutual company, not the individual securities that make up the fund portfolio. The mutual fund buys equities, bonds, or cash instruments that comprise a fund pool and report back to shareholders of the mutual fund on what is owned, performance, fees, and so forth. You do not have any control over when the fund buys or sells securities, nor have you any control over trading activity. The community environment greatly diminishes your control in managing your tax exposure (see Figure 2.1).

Although mutual funds have enjoyed great popularity among some investors, they enjoy even greater popularity among federal and state taxing agencies. Verifiable data from research about mutual fund tax bites were the primary reasons for the Securities and Exchange Commission (SEC) requirement that all stock and bond funds report their after-tax returns for one-, five-, and ten-year periods.

What does the research reveal? Morningstar, Inc. has found that over the five-year period ending July 31, 2000, investors in U.S. stock funds have paid about seventeen percent of their annual returns in taxes from fund distributions alone. (See Figure

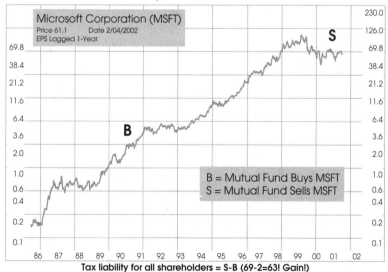

Source: Robert Jorgensen. Microsoft Corp. is used to illustrate embedded capital gains and should not be viewed as a recommendation.

Figure 2.1 How investing in the mutual fund "community pool" affects investors.

2.2.) Two other research projects conducted in 2000 provide further proof that mutual funds can't effectively deliver tax-advantaged investing. Eaton Vance commissioned KPMG to study the pretax and after-tax performance of more than 500 U.S. stock funds for the ten years ending December 31, 1998. Using mean individual tax rates over that period for a basis, the median fund's after-tax return was 13.2 percent. The pretax return was 15.7 percent. In other words, an after-tax return was only eighty-four percent of the pretax return.

A further study released in 2000 by the investment management firm First Quadrant looked at actively managed stock funds over a twenty-year period ending December 31, 1998. Had you put $1,000 into the average actively managed fund and cashed out at the end of twenty years, you would have earned $19,600 before taxes. After adjustments for capital gains and dividend taxes, this amount was reduced to $11,300. When the researchers looked at the return on the same amount over the same period in a Vanguard Index fund, the pretax amount was $24,000 and the after-tax return was $16,200.

5-Year Average Tax Efficiency

Mutual Fund	Pre-tax Return	After-tax Return	Tax Efficiency
AIM Weingarten	30.7%	26.6%	86.6%
Putnam G&I	13.4%	10.6%	78.3%
Vanguard Windsor	13.1%	9.2%	70.5%
Fidelity G&I	21.8%	19.7%	90.7%
Am. Century Ultra	28.8%	25.9%	90.1%
Janus	31.3%	27.9%	89.0%
Average Fund			84%

Source: Morningstar, thru December 1999

Figure 2.2   Tax efficiency of some funds.

Regardless of how well the respective investments were managed, taxes reduced the return of both funds significantly.

In April 2001, *The Wall Street Journal* reviewed the performances of Fidelity's Magellan Fund and Vanguard's Growth and Income Fund. For the five- and ten-year periods ending December 31, 2000, the annualized after-tax returns from both funds were about twenty-two percent less than the annualized pretax returns

AN SEC MANDATE

And so it goes. The SEC finally mandated that mutual fund companies must list in their prospectuses their after-tax returns for one-, five- and ten-year periods so that investors would have some idea of the tax consequences. These after-tax returns are now required by law:

- *Tax-adjusted returns on fund distributions.* This computation is for investors who intend to hold on to their shares. This calculation of tax liability illustrates tax efficiency, because it is based on capital gains and dividend distributions for the fund's accounting year.
- *Tax-adjusted returns on distributions and the sale of shares.* This computation represents the after-tax return for those who will get taxed while they hold shares, as well as the taxable gain (or loss) they incur when they sell a share.

In a fund's computations, the SEC wants fund companies to use the highest federal income tax rate in existence at the time the disclosure is published. This mandate is to assure that the funds disclose the worst-case scenario. Note that all the computations include the impact of income and capital gains.

TWO DISTINCT TAXES

Let's look closer at the impact of income and of capital gains taxes on your money. These two distinct taxes on different streams of income are what compound this diminishment of investment returns. The tax on capital gains is most harmful with respect to mutual funds.

The Community Pool and the Capital Gains Nightmare

Remember that when you buy a mutual fund, you're placing your investment into a common pool. Owning shares in a mutual fund, by definition, precludes your ownership being considered as a personal investment. Your money is anonymous, so to speak. It's being handled by an investment manager, or team of managers, who know nothing about your specific tax situation.

The Community Swimming Pool and the High-net-worth Investor

Over the years I have been asked many times what is the best way to describe the difference of investing in IMAs versus mutal funds. The easiest and simplest analogy which I mentioned earlier is that a mutual fund portfolio is like a community swimming pool. If the markets are doing well and the fund is going up, everyone jumps "into the pool." By jumping in, the water level rises and a fund manager must buy stocks at higher levels as the new cash coming in from investors jumping in must be put to work.

Conversely, when the fund starts performing poorly, the investors "leap out of the pool" and the fund manager is forced to sell stocks at levels he or she may not want to. These fluctuating flows of money in and out of the community mutual fund pool are the main reason high-net-worth investors get disappointed with returns from their mutual funds.

You see, if you are a long-term investor you may not want to report each year capital gains and/or losses as a result of the activities of other investors who jump in and out of the market.

Most high-net-worth investors are interested in investing in their own pool. You generally find that they in fact are interested not only in long-term capital gains, but like their own private swimming pool, they want the water a certain temperature. In the case of an IMA, they can restrict the purchase or sale of specific securities or industry groups. The bottom line is that if you have $50,000 to $100,000 to invest, get your own IMA account!

Fund managers are paid to generate returns, not to minimize anyone's taxes. Regardless of when you buy into a mutual fund, you assume the potential capital gains liabilities of the stocks in that portfolio. The fund's basis of the shares held is a mutual basis for all shareholders. You, as a shareholder, most likely have bought into embedded capital gains. Remember that a fund is required to pay taxes on the capital gains it realizes when it sells some of its holdings, and those gains are distributed among you and the other owners of the fund, without regard for how long you have owned shares. In other words, *with a mutual fund, its possible you could be paying taxes on capital gains you didn't incur.*

Long-term and Short-term Capital Gains

Whether the capital gain on a sale by a mutual fund is categorized as a long-term or a short-term gain is determined in the same way as a gain earned by an individual. If the stock was held for a year or less, the gain from the sale is taxed at your ordinary income tax rate. If the stock was held for over a year, the gain from the sale is taxed at the long-term capital gains rate of twenty percent. You can readily infer that some fund managers' trading habits could prove to be very expensive for you. The difference in the tax rates between long-term (eighteen to twenty percent) and short-term capital gains can be as great as twenty percent. Mutual fund distributions subject to just long-term (as high as thirty-nine percent federal) capital gains taxes can themselves be living nightmares.

When a lot of investors buy into a popular fund during a year, the capital gains distribution is spread among a lot of people. If, toward the end of the year, a large number of investors liquidate their shares, the fund might have to sell some stocks, at a gain, in order to raise money to pay off those people who have sold their shares. The proceeds then have the potential to become a big capital gains distribution for remaining shareholders. There are instances in which moderate-income investors who diligently invested a few thousand dollars a year in a fund have been hit with a five-figure taxable distribution. Yet these people never sold a share of the fund.

There is now sufficient evidence to show that there can be hideous tax traps when mutual fund managers face an overall market decline. In 2000, the Standard & Poor's (S&P) 500 index lost 9.2 percent of its value and the Russell 1000 index of large capitalization stocks declined 22.4 percent. The average U.S. diversified stock fund lost over 4.5 percent of its value, yet taxable capital gains distributions to shareholders of U.S. funds amounted to $345 billion! One small company growth fund declined in net asset value (NAV) by 21 percent in 2000, although shareholders who owned the fund had to pay 11 percent in capital gains taxes at year end.

The *Barron's* Reader

In 2000, those investors who bought a growth-style mutual fund in the last half of that year got hit with distribution tax liabilities, even though the NAV of the fund was significantly less than what they had paid. In the April 16, 2001 (Tax Day) issue of *Barron's,* Michael Santoli's "Fund of Information" section ran a letter from a reader detailing his "calamitous experience with money-losing mutual funds that nevertheless served him a towering tax bill." In August 2000, the reader received a short-term capital gains distribution from a fund of $89,221. The reader had invested $200,000 in the fund the previous April. At the time the reader received notice of the distribution, the investment was worth about $160,000. When he bought the fund, he inherited the short-term gain. He accepted this by consoling himself that he could offset the distribution with the realized loss from the sale of his underwater shares in the fund. Sorry! The IRS taxes short-term capital-gains distributions from mutual funds as ordinary income. Moreover, short-term capital gains distributions can't be offset with realized losses.

What is the likelihood that the managers of the fund would have altered their strategy if they could have foreseen this investor's dilemma? None whatsoever. Mutual fund managers are paid to generate returns, not maximize tax efficiency.

VARIABLE ANNUITIES AREN'T THE ANSWER

The crowning feature that sellers of variable annuity contracts tout is their tax advantages. The bottom line advantage is that taxes on earnings and capital gains are deferred. When you cash in your annuity, typically after age 59$\frac{1}{2}$, you will pay ordinary income tax rates on your income *and* your capital gains. The purported tax advantage is that you will be in a lower tax bracket at that age so long as the law remains unchanged. Who wants to aspire to that circumstance? If you withdraw your money before you reach 59$\frac{1}{2}$, you pay the taxes plus a ten percent early withdrawal penalty and you may also be subject to a state tax on your proceeds.

THE IMA APPROACH

IMAs don't pool assets. This means you aren't liable for taxes on gains accumulated before you put money in. You aren't at the mercy of fellow investors who may pull out at any time and leave you with a nightmare tax liability. You have a say over how and when a manager makes a decision that could impact your tax-avoidance plans. And tax-efficiency strategies can be enhanced with a multiple-manager IMA, because gains from one manager can be offset by losses incurred by another manager.

Unlike mutual funds, IMAs permit you to fund your accounts with the "currency of your choice." In addition to cash, you can use securities you own. These securities will most likely have different values relative to their purchase prices. Some may be traded at a price less than what you paid, while some may be trading at prices higher than your cost basis. You can turn these securities over to a professional money manager or team of managers, with documented proof of the respective costs of each security, stipulating that your account be managed in a manner that employs those securities in a tax-efficient manner.

Tax efficiency is one of the primary service advantages of an IMA. One of the independent money managers featured in Chapter 10, John Springhouse, of 1838 Investment Advisors, typifies the conscientious mind-set of the independent investment manager:

> We have to be vigilant about transaction costs and in many cases the biggest transaction costs are taxes. Every individual's potential tax liability is different. When you manage tax-efficient portfolios, you have to look at each individual portfolio and each individual security right down to the tax lot level. Tax lots are bundles of the same security purchased at the same price, and that purchase price is documented. You could hold a $5 tax lot of a stock presently trading at $30. If another client holds the same security purchased at $27, in the context of tax liabilities,

they're not holding the same security. The situation can be more complicated because of a difference in the holding period. Now we have to consider using different tactics with the same listed security. Mutual funds can't do that.

Taxes As Transaction Costs

As John Springhouse notes, taxes can account for a significant portion of total investment transaction costs (see Figure 2.3).

Measuring Tax Efficiency

The tax-avoidance efficiency of a manager or a strategy using multiple managers is most commonly measured by the amount of taxes paid as a percentage of total return. Zero percent may or may not be the optimum measurement, because there could be

They kill compounding power!

Let's look at an example from 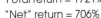 Journal of Investing (Spring '97)

- Time Period : 1971-95
- Assumptions:
  - **Returns = S&P 500 actual**
  - **Expenses =** 1.0%
  - **Turnover =** 80%
  - **Cap Gains =** 28%
  - **Income tax =** 36%
- Total return = 1721%
  "Net" return = 706%

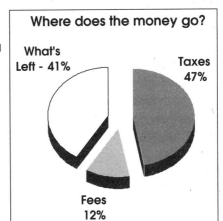

Source: *Journal of Investing (Spring '97)*

Figure 2.3   How turnover and taxes effect compounding.

some carryover losses that could create a refund circumstance. I use a simple measurement referred to as the tax efficiency ratio (TER), which is expressed as a percentage. After-tax returns are divided by pre-tax returns. Professional money managers can work with you and your advisors with the goal of reaching a TER of eighty percent or higher.

One of the most common tax challenges is that of the individual who owns thousands of shares of his employer's stock with several different cost bases. The holdings in this one stock may account for over three fourths of the client's net worth. A great deal of planning is necessary to avoid incurring a huge capital gain in the attempt to diversify the client's investments. This is a challenge that can be met only with an IMA. A team of managers would not aim for an immediate TER of over eighty percent for someone with such a concentrated holding, but having an achievable TER goal of over eighty percent within three years helps the client's managers craft a workable investment strategy.

WHAT A PROFESSIONAL MONEY MANAGER CAN DO FOR YOU

The most common and easiest tax-efficient strategy for any equities investment manager is to employ a very low turnover strategy and not make any trade that would incur a short-term capital gain liability. Of course, there are few investors whose financial circumstances can accommodate such a strategy. As an investor with a significant net worth composed of many asset classes, you have tax and dispersion problems that are unique to you.

Take, for example, the common problem of an investor with a heavy concentration of her employer's stock. She might experience a steep decrease in that stock's value in less than a year from when she acquired it. Say these circumstances required her to sell some shares at a loss; a short-term loss. The decrease in her net worth and her discretionary income might further prompt her to sell some other stocks held for less than a year, at a gain. Were she to turn her stocks over to a professional money manager, he would study her entire portfolio to see if he could "harvest" her short-term loss to offset any incurred short-term gains.

Professional money managers have the flexibility, the experience, and the opportunities to employ tax-efficient strategies for both common and unique financial planning problems.

IN THE NEXT CHAPTER

A keen interest in and understanding of your tax exposure is a major reason for investing with professional money managers. Just as important, you'll know precisely what you are being charged for the investment management service, and you won't have to spend hours reading the fine print accompanying pooled investments. Time is money, and you have better things to do with yours.

CHAPTER 3

The Impact of Expenses

The greatest concentration of wealth in America today is in professionally managed portfolios primarily because of their superior risk control and their tax efficiency.
—James Kuntz (CIMA, Pacific Wealth Management)

Enhanced tax efficiency is one of two major goals in constructing an absolute return (after taxes, after fees) strategy. Some fees should not be reduced—they should be eliminated altogether. These are fees that *diminish your principal and return,* the subtlest of which are "loads" charged by certain classes of mutual funds. The pitch by someone selling a front-end loaded mutual fund goes something like this: "This is a relatively insignificant charge. As your account increases in value, the impact of this load lessens." That's bogus arithmetic.

Actual arithmetic computes to greater impact over time. A four percent front-end load decreases a base principal of $100,000 to $96,000. Assume the fund still earns a respectable return of ten percent. A ten percent return after one year on $100,000 is $10,000. A ten percent return on $96,000 after one year is $9,600. So if you were to buy into this load fund, you would have paid $4,000 at the time you had invested your money.

ALL KINDS OF FEES

When you look closely at how some large mutual fund companies continued to increase some of their adminstration fees and other charges during the bull market of the 1990s, it's apparent that there was no "mutual" sharing between shareholders and the fund companies. Money poured into the funds during the decade and increased assets under management far beyond anyone's expectations. When you consider that the costs of managing large pools of money are mostly fixed, such as staffing, information accounting systems, research, and trading capabilities their infrastructures were already in place. These infrastructures were able to accommodate significant increases in dollar inflows with relatively little expansion. As the money poured in, fixed costs became a smaller and smaller percentage of the revenues. The simple arithmetic is that operating costs should have gone down when a mutual fund had more money under management. This certainly happened during the 1990s when mutual funds increased sevenfold from $1 trillion in assets under management to over $7 trillion. Even though mutual funds have enjoyed significant economies of scale, little has ever been passed on to investors. As these assets under management have risen, one would have expected internal expenses to have declined. But in fact, over the past twenty years the internal fees charged by mutual fund companies have risen by approximately thirty percent.

Mutual fund companies argue that they have invested these economies of scale surpluses into better services, such as check-writing privileges and around-the-clock automated deposit and withdrawal services. Financial professionals and some regulators have countered that these customer service infrastructures enhance the funds' operational efficiencies but they don't necessarily reduce expenses.

The issue of reducing investor costs becomes even more severe when considering load charges like the one described at the beginning of this chapter.

Load Charges

Loads are sales charges levied by mutual fund firms to compensate intermediary financial professionals for distribution and marketing. In addition to the front-end load, there are also back-end and level loads.

> *Front-end load* fees range from three to five percent of principal. As with the example at the beginning of this chapter, these charges may significantly reduce your principal and subsequent returns. You may even be required to pay this load fee when you reinvest dividends for additional shares of the fund.
>
> *Back-end load* fees are charged when you redeem or sell your shares of the fund. They can be a percentage of the money you are taking out, or they can be a fixed sum. Back-end charges could be as high as six percent of the money you withdraw.
>
> *Level load* fees are paid annually and can be as much as one percent on a continuing basis.
>
> Mutual funds are generally identified by the "class" of their investment fee. These categories or class of shares are most commonly broken into three categories:
>
> *Class A shares* are front-loaded shares for large institutional investors who are most likely to keep their money in one fund for a sustained period.
>
> *Class B shares* are shares subject a redemption fee when money is withdrawn to meet obligations such as pensions. B shares can be subject to other fees, as well.
>
> Class *C shares* are the level-loaded shares subject to higher annual fees to accommodate moving the money from one style

(type) of fund to another style within the same family of funds. There are other letter-designated funds to denote special load fees. F, M, and Y are designations that some fund firms use to signal that such designated funds have very high minimum investments.

Loads will cut into your returns. But so can expenses charged to your shares by no-load mutual funds (see Figure 3.1).

No-load Fees

Mutual funds with no load charges represent themselves as a less expensive alternative to load funds. But that's not necessarily true. No-load funds still charge annual fees, also known as operating expenses. Some of these expenses are appropriate because they cover the costs of trading transactions and the costs of adminis-

Fee Classification	Up Front Commission Paid	Annual Fee (%)	Assessed
A	5-6%	0.25%	Once, at time of purchase "Front-End Load"
B	5-6% "Deferred or Backend Fee"	0.25% (12-B1)	Once, at time of withdrawal "Back-End Load" or "Contingent deferred sales charge"
C	1.0%	1.00%	Once a year. Some funds impose an additional 1% fee on shares redeemed within a year.
D	0%	0.25% (12-B1)	Rarely utilized
F	0%	0%	Rarely utilized
I	0%	0%	Rarely utilized
L	1.0% + 1.0% Deferred Load	0.70% (12-B1)	Deferred sales charge of 1.00% if redeemed early

Source: Robert Jorgensen

Figure 3.1   Alphabet soup: common mutual fund fee.

tration and overhead, although there are funds that charge as much as two percent for operating expenses.

Most funds also add what is known as a 12b-1 fee. This is a means by which the fund can charge sales, marketing, and distribution expenses directly against the fund's assets. The designation 12b-1 refers to the 1980 Securities and Exchange Commission (SEC) rule that allows this practice. There is no legal limit to what a mutual fund can charge under 12b-1; however, if a fund charges more than one quarter of one percent, it cannot promote itself as a no-load fund. The typical annual 12b-1 distribution fee is 0.25 percent annually.

Other Fees

Some new fees have been introduced recently. Here are some of the commonly known fees you might pay if you invest in a fund, and some fees that are not so commonly known or understood:

- *Exchange fee:* a charge that can be as high as $25, assessed when you exchange shares of one fund for another within the same mutual fund family.
- *Account maintenance fee:* another charge that can run as high as high as $25. This is typically charged against accounts whose value is below a specified minimum.
- *Transaction fee:* a fee of as much as two percent assessed against your account when you buy or sell shares. These fees are over and above any load charges that you may have already incurred (see Figure 3.2).
- *Contingent deferred sales charge:* a convoluted way of saying, "We will get our sales charge from you at some point to be determined at our discretion."
- *Incentive fees:* These charges are typically disclosed somewhat surreptitiously in a mutual fund prospectus. For example:

All potential securities investments have two basic expenses whether investing through "no load" Mutual Funds or through Separately Managed Accounts:

1. General administrative expenses (expense ratios)
2. Trading costs

The Cost of an Average Equity Mutual Fund is			
Average Expense Ratio 1994*	1.44%	1.44%	1.44%
Average trading costs @ 75% turnover*	0.90%		
Average trading costs @ 100% turnover*		1.20%	
Average trading costs @ 150% turnover*			1.80%
Total basic expenses of an Equity Mutual Fund	2.34%	2.64%	3.24%

versus

"Fee for Service" of 1.3 - 3.0% depending on size and negotiation

Source: Bogle on Mutual Funds, *John Bogle, page 206.*

Figure 3.2   Average mutual fund fees.

We will from time to time provide additional incentives or payments to dealers that sell our funds. These incentives or payments may include payment for travel expenses, including lodging, incurred by invited registered representatives and their guests to locations within and outside the United States for meetings and seminars of a business nature. In some instances, these incentives and payments may be offered only to certain dealers who have sold or may sell significant amounts of shares.

Incentive payments are in addition to any 12b-1 charges.

THE SUPERMARKET QUESTION

Some prominent brokerage firms have developed an asset accumulation strategy commonly referred to as a "mutual fund supermarket." This strategy permits investors to buy any number of mutual funds from any number of fund companies through the brokerage firm. The opportunity to do so is afforded investors at a "reasonable fee." The brokerage profit shortfalls from offering these reasonable fees are recouped through payments by the mutual funds to the brokerage firms. The funds do this because they believe they have to be in the supermarket or will lose investment dollars to competing funds that are members. The practice begs the question: "Where do mutual funds get the money to make payments to the brokerage firms to participate in the supermarket?" How about the existing mutual fund shareholders?

Whether the "pay to play" monies are labeled 12b-1 fees or management expenses, they are still being passed on to existing shareholders. They are not absorbed by the fund as expenses necessarily incurred while conducting business. More aggravating is how these fund companies encumber their shareholders with yet another charge. If you bought your shares directly from the mutual fund company, why should you have to help subsidize the investor who decides to buy the same class of the same fund from a brokerage firm?

THE "CHUTZPAH" FEE

Since the market decline of 2000, many mutual fund shareholders have been assessed an annual fee because the value of their accounts fell below a specified minimum amount, even though their initial investments were well above the minimum when the money was invested.

"SOFT-DOLLAR" FEES

Soft-dollar fees are designed to recover "transaction" costs paid by a fund to brokerage houses for their research help. These fees are typically higher than prevailing competitive rates for executing buy and sell orders. The question that should be asked is, "Why shouldn't funds pay for their research using the fees they already charge to their shareholders?"

THE REAL IMPACT OF FEES

Let's look at real expenses as a percentage of an initial investment over a period of ten years. A fund's expenses are expressed as an *expense ratio.* This ratio is the fund's total expenses expressed as a percentage of total assets. Assume a reasonable compounded annual return of 8 percent. Calculate the net return if the fund has an expense ratio of 1.36 percent. This reduces the annual return to 6.64 percent. If you do the compounding, you'll see an alarming diminishment on your investment over ten years. Remember, expenses do matter. Seemingly small leaks can sink big ships (see Figure 3.3).

John C. Bogle, founder of the Vanguard Group, brings another perspective to fund expenses: *costs as a percentage of the equity risk premium.* The equity risk premium is accepted as the return required by investors to compensate for not taking the risk-free rate of return from treasury bonds. If treasury bonds are returning five percent and the current annual rate of return on stocks is eight percent (including reinvested dividends), then the risk premium is three percent. If a mutual fund over the same period has an expense ratio of 1.36 percent, what's the return over the prevailing risk premium? Expenses matter.

Not surprisingly, Bogle makes his point in the context of what Vanguard offers: low-cost index funds. I will discuss index funds in the next chapter, where I will examine some other mutual fund industry features and practices.

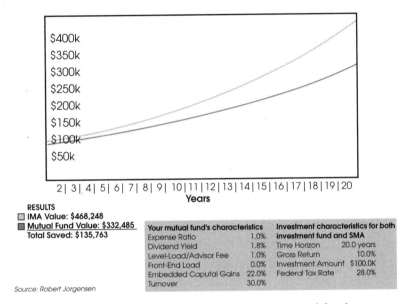

RESULTS
☐ IMA Value: $468,248
☐ Mutual Fund Value: $332,485
   Total Saved: $135,763

Your mutual fund's characteristics		Investment characteristics for both investment fund and SMA	
Expense Ratio	1.0%	Time Horizon	20.0 years
Dividend Yield	1.8%	Gross Return	10.0%
Level-Load/Advisor Fee	1.0%	Investment Amount	$100.0K
Front-End Load	0.0%	Federal Tax Rate	28.0%
Embedded Caputal Gains	22.0%		
Turnover	30.0%		

Source: Robert Jorgensen

Figure 3–3   Tax efficiency of IMAs vs. mutual funds.

THE REAL ISSUE ON FEES

Is the average expense ratio for mutual funds significantly greater than that of a professional money manager? Not necessarily. Mutual fund fees may or may not be more expensive than IMAs. It's just that with IMAs the fees are a little easier for the average investor to identify. It's also important to note that with IMAs annual management fees are lower if you invest large sums of money (generally more than $500,000). With mutual funds the annual expenses remain constant no matter how much money you invest.

When you compare the annual fees of a mutual fund to those of a professional money manager, remember that mutual fund trading costs and commissions are not disclosed in advance.

Conversely, professional money management trading costs are almost always disclosed in Form ADV (see glossary), which must be filed for public access by the SEC.

Greg Horn, CEO of Persimmon Research Partners had this to say about fees:

> When you examine mutual fund expenses over the past ten years you can see that their internal annual expenses have actually risen whereas IMA expenses have steadily declined about 35% over the same time period. These lower fees, the lower account minimums, improved tax-efficiency, and the simplicty of delivery (e.g., MDAs, see Chapter 14) are just a few of the reasons we are seeing a shift of capital out of funds and into IMAs.

IN THE NEXT CHAPTER

I've brought two distinct disadvantages of mutual funds to your attention: the absence of any concerns about a shareholder's tax planning strategies, and a plethora of fees, many of which might not be adequately disclosed. In Chapter 4, I talk about some other aspects of mutual funds that make them less than suitable for making the most of your investment portfolio.

CHAPTER 4

The Feeling Isn't Mutual

The mutual fund industry has over $7 trillion in assets and generates approximately $100 billion in fees annually without generating a single invoice.

—R.B.J.

I want to begin this chapter by stating that professionally I feel mutual funds are excellent investments for the average investor. They are nicely packaged, easy to buy and sell, offer complete diversification, and they allow for incremental investing (dollar cost averaging) with low minimums. They have become the vehicle of choice for 401(k) retirement plans for almost every plan in America. However, they do have some drawbacks that I will discuss in some detail:

1. Investors have no discretion or control as to when individual securities are bought and sold by the fund manager, or what type of securities are selected for the mutual fund portfolio.
2. Fund transactions may expose taxable investors to very high tax liabilities. In some instances, taxes might erode as much as forty percent of investment gains. The tax

dilution of mutual fund investment returns are so severe that in early 2002, the Securities and Exchange Commission (SEC) began requiring mutual fund companies to show (in two ways) their annualized after-tax returns in the prospectus of any specific fund. And remember, if you need some offsetting capital losses, even the most tax-efficient mutual fund *cannot pass capital losses on to you.* This is because you are part of a "pool of investors, rather owning your own securities, as in an IMA.

3. Mutual funds charge a variety of fees that are sometimes difficult to discern. I call this mix of fees "alphabet soup." These fees can compound to significantly reduce an investor's total return over long periods of time.

There are other aspects of mutual funds that make them less attractive than some other means of investing. What these other aspects have in common with the three major disadvantages is the *control over your money that you forfeit when you buy shares in mutual funds* (see Figure 4.1).

WHAT'S HAPPENING WITH *YOUR* MONEY?

You can now shop for an automobile among regional dealers or you can shop and compare on the Internet. Either way, a diligent car shopper can discover all the components and features that distinguish one model from another. You can compare features such as horsepower, acceleration, interior appointments, and price. You can also shop around for a mutual fund through your broker or on the Internet, but there is a difference. Regardless of how diligent you are in shopping for and selecting a mutual fund, you can never really discover all the individual components (equities, bonds, or cash) of which a fund is composed.

There is a simple reason for this. A mutual fund is only re-

Feature	Buying Stocks Yourself	Buying Shares of a Mutual Fund	Investing in an Individually Managed Account
Individual ownership of stocks	✓	✓	
Professional money management and research services		✓	✓
Professionally customized to your portfolio specifications	✓		✓
Cost Basis for stocks set on purchase date	✓		✓
Timing of capital gains realization planned to minimize your tax liability	✓		✓
Tax-Efficient Investment Approach	✓	Occasionally	✓
Funding the portfolio with low cost basis stock			✓
Manager independence from "herd instinct" of buyers and sellers	✓		✓
Volume fee discounts	✓		✓
Separately held individual securities	✓		✓
Time-weighted performance monitor			✓

Source: Robert Jorgensen

Figure 4.1 Individually managed accounts: the differences your choices can make.

quired to disclose their actual holdings in the portfolio twice each year, and only those securities held at the time of disclosure. Moreover, these printed disclosures may not be available until thirty days to three months at the end of a reporting period. You also can't tell what securities were bought, sold, or held at other times of the year, or during the times after which the semi-annual reports or prospectuses were produced. How much risk was taken? How much cost was incurred in buying and selling these securities?

This lack of disclosure, which I refer to as lack of visibility as to what is going on with your investments, highlights one of the major benefits of owning an IMA. IMA transactions are reported daily. All of your holdings and activity can be viewed through your custodian's on-line service.

No Investment Manager Is Infallible

Every investment management company, professional money manager, and mutual fund prominently displays the following statement in their marketing materials, in their prospectuses or in their Form ADV (a disclosure document that the SEC requires independent investment managers to file) "Past performance is no guarantee of future results." This is the one and only validated truth about investment performance. Regulators realized a long time ago that hope often overrides experience, and hence mandated that the above caveat be appended to any information about investment performance.

Investment professionals assign securities to specific market categories, such as large companies, small companies, newly emerging companies, international stocks, bonds, and so forth. None of these categories increase (or decrease) in value over the same periods. In academic jargon, their respective performances "co-vary". This prevailing condition forms the bedrock of that one and only truth about performance: past investment performance provides no guarantees for future performance. Take, for example, the performance of international stocks in the 1980s, and compare their performance to the 1990s.

From 1985 to 1990, international stocks outperformed all other styles of investing. The performance of international stocks was in great part driven by Japanese stocks. In the early 1990s, Japan experienced its worst recession since the end of World War II, and the subsequent plunge of its stocks adversely affected the stocks of other foreign markets. The performance of emerging company (small growth) stocks from 1996 to early 2000 created a "microcap mania" that eventually pushed many investors off the cliffs in 2001. Stocks in the telecommunications sector generated attractive investment returns in the mid-1990s before their valuations decreased to levels lower than at the beginning of their run-ups.

The instances just cited are some historical samples illustrating the nature of stock market cycles, and how certain stocks come in and out of favor over time. History shows that when one category of stocks is trading low over some period, investors at some point will find those stocks attractively priced, rush to them, and bid their prices up. The result is that over time, an out-of-favor category of stocks turns into a category that outperforms other securities.

Most mutual fund managers and independent investment managers will concentrate their investment strategy on one category of securities. These individual strategies are referred to as *investment styles* in the world of finance. Investment styles evolved out of the concept of diversifying investments because of the ongoing cyclic changes among different kinds of securities (they co-vary). I will discuss investment styles in more detail in Chapter 5.

Again, no investment professional is infallible. Professional money managers are as subject to the vagaries of varying returns and market cycles as are the managers of mutual fund portfolios, but there is a definitive distinction. The organizational structure of a mutual fund company puts its funds' shareholders at some critical disadvantages compared with the structure of a professional money management firm. The major disadvantage is the *absence of transparency* through which mutual fund investors can observe how their mutual funds are run. In addition to the manner in which they devise and levy fees, there are some other practices that impact the value of your mutual fund investments:

- Fund family simply closes down a poorly performing fund
- One fund may be merged with another fund within the same fund family
- Merging of two mutual fund companies
- Advertently shifting out of the stipulated fund to a more successful and advertised fund

- Changing investment strategy of a fund (e.g., from small cap to large cap)
- Fund manager of management team is changed

When Mutual Funds Close

Over the 24-month period ending December 31, 2001, 304 mutual funds were closed. They were closed because their returns were very poor, and/or they were not able to attract new money. If a shareholder of a fund being closed declined to assign his assets to another affiliated fund, the fund company wrote the investor a check for his shares: net of all the expenses, fees, and transaction costs incurred from closing the fund. Moreover, the ex-shareholder was liable for the capital gains taxes generated by the transactions that garnered returns in excess of the original purchase prices. It is almost impossible for an independent investment manager to close out his portfolio.

The professional who runs your IMA is dedicated to one specific *style* of investing (see Chapter 5). Unless they choose to close their firms, these professionals have no alternative place to direct your assets. The structure of their business model dictates prudence and stewardship as a means of survival.

When Mutual Funds Merge

The steep decline in investment returns at the turn of the new century also resulted in the merger of some mutual fund companies, as well as the consolidation of funds within mutual fund companies. These mergers sometimes involved merging a poorly performing fund with a fund with much better returns. The objective of this strategy is to retain the assets of the shareholders of the poorly performing fund.

These consolidations were also expense-reduction strategies. Cost cutting is now an acceptable business practice when a company is faced with a decrease in income. But good business practice dictates that the business managers ask themselves, "How will a merger impact our customers?" If customers have entrusted some of their money for investing, you would think that such an arrangement would heighten fund manager concern for investor well-being. Such concern was not much in evidence among some mutual fund companies that were merging or consolidating specific funds.

Prior to the merging of funds, some fund managers were required to liquidate some of their holdings. These transaction costs were absorbed by the existing shareholders of those funds. And yes, these shareholders incurred unrealized capital gains exposures from the transactions that yielded investment gains.

Truth in Labeling

Some mutual funds have shifted their investment style without adequately disclosing that they have done so. Some shareholders have discovered that a fund they own has holdings that don't match the profile of the stated investment objective. An egregious example I encountered was a corporate bond portfolio I analyzed I found had over twenty percent of the fund was actually composed of high-tech growth stocks. We call this "tracking error."

How extensive is this problem of "tracking error?" In 2002, the SEC mandated that at least eighty percent of a fund's assets must match its name and stated objective. Funds out of compliance with the new rule can correct their portfolios or else they must change their names.

There is a prevailing situation that compounds the problem of style labeling. Style criteria differ among the mutual fund rating companies, of which the two most prominent are Morningstar and Lipper. Of the over 1,100 domestic funds tracked by these two firms, twenty-two percent of them were characterized differently. Both companies have plans to categorize and rate individual money managers. Such a state of affairs reinforces my strong recommendation that you should retain an investment advisor to help you choose where to invest your money (see Chapter 9).

Who's There?

Many people who invest with mutual funds have an unrealistic image of the person they believe is managing the fund. Investors might imagine a financial guru whom they have seen on television, whose image is carefully crafted by the fund company. Such a "guru" campaign makes for great advertising, but doesn't represent reality.

Over ninety percent of current fund managers were not running their respective funds ten years ago. Why is this relevant? Any measure of investment acumen should be measured over at least a decade. Most professional money managers have been overseeing their portfolios for longer than ten years. They have the hands-on experience of several market cycles. If the fund managers change frequently, then the fund's underlying portfolio performance may vary as well.

Here's another fact about mutual fund managers: It isn't uncommon for a fund manager to run a half-dozen other funds in the parent company. How do you find out if this is the case with the fund whose shares you own? It doesn't have to be disclosed in the fund prospectus, so it isn't. What is the likelihood that the manager of multiple funds creates conflicts of interest? Where are the best ideas or opportunities going to go? These are real questions that should be posed to the fund companies.

In addition to these perplexing dilemmas, the company that owns the fund you bought might not be running that fund. The fund you own might be "sub-advised." In other words, the fund company has farmed out the investment decisions to an independent investment professional outside the company. You may be informed about this arrangement, but you will not have a voice as to who manages your money.

Most importantly, the professional money manager is going to charge the fund company a management fee. How likely do you think it is that the fund company will pass that expense on to you in some manner?

One counter-response to my argument for IMAs runs, "Buy shares of an index mutual fund. You won't have to deal with high fees. Besides, there's evidence that the best you can expect is to match the overall market's returns." But as you'll see, there's more to it than that. Now let's discuss index investing.

INDEX MUTUAL FUNDS: THE REAL STORY

Index funds have been touted in recent years as one of the best ways to invest in stocks. Index funds are run by fund managers commonly referred to as *passive investors* by academics and professionals. The dominant index mutual fund company for individual investors is Vanguard. At one point in 2000, Vanguard's 500 Index Fund had assets in the neighborhood of $100 billion. Yes, passive investment strategies play significant roles in global capital markets. Proponents stress their low fees and tax efficiencies. These are attractive index fund features—some of the time. However, indexing isn't the last word on investment strategies, it's just the latest.

Just What Is Indexing?

Most academics believe that any investment return in a given market will, over time, revert to the mean of all the other investment returns in that market. The argument runs that since every investor is part of the market, their collective actions will cancel each other out. Market indices were devised to provide mean benchmarks against which investors could measure investment performance. That is, market indices are used as broad-based measurements of market trends.

Any particular index is composed of *selected securities* that should have features common to all the securities traded in the market that the index is intended to measure. There are indices composed to represent the stocks of large capitalized companies, such as the Dow Jones Averages and the Standard & Poor's (S&P) 500. Other indices have been developed to replicate other specific securities markets. The Russell 2000 is constructed to represent smaller capitalized stocks. The Lehman Brothers Aggregate Bond Index is intended to provide a measure for long-term fixed-income securities. There are indices intended to mirror securities in foreign markets.

The case for indexing is stated like this: "If all investment returns in a given market will revert to a mean, then one should just invest in portfolios composed of securities that replicate the respective market benchmarks." Indexing proponents follow this argument with:

> There are two benefits for investors who invest with index mutual funds.
> 1. There are lower fees, because index fund managers don't incur as much transaction costs as active investment managers. They hold the securities in their portfolios throughout different market cycles.
> 2. Because there is almost no turnover within an indexed mutual fund, shareholders enjoy greater tax efficiency. There will be no realized capital gains surprises at the end of the year.

The underlying structures of index funds and the basis for the foregoing arguments are easy to understand. That's why the media reports so enthusiastically on index funds. Media interest was obviously heightened by the performance of Vanguard's 500 Index Fund. If all you've studied in terms of educating yourself about investing are articles in the popular press and financial news shows, you'd believe that index funds are the perfect means by which you must invest. We must recall the classic adage: "If it's too good to be true, it probably is."

The Real Story of an Index Composition

Only the media represents index funds as "mirrors" of the markets. No index fund would represent itself this way in good conscience. The fluctuating market capitalization of any one stock makes it impossible to weight any index precisely to its market. What you get from an index fund is an approximation of its respective market. And many index funds don't hold equal proportions among the "representative" stocks in their portfolios. The media most commonly refers to the Vanguard 500 Index Fund, unintentionally misrepresenting it as a fund that mirrors the mean market valuation of all the stocks comprising the S&P 500 Index. However, S&P 500 stocks are *periodically selected* by McGraw-Hill's Standard and Poor's to represent the largest capitalized stock issues in the United States. And the S&P 500 is not weighted equally among all 500 companies. Did you know that?

Each of the 500 stocks is proportioned within the index by the size of its market capitalization. Here's what you'll get when you buy a fund indexed to the S&P 500. You'll get a preponderance of stocks that have likely peaked in value. You are neither a growth investor, nor a value investor. Instead, you are a momentum investor, chasing the monster corporations, but where? There are other index funds that weight the composition of their portfolios other than by an equal number of shares. This is okay, but any other weighting mandates a weighting adjustment. Adjusting the weightings means selling some shares and buying others. And remember, selling and buying incurs transaction costs. You do know that.

The Real Story on Index Fund Transaction Costs

Transaction costs can be incurred by index funds just as frequently as by professional money managers. The S&P 500 managers have often had to retool. Not too long ago, the Standard

& Poor's committee that selects the companies comprising the 500 Index was faced with the likelihood of replacing thirteen stocks. That was because several of the representative companies were being acquired or were consolidating. When index composition changes, index fund managers have about a week to shift stocks, so that their indexed portfolios are back in line with the benchmark.

Index changes create significant, if not readily apparent, costs for index managers over and above transaction costs. Changes in indices are announced publicly before the changes are made. Savvy investors quickly buy the stocks to be added to an index, and sell those stocks being dropped. Thus, nimble investors front run the index fund managers. These managers now incur what the investment professionals call *market impact costs*. They will be selling into a declining market for the stocks they have to drop, and chasing the stocks they must buy behind the smart money that has bid the stocks up.

The Real Story on Index Fund Taxes

Alert readers are now realizing another result of this buying and selling. Yes, there are tax liabilities. Don't ever assume that investing in index funds is more tax efficient than other means of investing. Some people often overlook the obvious: there is almost always an embedded capital gain when you buy an index fund.

One of the reasons index funds have not been tossing out a lot of capital gains hits is because they have been taking in lots of new money for a long time. When (not if) the index funds encounter a climate of redemptions, they will first raise the redemption money by selling off some of the lower cost stocks. The consequences for shareholders are obvious.

The Real Story on Some Overlooked Index Fund Costs

One of the overlooked costs of an index fund is what financial professionals and academics call *opportunity cost*. A true index fund must stay fully invested in its representative stocks, regardless of how the holdings are weighted in the fund. The manager loses the opportunity to buy undervalued stocks and foregoes capturing possible returns. Just as important, being fully invested precludes an indexer from protecting his shareholders from a market correction. He has no cash cushion.

Index funds of any size carry large personnel and information technology costs, just as great or greater than professional money managers. One of my close friends served on a study group composed of eighteen people from all the areas of finance. One of the members of the group was a vice-president for one of the largest index fund companies in the world. This vice-president confided to my friend that she had a group of over twenty people whose sole function was to deal with the corporate governance and proxy issues of the over 1,000 companies whose shares were in the fund. I know of no independent professional money manager who comes close to owning shares in over 1,000 companies. Here again is evidence of how a major mutual fund company let red tape and a misapplication of a reasonable investment strategy get in the way of properly stewarding its shareholders' money.

CLOSED-END FUNDS AND EXCHANGE TRADED FUNDS

There is yet another investment company structure permitted by the SEC known as a *closed-end fund*. Shares of a closed-end fund are issued in a fixed amount. These shares also represent mutual ownership of a designated portfolio of securities, but they are not redeemable by the issuer at your option. Redemption takes place through secondary auction markets. Investors buy and sell the shares of closed-end funds on a stock exchange. This exchange-trading activity results in shares often being traded at a discount or a premium to the computed value of the shares in the portfolio, more often at a discount. Closed-end funds are not popular, but they do have a very attractive feature, which is the ease with which their shares can be traded.

Remember the primary appeal of an index fund? If constructed properly, the fund can come close to replicating a given stock or bond benchmark. Wall Street has introduced a new class of investment that permits you to acquire a benchmark portfolio and mitigate the burdens of unexpected expenses and tax surprises: closed-end index funds called *exchange-traded funds* (ETFs). There are now hundreds of ETFs traded on the major exchanges. The funds have names like Spiders, Webs, Diamonds, and QQQ (or cubes). ETFs are being constructed to track any market: domestic stocks, specific sectors, foreign securities, and even real estate investments.

ETFs are not exact replicas of a benchmarked index. They may closely follow the composite value of the index they are representing, but maybe they won't. Why not? ETFs require a market maker (called a specialist) like any exchange-traded stock. The market maker will bid under the current level of the index if he has an order to sell shares, and will offer it at above the current level if he has a buy order. These funds have not been traded during a sustained period of overall market volatility. Nobody knows what will happen if there is a deluge of buy or sell orders, so nobody really knows anything of consequence about the long-range viability of these unique funds.

CONCLUSION

If you are willing to invest a minimum of $50,000, you have a more versatile money management option than traditional mutual funds. An IMA permits you to direct how your and your family's money is invested, with specific attention paid to your tax situations.

Robert's 10 Commandments of Professional Money Management

1. Thou shalt not hire inexperienced mutual fund or IMA managers to manage your securities portfolio.
2. Thou shalt not pay an upfront commission to buy a mutual fund or mutual fund type product.
3. Thou shalt not put more than $250,000 in a mutual fund if the internal expenses exceed 1.00% annually (no price breaks for large purchases only with IMAs).
4. Thou shalt not buy mutual funds or hire IMA managers if you do not understand their investment process.
5. Thou shalt not buy a mutual fund with a large imbedded capital gain (unless it is in a non-taxable account such as an IRA).
6. Thou shalt not buy a mutual fund at the end of the year in a taxable account just prior to their year-end dividend declaration.
7. Thou shalt only buy mutual funds or IMA managers that stick with their stated investment style.
8. Thou shalt not make your find or IMA purchasing decisions based *solely* on past investment performance.
9. Thou shalt not put all of your investments in index funds.
10. Thou shalt know what your mutual fund or IMA manager invests in.

I have said all I have to say about mutual funds. The remainder of this book addresses what you need to know in order to select the most appropriate professional investment manager for your money.

IN THE NEXT CHAPTER

The last three chapters have been devoted exclusively to the investment and administrative practices of the mutual fund industry. In the next chapter, I will describe and explain how the independent side of the investment management industry is structured. I will discuss further the distinguishing investment styles, and conclude by explaining how independent investment managers work with investment advisors.

The Key Ingredients to Building a Professionally Managed Portfolio

The Business of Investment Management

Do not hire a man who does your work for money, but hire a man who does it for the love of it.
                              —Henry David Thoreau (1817–1862)

When people talk about investing, they typically use the term *market* incorrectly. The business of investment management is conducted in the market, but financial professionals are more precise in how they use the term. Within the general framework, it refers to all exchanges and systems with listing requirements, including disclosure of relevant information about all company securities.

In practice, the market is the arena in which company securities of like characteristics are traded, for example, the government bond market, the corporate bond market, the large-capitalization (large-cap) stocks market, the small-cap stocks market, the foreign markets, and so forth. Most professional money managers specialize in one specific market. This specialization is known as a manager's *investment style.*

STOCK INVESTMENT STYLES

For reasons already discussed in the earlier chapters of this book, I will devote this examination of styles to active investment strategies. The primary concern for investors is how a professional money manager's style adds to the value of their portfolios. And remember, the overall goal includes risk management in addition to maximizing tax efficiency and returns.

Professional investment managers believe that the market prices of different assets move in different directions at different times, depending on overall global economic environments. Professional investors who are responsible for large pools of money, such as pension funds, endowments, and trusts, seek diversification even within asset classes. Typically, they will assemble a "portfolio of portfolios," each of which represents a different configuration within the same asset class, particularly among stocks. These distinctive configurations may be arranged by market capitalization, valuation methods, global regions, or business types. A manager focused on just one particular industry group is referred to as a *sector-style* manager.

The two most common styles of stock investment management are based on the valuations of the companies issuing their respective common stocks. These two styles are known as *value* and *growth*. Most growth-style and value-style investment managers specialize even further, with focus on stocks of a specific range of market capitalization or size. In your search for a professional money manager for your individually managed account, you'll find listings for:

Large-cap growth
Mid-cap growth
Small-cap growth
Large-cap value

Mid-cap value

Small-cap value

Core

International

Global

Fixed

There are significant distinctions between growth and value investing. In the five-year period between 1997 and 2002, the covariance between value stocks and growth stocks has been very discernible. Let's look at each style.

Value Investment Managers

Value investing concentrates on a company's *book value*, calculated as total assets less total liabilities and intangibles, such as goodwill. The other commonly accepted terms for this measurement of company worth are *net tangible value* and *liquidating value.*

Value managers calculate the book value of a selected stock and compare it with the present market price. If the market price of a stock is significantly lower than the book value, that particular stock is a candidate for a value portfolio. The manager further researches reasons why a particular stock appears to be undervalued. A good example of a "value" stock would be an old-line manufacturer like Ford Motor Co. A value stock like Ford has very steady and somewhat predictable earnings.

The rationale for value investing is based on the assumption that other investors will eventually recognize that the stock is undervalued. Subsequent purchases will increase the value of the shares. Remember that value managers usually restrict their research and investments to a specific market capitalization grouping.

Growth Investment Managers

Growth managers pursue sustained growth in earnings, seeking companies with annual earnings increasing at a rate greater than the market as a whole. They devote substantial time and money to extensive research and analysis to identify companies with current and projected growth rates not fully reflected in their stock prices.

High potential growth opportunities are harder to identify than value stocks. Part of the challenge with growth is identifying the stock before other investors drive the stock price higher. In addition, growth investing is more popular among investors than value, creating a premium for these companies. Naturally, growth investing is more costly than value investing. A good example of a growth company would be a technology stock like Cisco Systems. A growth stock like Cisco is highly leveraged and can create quick growth in a short period of time.

Growth portfolio managers devote considerable resources in the forms of time and money toward capturing an early position in a promising stock and also restrict their styles to a specific market capitalization group.

Comparing the Costs of Growth and Value Investing

Fees charged by growth managers are generally higher than those charged by value managers, since it's more costly to trade growth stocks. Growth is an aggressive style, and growth managers could be characterized as the proverbial hunter. In contrast, value managers are like collectors in pursuit of the best available gems at the best bargains.

Investment style and market capitalization impact transaction costs. The smaller a stock's market cap, the fewer available shares, the higher the demand, and the greater the cost. The Plexus

Group, a prominent research and consulting firm, has studied and compared the transaction costs associated with market-cap size and between growth and value styles. Not surprisingly, the research shows that large-cap value managers enjoy a definite cost advantage of about one percent over large-cap growth managers, and a three percent cost advantage over small-cap growth managers.

The Socially Conscious Approach

Some investors are very selective about the companies in which they invest. They do not want to own stocks of companies with whose businesses activities they disagree. Some investors object to the practices of energy or natural resource firms. Some object to the nature of the defense industry, and others have strong feelings against companies making or distributing tobacco or alcoholic products.

There are investment managers who run portfolios dedicated to "social awareness" investing. This approach was introduced in the late 1980s. Since these socially aware investment managers have a distinct style, your investment advisor will know about them. These managers benchmark their performance against a socially conscious version of the Standard & Poor's (S&P) indexes known as the *Domini Indexes,* the most well-known of which is the Domini 400.

Other Styles

Core or *blend* managers don't restrict their investing to any particular style, sector, or market capitalization. These are highly skilled opportunists who chafe at any restriction as to what they can buy and sell, seeking to invest in whatever stock or asset class has the greatest potential for meeting and exceeding an investment objective.

Regardless of style, IMA managers typically invest in portfolios of between thirty and eighty holdings. Broad, well-diversified positions protect an investor from excessive volatility and the poor performance that can affect an individual stock. But with each position making up no more than two percent of a portfolio, a large run-up in one of the stocks will have only a small overall effect.

Concentrated investment managers attempt to leverage their training, experience, and judgment into holding just a dozen or so stocks, which they believe will increase value at a rate higher than the overall market.

Top-down and Bottom-up Approaches to Stock Analysis

The majority of stock investment managers appraise each stock's value individually on some measure of worth reflected in the issuing company's financial statements. With this approach, commonly referred to as *bottom-up investing*, a manager actively builds a portfolio security by security, based on extensive research and analysis of a company to determine whether its market price is undervalued compared with the intrinsic value of the stock. This approach is based on the belief that the stock market is inefficient by nature and thus offers good investment opportunities.

Other managers analyze stocks based on their relationships to the market or prevailing economic conditions. This is known as a *top-down* approach, which focuses on all events, nationally and globally, that could affect a specific industry sector. An example would be a manager who searches for attractively priced energy stocks during periods of Middle Eastern turmoil. Another would be a manager who looks at the stocks of leisure activity companies during times of high employment and salaries.

Some portfolio managers do not rely on accounting measures

or prevailing political-economic circumstances to value a stock. *Technical analysts,* known also as *chartists* and *technicians,* focus on the direction of price and the transaction volume changes of a particular stock. By charting these patterns of change, these managers forecast stock prices over the short term, trading the stocks in their portfolios on these indicators without regard to sector, industry, value features or growth prospects (see Figure 5.1).

FIXED-INCOME INVESTMENT STYLES

Investment managers specializing in fixed-income securities aim to provide steady interest income for their clients while using the market value of bonds to increase principle value. These managers use different instruments, depending on an investor's tax situation. There are two commonly used fixed income investment strategies, each having some variations.

The first strategy focuses on predicting the direction of interest rates. Since market prices move in the opposite direction of interest rates, a manager using this strategy builds a portfolio with bonds of different maturities. If interest rates rise, short-term bonds are advantageous because their close maturation dates permit the manager to sell at close to face value and buy bonds with higher rates of return. Meanwhile, market prices of long-term bonds are good hedges against falling interest rates.

The other strategy focuses on arbitrage opportunities among price differences of bonds of comparable quality and characteristics. This method does not focus on interest rates and yield, but rather on the price differences of bonds of comparable quality. Gains from this strategy tend to be more modest, although this is offset by lower risk exposure.

The MARKET CYCLES chart ranks the best to worst performing indexes per calendar year from top to bottom. This chart represents the importance of being diversified by manager style (growth and value) and displays the fluctuations in market cycles.

1987	1988	1989	1990	1991	1992	1993	1994	1995	1996	1997	1998	1999	2000	2001	1Q02
EAFE 25.0%	Russell 2000V 29.5%	Russell 1000G 35.9%	LB G/C Interm. 9.2%	Russell 2000G 51.1%	Russell 2000V 29.1%	EAFE 33.0%	EAFE 8.1%	Russell 1000V 38.4%	Russell 1000G 23.1%	Russell 1000V 35.2%	Russell 1000G 38.7%	Russell 2000G 43.1%	Russell 2000V 22.8%	Russell 2000V 14.0%	Russell 2000V 9.6%
Russell 1000G 5.3%	EAFE 28.6%	S&P 500 31.7%	Russell 1000G -0.3%	Russell 2000V 41.7%	Russell Mid Cap 16.3%	Russell 2000V 23.9%	Russell 1000G 2.7%	S&P 500 37.6%	S&P 500 22.9%	S&P 500 33.4%	S&P 500 28.7%	Russell 1000G 33.2%	LB G/C Interm. 10.1%	LB G/C Interm. 9.0%	Russell Mid Cap 4.3%
S&P 500 5.2%	Russell 1000V 23.2%	Russell Mid Cap 26.3%	S&P 500 -3.1%	Russell Mid Cap 41.5%	Russell 1000V 13.8%	Russell 1000V 18.1%	S&P 500 1.3%	Russell 1000G 37.2%	Russell 1000V 21.6%	Russell 2000V 31.8%	EAFE 20.8%	EAFE 27.9%	Russell Mid Cap 8.3%	Russell 1000V -5.6%	Russell 1000V 4.1%
LB G/C Interm. 3.7%	Russell 2000G 20.4%	Russell 1000V 25.2%	Russell 1000V -8.1%	Russell 1000G 41.2%	Russell 2000G 7.7%	Russell Mid Cap 14.3%	Russell 2000V -1.6%	Russell Mid Cap 34.5%	Russell 2000V 21.4%	Russell 1000G 30.5%	Russell 1000V 15.6%	S&P 500 21.0%	Russell 1000V 7.0%	Russell Mid Cap -5.6%	EAFE 1.0%
Russell 1000V 0.5%	Russell Mid Cap 19.8%	Russell 2000G 20.2%	Russell Mid Cap -11.5%	S&P 500 30.5%	S&P 500 7.6%	Russell 2000G 13.4%	LB G/C Interm. -1.9%	Russell 2000G 31.0%	Russell Mid Cap 19.0%	Russell Mid Cap 29.0%	Russell Mid Cap 10.0%	Russell Mid Cap 18.2%	S&P 500 -9.2%	Russell 2000G -9.2%	S&P 500 0.3%
Russell Mid Cap 0.2%	S&P 500 16.6%	LB G/C Interm. 12.8%	Russell 2000G -17.4%	Russell 1000V 24.6%	LB G/C Interm. 7.2%	S&P 500 10.1%	Russell 1000V -2.0%	Russell 2000V 25.7%	Russell 2000G 11.3%	Russell 2000G 12.9%	LB G/C Interm. 8.4%	Russell 1000V 7.4%	EAFE -13.8%	S&P 500 -11.9%	LB G/C Interm. -0.2%
Russell 2000V -7.1%	Russell 1000G 11.3%	Russell 2000V 12.4%	Russell 2000V -21.8%	LB G/C Interm. 14.6%	Russell 1000G 5.0%	LB G/C Interm. 8.8%	Russell Mid Cap -2.1%	LB G/C Interm. 15.3%	EAFE 6.4%	LB G/C Interm. 7.9%	Russell 2000G 1.2%	LB G/C Interm. 0.4%	Russell 1000G -22.4%	Russell 1000G -20.4%	Russell 2000G -1.9
Russell 2000G -10.5%	LB G/C Interm. 6.7%	EAFE 10.8%	EAFE -23.2%	EAFE 12.5%	EAFE -11.8%	Russell 1000G 2.9%	Russell 2000G -2.4%	EAFE 11.6%	LB G/C Interm. 4.1%	EAFE 2.1%	Russell 2000V -6.3%	Russell 2000V -1.5%	Russell 2000G -22.4%	EAFE -21.2%	Russell 1000G -2.6%
35%	22.8%	25.1%	32.4%	38.6%	40.9%	30.1%	10.5%	26.8%	19.0%	33.1%	45.0%	44.6%	45.2%	35.2%	?

Greatest annual dispersion = 45.2% (2000); Least annual dispersion = 10.5% (1994); Average annual dispersion = 32.3%

EAFE - (Europe, Australia, and the Far East) Index. A market capitalization index representing all of the MSCI developed markets outside North America.
Source: Morningstar
Lehman Brothers Interm. Govt/Corp. - A measurement of the movement of approximately 3,500 bonds from the Lehman Brothers Government/Corporate Index with maturities between 1 and 9.99 years.
Russell 1000 Growth - Represents a segment of the Russell 1000 with a greater-than-average growth orientation, higher price-to-book and price-earnings ratios, lower dividend yields and higher forecasted growth values than the Russell 1000 Value index.
Russell 1000 Value - Represents a segment of the Russell 1000 with a less-than-average growth orientation, lower price-to-book and price-earnings ratios, higher dividend yields and lower forecasted growth values than the Russell 1000 Growth index.
Russell Mid Cap - Consists of bottom 800 securities in the Russell 1000, ranked by total market cap, and representing over 30% of Russell 1000 total market cap.
Russell 2000 Growth - Represents a segment of the Russell 2000 index with a greater-than-average growth orientation, higher price-to-book and price-earnings ratios, lower dividend yields and higher forecasted growth values than the Russell 2000 Value index.
Russell 2000 Value - Represents a segment of the Russell 2000 index with a less-than-average growth orientation, lower price-to-book and price-earnings ratios, higher dividend yields and lower forecasted growth values than the Russell 2000

Figure 5.1   Style allocation.

Bond managers typically specialize in municipal bonds or in non–tax-free fixed-income securities such as government and corporate bonds.

Municipal Bonds

Interest income from *municipal bonds* is free from both federal and state taxes, making them highly attractive to individuals in the highest tax brackets. Although their interest rates are lower than for taxable bonds, net income after taxes can quickly become higher as incomes get larger. They are obviously redundant and inappropriate for portfolios structured for retirement plans or charitable trusts. Municipal bonds are ideally suited for the investor seeking tax-free returns and active portfolio management.

Taxable Bond Portfolios

Taxable bond portfolios are intended primarily as capital preservation tools structured with issues of differing maturities. In addition, they can provide some guaranteed, incremental cash flow. These conservative portfolios are composed of mostly government bonds and high credit-rated corporate bonds. They are well suited for deferred taxation accounts requiring the highest level of safety for their assets. Government bonds are the safest investment, because as long as the IRS is in business, there will always be money to redeem them. Bonds issued by large, well-established corporations are a close second, and offer slightly higher interest rates to make up for added incremental risk. The significant feature of these bonds is that the income they provide is taxable at the federal level, hence their attractiveness for tax-deferred accounts or for institutions requiring the highest level of security for their assets.

High-Yield Bond Portfolios

Some fixed-income securities carry a high degree of credit risk and therefore carry higher coupon rates than bonds with good credit ratings to increase their investment appeal. These bond portfolios are not designed with capital preservation in mind. They're most often composed of bonds with market prices far below face value, based on the high likelihood of the issuers defaulting on their payment obligations of interest and principal—hence the oft-heard colloquial name "junk." The instruments of these portfolios are classic examples of the inverse degrees of relationship between risk and return. They are appropriate only for money specifically earmarked for discretionary, speculative investment strategies.

Other investment managers specializing in strategies for designated speculative investments include *hedge fund partnerships*, *emerging market funds*, *micro-cap stocks funds*, and *commodity trading advisors*.

HOW PROFESSIONAL MONEY MANAGERS EARN THEIR MONEY

As I've mentioned already, having your professional money manager's financial interests aligned with yours is one of the great benefits of IMAs. Money managers are compensated with an annual fee (typically between 0.20 percent and 1.0 percent), which is openly disclosed to you. The fee is based on the overall value of your portfolio and is generally billed quarterly and in advance. Hence, the better your IMA performs, the better your professional money manager is compensated. Billing occurs quarterly and is typically deducted from your account. Because your manager's compensation is based on the value of your portfolio, it's easy to see why his primary objective is to sustain an increase in your overall worth.

Of course, your professional money manager doesn't work alone. A brokerage firm processes your portfolio transactions. The brokerage firm or a designated custodian holds the securities. Your investment advisor, with whom you work to identify and select your professional money manager, oversees all of these activities for an all-inclusive fee, commonly referred to as an advisory fee. Professional money managers discount their fees to financial advisors, so the all-inclusive fee amounts to no more than what you would pay if you hired the manager on your own.

Because professional money managers aren't listed in newspapers like mutual funds, you track their progress using a monthly statement and confirmation of trades provided by the brokerage firm holding your securities. In addition, you have immediate access to your account on-line for up-to-date information on how

What should I expect from my money manager?

A manager with a clearly defined investment style and discipline
A manager who adheres to that style and discipline under all market conditions
A manager who outperforms the applicable benchmark over the long term
A manager with a commitment to timely and ongoing communication

What should I NOT expect from my money manager?

To make a profit on every investment
- some manager selections will decline in value and may be sold at a loss

To perform in-line with the market in every period
- styles fall in and out of favor
- performance should be measured over a reasonable time frame

To be in the top quartile of managers for every period
- no manager can be expected to to be in the top quartile every quarter

To change styles to perform at the top of each market
- managers are hired for a specific niche or investment style

Source: Robert Jorgensen

Figure 5.2 Steeting realistic expectations.

your money is invested and how those investments are performing. Bear in mind, however, that your IMA is a product for working toward your long-term financial goals and therefore requires measurement criteria beyond a daily check of account values (see Figure 5.2).

Enter the quarterly performance monitor, which I like to call the report card. This performance monitor is one of the best financial tools I've ever encountered in my two decades in the financial industry. It provides you with extensive, in-depth data with which to evaluate your progress, including year-to-date and quarterly percentage returns since inception, asset allocation, and comparisons against applicable benchmarks and indices.

The performance monitor (see Figure 5.3) is really the most

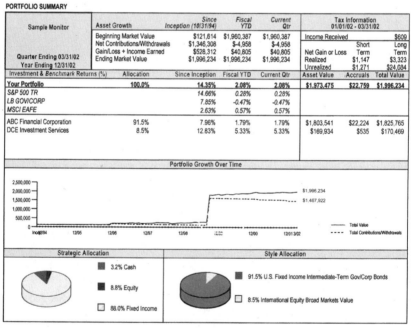

Figure 5.3 Sample performance monitor.

effective tool you have to measure how well your professional money manager is performing for you over time, the risk level he or she is maintaining, and whether or not he or she is bringing you closer to your objectives. This is far more valuable than statements issued by mutual funds, which disclose only how many fund shares you own and their value at the time of the report.

Expertise of any kind is a difficult commodity to define, although this particularly applies to professional money management. Anyone who generates good results over even a short period, either by applying various systems or perhaps even just plain luck, is often called an expert, especially by the financial trade media. While success is good, professional money managers do far more than inspire confidence with their methodology and short-term results.

Most managers readily explain their philosophies and their basic parameters for portfolio building. However, some screening practices and particularly technical methods are considered proprietary information. Many professional money managers apply sophisticated computer applications to help distinguish the most attractive opportunities from the tens of thousands of securities available. Other managers rely on old-fashioned, diligent research and company fundamentals to identify potential. Whatever the methodology, a professional money manager uses, you can be certain it aligns your interests with his toward achieving the most favorable outcome.

IN THE NEXT CHAPTER

Chapter 6 is one of the most important chapters in the book. Many readers will consider it the most challenging, and others will find it the most interesting. The subject is the nature of investment risk and how professional investors go about managing it. I will define risk and the types of risks as categorized by academics. I will discuss personal levels of risk tolerance and their relationship to each person's investment time horizon. I will conclude with a description of how investment risk is managed by professional money managers.

CHAPTER 6

The Reality of Managing Risk

Don't gamble; take all of your savings and buy some good stocks, and hold them until they go up, then sell them. If they don't go up don't buy them.

—Will Rogers

Investment manager and eminent financial historian Peter L. Bernstein states with his customary eloquence:

> Investing is a process of making decisions today whose results will not be known until tomorrow. Nobody knows what tomorrow will bring, because nobody can control everything that is going to happen tomorrow. The overarching reality, the launching pad from which investment theory takes off, is that being wrong on occasion is inescapable, even for people who are very smart. The subject matter of investment theory, then, is about why being wrong is inescapable and then about how best to manage our affairs in the face of that disagreeable reality.[1]

Bernstein's "disagreeable reality" describes investment risk perfectly. Another accepted definition of investment risk is the possibility that an asset will sell for less than the price at which it was purchased. The other most commonly accepted investment risk is the possibility of not being able to convert an asset back into cash in order to meet a financial obligation on time. This is the risk every defined-benefit pension manager keeps in the back of his or her mind.

You should consider risk in relative terms. An investment could be earning the highest return among several alternatives, but the probability of earning that greater rate is much less than the probability of earning lower rates of return among the other opportunities. In other words, the risk is greater. If you've ever been to the racetrack, you've been exposed to the logic of relative risk. The payoff from a 30-to-1 bet is fifteen times greater than the payoff from the 2-to-1 bet, but the probability of your winning the 2-to-1 bet is fifteen times better than winning the 30-to-1 bet. We'll discuss measuring risk in relative terms later in this chapter.

Risk tolerance varies greatly among investors, and among those who like the horse races. Typically, as an investor approaches retirement, tolerance for risk is low. Younger investors tend to accept higher degrees of risk because of their long-term financial horizons. A short-term loss is not as likely to affect your quality life if you aren't going to need your money right away. For those on a fixed-income, a short-term loss can have significant consequences.

The risk of any asset decreasing in value is a fact of life. Even United States Treasury securities, practically the most stable investment available, have some embedded risk. As interest rates fluctuate, the market value of any traded bond changes. If interest rates rise above the coupon rate of an existing treasury bond, the market value of that particular bond falls below its face value. And market value will vary until the bond matures.

As an investor interested in professional money management, understanding the different types of risk that IMA managers take is critical to your overall long-term success as an investor. Let's begin by understanding risk associated with individual securities. If you're an investor in common stocks, you need to understand their risk characteristics. The market value of any stock can be influenced by several factors besides the financial prospects of the company issuing the stock. These include overall economic condition, market capitalization, the amount of stock available in the market, financial prospects of other companies in the same industry, the consensus of opinion among investors of the company's future, and outright rumors. These conditions that affect stock value remind us that there are a lot of categories of risk we need to know about.

TYPES OF INVESTMENT RISK

William F. Sharpe earned the 1990 Nobel Prize in Economics for his work in analyzing investment portfolio risk. Sharpe assigned risk to one of two categories: systemic and unsystemic. *Systemic risk* is market related, and also called nonspecific risk. *Unsystemic risk* is specific to a single stock.

Nonspecific (Market) Risk

This risk entails the variation of a stock's market price due to overall market changes. These changes could be due to prevailing macroeconomic conditions, perceived or real threats to national security, a natural disaster, or investor consensus that the stock market is overvalued. You could also call many of these commonly encountered market risks *event risks*. A few people argue that some of these risks are predictable, but few could argue that they're controllable. You can't reduce market risk by changing the mix of your portfolio. Experience and informed investors have learned to live with nonspecific risk.

Specific Risk

There are risks specific to every stock, and they are typically founded on investor concerns and opinions about an issuing company's present and/or future financial health. Unlike market risk, you can reduce your specific (unsystemic) risk with a diverse portfolio of many different stocks. Scholars and investment professionals alike agree that diversification among several stocks affects the trade-off between risk and return.

As you've learned from the study on indexing, there are plenty of scholars and financial professionals who recommend a portfolio replicating an entire market as the best way to mitigate the risks of stock investing. They don't outright claim this will eliminate risk, although they do argue that indexing limits investors to a level of risk no higher than that faced by the overall market.

I've made no secret of my skepticism of index investing strategies, although I have no argument with diversification strategies. Consider two capricious hypothetical stocks. Say stock A's market price goes up when it snows and is lower when it's not snowing. Stock B's price goes up when weather is warm and is lower when it's snowing. So while one, in effect, is winning, the other is losing. The return from a portfolio that holds just these two stocks, bought at the same price, still depends on the weighted holdings between the two. But there's always some payoff. The risk of holding one stock is reduced by the reward of holding the other. Diversification has reduced (not eliminated) the overall risk of this two-stock portfolio. So the overall risk of a particular stock isn't as much of a concern as how it affects the overall risk of the portfolio.

The real challenge is picking the right stocks for your portfolio from the entire universe of available stocks, particularly when you have to account for differing degrees of risk tolerance among investors. All investment managers recognize that these differing degrees exist, whether they are professional money managers or mutual fund managers. While there may be agreement about their existence, professional money managers and mutual funds have dramatically different methods of dealing with the situation.

CONNECTING WITH INVESTORS

The distinction between professional money managers and mutual fund managers is one of connection with investors. It's all about relationship. As I've discussed, determining whether a particular mutual fund is right for your level of risk tolerance is all up to you to determine. You don't have the opportunity to sit down with the mutual fund manager to talk about it. Sure, there are some accepted measurements of the relative degree of risk a mutual fund manager undertakes (discussed later in this chapter), but you have to look up the ratings, and then verify and validate these measurements through outside sources. You definitely won't have any opportunity to visit the fund's managers.

Although professional money managers don't have time to visit with you either (after all, their job is to manage your money) you have far greater and timelier access to information as to how your money is being invested and managed in your personal portfolio. Additionally, your investment advisor often communicates directly with the money managers themselves. After you've identified your investment objectives and risk tolerance with your financial advisor, you're prepared to hire a professional money manager to oversee your personal IMA portfolio built with the express purpose of helping you attain your financial goals in the most effective manner. And unlike a mutual fund, you can access your holdings and track their performance with a few mouse clicks on your home computer.

Your Personal Risk Tolerance

When you examine your risk tolerance, the first thing a sharp financial advisor seeks to determine is which of two concerns overrides the other in your mind: a fear of being poor or a desire to be well off. You not only have to answer these questions for yourself, you have to take into account the mind-sets of your spouse, other family members, and anyone else who depends on you for some degree of financial support.

The experienced advisor takes this information further to determine how you (and anyone who depends on you) define "poor" and "well off." Have you candidly thought it through? And how do you go about meeting your needs and attaining your wants? A professional money manager can help you manage your money in a tax-efficient manner to make the most of what you have and earn. A mutual fund company, on the other hand, won't have the slightest concern about your personal financial strategies except in the most general of terms. Because you know how a mutual fund operates and is managed, you can see that its ability to meet your financial goals is largely coincidental to its operation.

Professional money managers use the information you personally determine with your financial advisor to manage a personal portfolio designed specifically around your expectations. The nature of professional money management businesses rests in providing you with complete information about your money, where it's invested, and how those investments are performing relative to meeting your needs. They also make certain you're aware of the crucial, although ambiguous, role time plays in your investment activities.

About Time and Risk

Professional money managers have all encountered prospective clients with unrealistic goals, mostly about what returns can be achieved over relatively short periods of time. And any respectable and reasonable money manager has declined to work for a client who wants to double an investment in a year. It happens, but mostly in fairy tales. Prudent money managers don't deal in fairy tales. They help you make the most of your money over time.

The Real Advantage of Long Time Horizons

Now, let's take a look at long-term investing. You might think that the longer you own a common stock, the smaller the chance of that stock selling for less than what you paid for it. That's just not true and that isn't what I've been saying.

Unless held to maturity, even U.S. Treasury bonds can incur a loss at some point over a long holding period, depending on interest rate risk, as discussed at the beginning of this chapter. Any asset can decrease in value at some point over any given period. Sure, there's a marked advantage to having longer time horizons in your investment plans, but a long-term investment plan doesn't reduce the risk of a decrease in value. The advantage of operating with a long-term mind-set provides you with more opportunities to decrease the likelihood of loss. Yes, the mutual fund manager and the independent money manager operate in the same market and encounter the same peril of investment loss (and job loss, for that matter). But, who's more likely to enjoy the flexibility and "wiggle room" benefits of a longer time horizon? The mutual fund manager operating in a highly structured, bureaucratic organization, or the professional money manager? Who's more likely to be pressured to meet redemptions by selling stocks from the portfolio? Who's more likely to take the time to be deliberate? That brings up the next risk you need to consider.

OPERATIONAL RISK

There's another kind of risk not normally considered in the context of investing. I'm talking about risk associated with the administrative activities undertaken by any organization, the risks incurred in operations.

Operations are a vital part of investment organizations. Consultant James T. Gleason cites the significant risk aspect of these activities in *Risk: The New Management Imperative in Finance*:

> Financial institutions require high levels of technical and operational support to deliver information and analysis to their traders, brokers, and lenders for structuring and pricing deals. The same high level of support, including computing and technology, is needed to follow through on the dealing, for example, to confirm, account for, settle, and manage the deals, and portfolios. Entities on the buy side require significant operational support as well.[2]

Gleason then goes on to talk about some huge losses from operational failures where "lax oversight was a key contributor."

When would you have the opportunity to talk with an officer of a mutual fund company about their oversight policies and procedures? Conversely, when you select a professional money manager, you can learn about operational procedures. It's all about accessible information. A professional money manager doesn't necessarily have better operational control than one would expect from a mutual fund company. That's not my point. I'm saying that if you have risk concerns about how your money is administered, a professional money management company is more readily able to provide this information to you or your financial advisor. There's always a bureaucracy of intermediaries between you and any mutual fund company. Just try getting hold of an operations executive of a mutual fund company by phone, letter, or e-mail. With a professional money manager overseeing your investments, you'll typically have only one intermediary between you and your manager, and that's your advisor.

Earlier in this chapter we discussed how to determine your risk tolerance. How do you determine how much risk an investment manager takes in the course of running a portfolio?

MEASURING INVESTMENT RISK

No experienced investor judges an asset or a portfolio by return on its own. One has to consider risk, because high returns are usually the result of taking a big risk (like betting on that 30-to-1 horse at the track). One way to think about risk is to consider how much the return for one year of a given investment differs from the average of a series of that investment's returns. Consider the annual rates of return over a five-year period for portfolios A and B in Table 6.1.

You can see that B is a riskier portfolio by looking beyond the arithmetic mean (average) of five years of returns. In those five years, the average rate of return on portfolio B varies significantly from that of any of its single year rates of return. In years 1, 3, and 5, the annual rates of return were well below 10 percent. If you exited from portfolio A at the end of year 3, your annual rate of return would be 9.97 percent. If you sold out of portfolio B at the end of year 3, your annual rate of return would have been 7.27 percent.

Volatility and Investment Risk

Looking at B's return pattern over five years, you can see significant differences between any two of the annual return rates, as well as between the average return of ten percent and any single year return. Which portfolio is more likely to have an annual rate

TABLE 6.1 Annual Ratres of Return

	Year 1	Year 2	Year 3	Year 4	Year 5	Average
Portfolio A	10.5%	9.75%	9.65%	10.85%	9.25%	10%
Portfolio B	5.0%	14.55%	2.25%	21.5%	6.7%	10%

of return close to ten percent in year 6? A's, of course. B's annual rates of return are more *volatile* than those of A. The most common definition of *volatile* is a *wide fluctuation* in market value over a given period. When experienced investors talk about fluctuation, they're talking about changes in value above and below the average value. Portfolio B is a good example of fluctuation of the yearly returns over a five-year period. This definition holds for a portfolio of securities, as well as for a single asset.

Beta

Over the years, some academics (including William F. Sharpe) have developed several methods of measuring relative risk among assets and portfolios. One of these involves assigning a "score" of returns volatility to a security (or a portfolio) relative to a designated market index, such as Standard & Poor's (S&P) 500. If the values of the security fluctuate in equal volatility to the values of the aggregate index, that security is assigned a score of 1. In other words, 1 means that the degree of value fluctuation for a security is neither more nor less than the degree of fluctuation in the value of the index. In theory, there is no greater or lesser risk in holding the security (or portfolio) than there is in holding the benchmark index. If the security/portfolio is assigned a score of less than 1, the inference is that the security is less risky than the benchmark index. A score higher than 1 implies that there is greater risk than the index.

What I'm calling a score is referred to as the *beta coefficient,* or more commonly as just *beta.* Professional money managers and mutual fund managers refer to the beta measurement all the time. So do organizations that rank and rate the performance of professional money managers and mutual fund managers. Beta is the most common measurement for assessing relative risk in the investment world.

TIME OUT FOR SOME MATH REVIEW

Beta is derived from an equation. All measurements of relative risk are derived from mathematics and statistics. Again, Peter L. Bernstein reminds us of this reality: "Without numbers, there are no odds and probabilities, without odds and probabilities, the only way to deal with risk is to appeal to the gods and fates. Without numbers, risk is wholly a matter of gut."[3]

Variance

In the investment world, the riskiness of an asset is commonly referred to as *variance*. Let me say it in another way: A degree of risk is determined by computing how much an asset's (or portfolio's) annualized rate of return is likely to *vary* from the average (mean) rate of its annualized returns. In the earlier example, portfolio B's variance is easy to see, because only five years of returns are measured.

You could even compute the average of the rates of return in your head. If the scores of years of returns were given, it wouldn't be as easy to determine the extent of how much riskier B is than A. There is a formula for calculating variance when a lot of annualized rates of return are known for a given asset:

1. Calculate the average (mean) rate of return.
2. Subtract each rate of return from the average rate.
3. Square each of the differences.
4. Add the squares of the differences.
5. Calculate the average from the sum of the square differences (see Table 6.2).

The higher the number derived from this five-step computation, the greater the variance. Think about that. The difference

TABLE 6.2 Calculating Variance

	Return	Average	Difference (Return–Average)	Squared (difference)
Portfolio A	10.5	10	0.5	0.250
	9.75	10	−0.25	0.063
	9.65	10	−0.35	0.123
	10.85	10	0.85	0.723
	9.25	10	0.75	0.563
Sum	50			1.722
Average	10			0.034 (variance)
Portfolio B	5.0	10.0	5.0	25.0
	14.55	10.0	4.5	20.25
	2.25	10.0	−7.75	60.06
	21.5	10.0	21.5	462.25
	6.7	10.0	−3.3	10.89
Sum	50			578.45
Average	10			115.69 (variance)

between the variances of asset A and asset B is 115.66. This is just simple mathematical confirmation of a common observation. Let's change portfolios A and B into people: acquaintance A and acquaintance B. Now think of B's differences in rates of returns as mood swings. B has a volatile personality. With whom would you rather take a month-long sailing excursion? A or B?

Standard Deviation

You've seen how a series of simple calculations are used to distinguish an asset's relative degrees of risk based on a series of annual returns. Computing variance is an acceptable method of measuring relative risk. But it doesn't provide us with a picture of a range (or band) around the mean return within which an asset's (or a portfolio's) annual returns are likely to be. We can get the picture of that probable range with one more step.

The square root of the variance provides the *standard* bandwidth within which the annual returns of a particular asset will *deviate* up and down from its mean returns. The *standard deviation* of the annual rates of returns for portfolio B is the square root of 115.67, or 10.75. For portfolio A, the square root of .034 is .184. It's also easier to compare the standard deviations of two assets, making the risk measurement easier to compute. B is about fifty-eight times more risky than A, (10.75 divided by .184). Again, we see a mathematical confirmation of a common-sense observation: *The wider the band of returns' fluctuations around the mean (its volatility), the riskier the asset is likely to be.*

A portfolio's standard deviation (SD) value that is higher relative to another stock doesn't mean that the stock with the higher SD is a worse investment relative to the other. It means only that the stock carries more risk, because it is more volatile.

Once you've computed the relative risks between alternative investment opportunities, you can move on to refining the measurement of risk and even to calculating beta. As a general rule, most professional advisors as well as consultants that work within the IMA industry prefer the use of standard deviation to best measure risk and volatility. [The Investment Management Consultants Association (IMCA) publishes an excellent book defining risk measurement techniques, and the method for calculating them. *The Consultant's Math Primer* can be ordered from IMCA at 9101 Kenyon Ave., Suite 3000, Denver, CO 80237.]

The Sharpe Ratio

Any discussion of investment risk is conducted in the context of investment return. People have always been curious about whether an investor who earned superior returns was smart or just took excess risk. William F. Sharpe turned his attention to this question and devised a simple formula to address this curiosity. He devised the *Sharpe ratio*. It is calculated by subtracting a risk-free rate of return (such as the return from a U.S. Treasury Bond) from the annualized rate of return from the investment and divided that difference by the standard deviation of the investment return.

Recall that the annualized rate of return for both portfolio examples A and B above was ten percent. Assuming a risk-free rate of four percent, the Sharpe ratio for portfolios A and B are computed:

A's Sharpe ratio: $10\% - 4\% = 6\%/.184 = .326$
B's Sharpe Ratio: $10\% - 4\% = 6\%/10.75 = .005$

Note that when you compare Sharpe ratio values, the value that is higher connotes that the investor has taken less risk. Not only do mutual fund and professional money managers monitor the risks they incur, they also use means to modify risk with common hedging strategies. Most of these strategies use risk management contracts commonly referred to as *derivatives*.

DERIVATIVES

There's a lot of misinformation and misunderstanding about using derivatives in managing investment risks. Sometimes referred to as "insurance" contracts, they get their name because they derive their value from the market prices of the underlying assets they insure. Derivative strategies are typically safe and cost-effective tools for reducing investment risks and are used by both mutual funds and professional money managers.

You've probably seen some of the highly publicized instances in which parties to derivative contracts have lost millions of dollars. The trouble in each of these instances was not with the derivative, but with people attempting to forecast future events. Believe what you will about fortune tellers, but they have no place in finance.

These people paid no regard to the odds or the likelihood that they could be wrong.

Prudent professional money managers or mutual fund managers would not stake their reputations and their portfolios on that level of risk. Financial professionals are in the business of managing risks, not taking them.

A Common Use of a Derivatives Contract

There's one common derivative risk management strategy applied to large- and mid-cap stock portfolios, which is selling a listed *call option* on a stock in the portfolio. A call option is a contract permitting the selling party of the contract to sell shares of a designated stock at a specified (strike) price within a prescribed period of time. Note the operative words *option* and *permitting*. The contract does not require the seller to sell the stock. The contract does require a buyer to take the stock at the specified strike price if it is offered by the selling party.

For example, a portfolio manager might enter into an option contract to sell a stock in the portfolio, which she thinks might decrease in value in the near future. Assume that the she bought the stock at $15 earlier in the year, and the stock is now trading at $20, clearly evidence of volatility. If its market price starts to decrease, it could quickly fall back to $15. The manager doesn't necessarily want to sell the stock, because its volatile characteristics could also lead to a rapid increase in market price. She could arrange to sell the stock only at a price above the price at which she bought. She could write a contract giving her the option to sell some or all of the shares of that stock at a specified strike price higher than $15 over the next six months. She would have to pay a relatively small price for the privilege of writing the contract, but she has bought the assurance that she can sell the stock without incurring a loss any time during the next six months.

This strategy is usually referred to as *writing a covered call.* "Covered" means that the seller (writer of the contract) owns the stock designated in the contract.

The scope of this book doesn't permit a more in-depth discussion of derivatives. There are hundreds of books and articles on the subject. The best nontechnical treatment is *Understanding Financial Derivatives: How to Protect Your Investments* by Donald Strassheim.[4]

IN THE NEXT CHAPTER

We've now studied how diversification is the most effective portfolio investment strategy for managing specific risk. There are many theories and opinions about the most effective mix of diversified securities for constructing an optimal investment strategy. In the next chapter we'll examine what people know, and what they *think* they know about investing and why they shouldn't try to go it alone.

NOTES

1. Peter L. Bernstein, ed., *The Portable MBA in Investment* (New York: John Wiley & Sons, 1995).
2. James T. Gleason, *Risk: The New Management Imperative in Finance* (Princeton, NJ: Bloomberg Press, 2000).
3. Peter L. Bernstein, *Against the Gods: The Remarkable Story of Risk* (New York: John Wiley & Sons, 1996).
4. Donald Strassheim, *Understanding Financial Derivatives: How to Protect Your Investments* (Burr Ridge, Illinois: Irwin McGraw-Hill, 1997).

CHAPTER 7

The Challenge of Asset Allocation

90% of the people in the stock market, professionals and amateurs alike, simply haven't done enough homework.
—William J. O'Neil

Diversification is crucial to the success of any investment plan, but remember that diversification only reduces risk. It doesn't eliminate risk. There have been times, most recently in the 1970s, during which investors experienced losses in bonds and stocks at the same time. High interest rates and inflation had a bad effect on both. Nevertheless, diversifying your assets is critical and requires your sustained thought and careful study.

Before I discuss allocation among diverse assets, let me list those assets and their respective categories. I do not include in this list any *tangible assets*, such as real estate, natural resources, collectables, or precious metals (see Table 7.1).

These asset classes differ from one another by their degree of risk relative to their return. The differences are shown in Figure 7.1. The values of the horizontal axis are returns and the vertical axis represents degrees of risk measured by standard deviation.

Asset allocation is simply the diversification of investments among stocks, bonds, and cash, as well as alternative investments.

Table 7.1 Assets and Their Categories

Cash Equivalents	Stocks*	Fixed-Income Investments	Alternative Investments
Currencies	Large-cap growth	U.S. Treasury bonds	Managed futures
Treasury bill	Large-cap value	Corporate bonds	Venture capital
Money market funds	Medium-cap growth	Agency bonds	Private securities
Certificates of deposit	Medium-cap value	Commercial paper	Hedge funds
	Small-cap growth	High-yield bonds	
	Small-cap value	Foreign government bonds	
	Micro-cap		
	Foreign stocks	Foreign corporate bonds	

*There are so many issues of common stocks from companies of all sizes that they are categorized by the market capitalization of their issuing companies: large caps (over $xxx in market capitalization), medium caps ($xxx–$xxx), small caps ($xxx–$xxx), and micro-caps (less than $xx). The returns of these different stocks do not correlate well in any given economics environment; therefore, they are considered as different asset classes and used in combinations to offset overall investment risk.

Asset allocation is the key element in personal financial planning. Asset allocation is easy to understand, although implementing an effective plan is easier said than done.

Risk Tolerance	Holding Period			
	1 year	5 years	10 years	30 years
Ultra-conservative (Minimum Risk)	7%	25%	41%	71%
Conservative	25%	42%	61%	90%
Moderate	50%	63%	86%	113%
Risk-taking	75%	77%	104%	131%

Source: "Stocks for the Long Run", Jeremy J. Siegel

Figure 7.1 Sample historical recommendation of stock allocation based on holding period.

DIFFERENT STROKES

The difficulty lies in your *investment time horizon* and your *level of risk tolerance,* which we studied in Chapter 5. The combination of these two factors marks the distinction between theory (the universally accepted principle that asset allocation is the appropriate approach to managing your money) and the practice of implementing asset allocation for you.

Older Investors

Investors who are retired, or within a few years of retiring, typically have a relatively short investment time horizon. They may have a moderately high level of risk tolerance, but their short time horizon dictates an investment strategy that focuses on preserving principal. Hence, their primary focus will be on an investment such as high-grade bonds. In doing so, they assume some interest rate risk. There could be an attendant decline in the market value of the bonds for a period, although that should not affect their overall portfolio because they aren't planning to sell the bonds. Their returns will come from interest and the compounding of that interest. Such investors have no particular need for a computerized asset allocation model created by a mutual fund company. What they need are experienced fixed-income professional money managers who can diversify two thirds of their assets among fixed-income portfolios that might include selected foreign bonds and bonds with differing maturities.

Note that I'm not suggesting that these investors forego putting some money into a stock portfolio. Failing to do so would mean missing out on some capital gains, and their attendant tax advantages. My years of experience in the investing world has lead me to be a staunch advocate of the intermediate- and long-term benefits of investing in common stocks. My point with respect to older investors is that their time horizon overrides their asset allocation strategy, because their primary goal is preservation of capital.

Young Professionals

Young professionals who have not yet started a family would be wise to consider investments heavily weighted in stocks. Stock returns consistently exceed bond returns over the long term (see Figure 6.2). Their portfolios should be diversified among stocks of different sized companies, as well as stocks of selected foreign companies. The weighting among these classifications depends solely on the investor's level of risk tolerance in attaining his or her financial goals. Bear in mind that I'm talking about weighting, not about excluding certain classes of stocks.

Such investors who have a low tolerance for risk would want to invest with a professional money manager who specializes in large company stocks that have a consistent record of paying dividends. If they are willing to incur a level of risk commensurate with that of the general stock market (represented by a broad market index), they could allocate fifteen to twenty percent of their investments to a manager who focuses on the stocks of small companies, fifteen to twenty percent with a manager who has a proven record with medium-sized companies, and the remainder with a large-cap manager. If such investors have a high degree of risk tolerance, they could have forty to fifty percent of their investments allocated among investment portfolios of small company stocks and stocks of selected foreign companies, which are those that show the greatest potential for growth, but also carry the highest degree of investment risk.

Established Professionals

Established professionals typically have numerous overlapping goals, two of which could be the intermediate-term objective of financing college educations for children, and building a retirement nest egg. In some ways, these investors are akin to their retired counterparts. The level of risk they are willing to tolerate is determined by their stage of life. Even those who have a high level of risk tolerance understand that they have assumed a lot of financial responsibility. They'll want the expertise of experienced fixed income and stock professional money managers to help them meet goals that don't share the same investment strategies.

Real Needs

These examples are typical of most common life cycle situations. There are, of course, several more (for example, widowhood and disability). To manage investments in the context of these situations requires specific personalized focus. Some financial advisors contend that mutual fund companies are well informed about all the aspects of asset allocation strategies for each individual investor's circumstances, based on models developed around the latest research conducted by professionals and academics.

I disagree. Off-the-shelf asset allocation strategies created by mutual fund companies are too generalized to apply effectively to the specific needs and goals of each investor, let alone yours. Their asset allocation models may coincide with some of your requirements, but there's no way all of their assumption will be appropriate for you.

THE ASSET ALLOCATION DIALOGUE AMONG PROFESSIONAL MONEY MANAGERS

Let's revisit the discussion of risk in Chapter 5. We studied how to compute the differing degrees of risk between assets A and B. Consider now two other assets, C and D. Asset C's market price goes up when it snows and is lower when it is not snowing. Asset

D's price goes up when the weather is warm, and its price is lower when it is snowing. Their values *co-vary* with the weather. The return from a portfolio that holds just these two stocks, bought at the same price, depends on the weighted holdings of the two, but there is always some payoff. The risk of holding one stock is reduced by the reward of holding the other. Diversification has reduced the overall risk of the portfolio. So it follows that the overall risk of a particular stock isn't as much of a concern as how it affects the overall risk of the portfolio.

The basis for asset allocation is diversification. The basis for diversification is this: Investing in a single stock is risky, but when that stock is combined in a portfolio of stocks with market values having a low correlation with that first stock, then that stock reduces the overall risk of the portfolio.

This also holds true for a collection of portfolios, each dedicated to a different investment style. A share in a portfolio of small-cap growth stock carries a considerable degree of investment risk. If the investor also holds an equal dollar amount of a portfolio of large-cap value stocks, the overall degree of risk is reduced. The operative word here is *reduced,* not eliminated.

Academics and financial professionals know that co-varying relationships, or low correlation of market values, reduce risk. This appears to be the only common area of agreement with respect to asset allocation.

The Asset Allocation Controversy

In 1986, a team of academics and investment managers conducted a controlled and focused study of the investment decisions made by ninety-one large pension plans.[1] They wanted to determine which area of oversight management had the greatest effect on a pension plan's investment portfolio: the actual securities held, market timing strategies, or the policy governing the type and weighting of securities held. At the end of the study, the team concluded that ninety percent of a portfolio's performance is determined by investment policy. Put another way, most of a portfolio's performance can be explained by the way in which the portfolio's assets are allocated. Many academics and professionals inferred that this meant that too much time was spent on picking investment managers, rather than concentrating on asset allocation strategies. In 1991, the study was repeated using a like number of different large pension plans. The findings were the same. The results of the studies remain controversial (see Figure 7.2).[2]

Apples and Oranges?

I've mentioned these studies (known as the Brinson-Beerbower studies) because they're often cited in the investment community. But just because they are often referred to doesn't make the design or implications of these studies any better understood.

When you think about it, it makes sense that results depend on how you decide to invest—that is, developing your personal investment policy. If you develop a policy that is right for your personal situation, you'll maintain a careful stewardship of your wealth. Again, your personal investment policy should be determined by your investment time horizon and your level of risk tolerance. With most investors, the time horizon is the dominant factor in developing a sound policy.

If a young professional built his or her policy with the same criteria as the older investor, she would be missing out on the historically well-documented higher returns that stocks achieve over bonds in the long run. They would have much less money at the end of 20 years if she only invested in bonds, regardless of how highly rated the bonds were or how high their compounded yields.

Were an older investor to put most of his money in stocks, he could experience a downturn in the equities markets over a couple of years, which could account for a greater percentage of his life

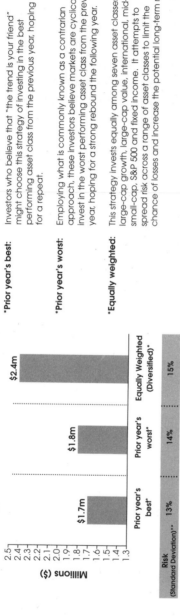

Diversification: Does It Really Work?
Growth of $60,000 invested annually: 1987-2001

*Prior year's best: Investors who believe that "the trend is your friend" might choose this strategy of investing in the best performing asset class from the previous year, hoping for a repeat.

*Prior year's worst: Employing what is commonly known as a contrarian approach, these investors believe markets are cyclical and invest in the worst performing asset class from the previous year, hoping for a strong rebound the following year.

*Equally weighted: This strategy invests equally among seven asset classes: large-cap growth, large-cap value, international, mid-cap, small-cap, S&P 500 and fixed income. It attempts to spread risk across a range of asset classes to limit the chance of losses and increase the potential long-term return.

Prior year's best: $1.7m, Risk (Standard Deviation) 13%
Prior year's worst: $1.8m, 14%
Equally Weighted (Diversified)*: $2.4m, 15%

**Standard Deviation (annual returns): *Standard deviation of returns measures the degree to which performance tends to vary from the mean of distribution. The greater the degree of dispersion, the greater the risk.*

The investment industry has a history of constantly selecting or switching to last years winners rather than adhering to a well designed program structured for long-term results.

Source: Harris Bretall Sullivan and Smith, L.L.C.

Figure 7.2 Asset allocation.

expectancy and severely affect his quality of life if he is using his money for income.

As you can see, your personal investment policy plays a critical role in how successfully you reach your investment goals. But does your policy really account for over ninety percent of your success (or failure)? The implications that proponents draw from the findings of the Brinson-Beerbower studies is that active strategies (stock picking) have been proved insignificant compared with the method you choose for asset allocation.

It's another spin on the indexing argument. If your personal circumstances dictate a heavy weighting in stocks, just buy some shares in a mutual fund that replicates a broad stock market index. If safety of principal is the driving force behind your investment strategy, invest in the appropriate mutual funds matched to a fixed-income benchmark.

But wait a minute! The subjects of the Brinson-Beerbower studies were large pension funds, not individuals. You can't overlook the considerable differences between huge pools of capital and the investment dollars of an individual. It is inappropriate to use these studies when developing asset allocation models for individuals.

To date, there have been no similar studies conducted of the impact of investment policy on private investors. All of the portfolios in the Brinson-Beerbower studies were huge and they were free of any tax obligations. Moreover, every fund had the same objective, which was to manage its assets in order to meet specific future pension obligations. There are as many combinations of investment time horizons and levels of risk tolerances as there are individual investors. Not only that, investment opportunities change over time. And so do your situations. You can't rely on cookie cutter strategies to meet your specific needs. A mutual fund manager isn't focused on:

1. your investment time horizon
2. your level of risk tolerance

3. your occupation
4. your present income
5. your future earnings prospects
6. your personal tax exposure
7. your marital status
8. the size of your family
9. your retirement plans

I won't dispute the importance of your personal investment policy to your overall investment success, but you shouldn't think that it's a ninety percent preponderant factor. As we've already learned, you'll need more than indexed portfolios to make the most of your money. I intend to talk about asset allocation again when I talk about the three investment traps in the next chapter.

IN THE NEXT CHAPTER

I believe that investors need the services of professional money managers. In the next chapter, I'll tell you about the inherent risks you face as an investor, how to determine your risk tolerance, and how you can achieve more with a professional money manager than by attempting to manage your own investments.

NOTES

1. Gary Brinson, Randolph Hood, and Gilbert Beerbower, "Determinants of Portfolio Performance," *Financial Analysts Journal* (July–August 1986).
2. Gary Brinson, Brian Singer, and Gilbert Beerbower, "Determinants of Portfolio Performance II: An Update," *Financial Analysts Journal* (May–June 1991).

CHAPTER 8

The Folly of Self-Investing

In modern business it is not the crook who is to be feared most,
it is the honest man who doesn't know what he is doing.
— William Wordsworth

By now, you should have a good understanding of why mutual funds are not the most effective vehicles for high-net-worth investors. However, I'm not saying you should attempt to take total control of how your investment dollars are allocated, unless you are a professional money manager yourself.

Yes, you should be the final determining factor of your investment policy, although by no means the only factor. I encourage you to periodically revisit and revise your policy, based on the nine factors listed at the close of Chapter 6. Throughout this book I've been stressing the importance of you having control over those to whom you entrust your money. But I haven't been implying that you should attempt to take charge of the investment process on your own. In all likelihood, you haven't time to do so and you don't have the necessary training and experience.

You know you're responsible for maintaining your health with proper diet, exercise, and a good balance of work, family, and leisure pursuits. But that doesn't mean you should try to be your own doctor. Allow me to take the analogy a bit further. With respect to choosing a doctor, you want to select one capable not only of diagnosis and treatment; you want someone who uses his or her education and years of experience to actively look after your well-being. The same criteria apply to a professional money manager when it comes to your fiscal health.

If I still haven't convinced you that you shouldn't be your own financial doctor, let me ask you this: If something were to happen to you, are you comfortable that all of your investments would be professionally managed to the advantage of your beneficiaries?

ESSENTIAL QUALITIES TO LOOK FOR IN AN INVESTMENT PROFESSIONAL

Three crucial qualities distinguish a successful professional: training, first-hand experience, and judgment. You've very likely recognized this yourself over the course of your career and possess these traits in your respective field. But how effective are your skills when applied to a discipline that isn't your area of expertise? Put it this way. If you were the CEO of a highly successful technology firm, would you want a medical doctor to fill in for you while you're on vacation? Would you feel confident in determining whether surgery or medication is the best course of treatment for someone?

Training

Chapter 7 opened with a quote from the eminent financial historian Peter L. Bernstein, which said, in part "The subject matter of investment theory . . . is about why being wrong is inescapable, and then about how best to manage our affairs in the face of that disagreeable reality." Managing money "in the face of that disagreeable reality" requires considerable formal and continuing education administered by reputable associations of investment professionals.

Someone who aspires to a successful career in finance needs to have studied and mastered the operation of global economics, structures of capital markets and financial institutions, fundamentals of corporate finance, principles of accounting, and, most importantly, the statistical analysis of data. Many successful investment managers didn't major in finance as undergraduates, having earned degrees in mathematically based programs such as engineering, physics, or computer science. They've learned economic and financial disciplines through an MBA program, or within a professional association's certification program.

Every bit as important to the development of competent investment professionals is hands-on industry training. Their first employers will train them on policy, procedures, and, most importantly, regulatory compliance practices governing investment management. In addition to company training programs are numerous professional investment associations. Each of these associations offers certification programs requiring completion of a succession of rigorous courses in the practical aspects of securities analysis, regulatory practices, taxes, and asset allocation. Appendix A describes the most common certification programs, the designations they confer, and the sponsoring associations, which award the respective designations.

Anyone who manages investment portfolios of any significant amount is legally required to be registered in the states in which he or she does business. To be so registered requires demonstrating thorough knowledge of generally accepted investment practices as well as federal and state regulations governing investment management. You should be aware that there are plenty of successful, registered investment managers without formal financial educations or a professional designation who are qualified for registration in every state in which they want to do business. This is not to say they aren't very good at what they do. They have attained their knowledge for qualifying to practice by an intensive program of disciplined self-education. They've also learned from years of hands-on experience and professional mentoring.

You want to make sure your professional investment manager knows his trade inside and out. Don't be too quick to dismiss someone who doesn't have a long line of designations following his name on his business card. Next to integrity, I believe experience is the most important attribute a professional money manager can possess.

Experience

Professional money managers are not typically employees of major financial institutions, although they most likely gained their initial investment management experience with one. They started off under the close supervision and mentoring of experienced money managers and thereby learned how to work in the real world of imprecision and fluctuating values, a considerably different environment from the armchair investment world of financial magazines and television.

The true measurement of *relevant* experience is whether or not the professional money manager has controlled money *over the course of several different market cycles.* When I talk about market cycles, I'm not referring to just the U.S. securities markets. You don't want to pick a professional money manager based solely on his record of incredible successes, either. You want a manager who has experienced the market slide at the beginning of the twenty-first century, the global disruption in 1987, the turmoil of the bond markets in 1995, and the blow-up of Japanese and emerging company stocks in the mid-1990s. A manager's mettle is measured by how he's performed in good and bad markets.

The experienced professional manager knows two things for certain:

1. A dramatic rise or fall of any asset class doesn't mean that the value of that asset class won't change over time.
2. The collective actions of investors don't always drive markets to fair values. There will always be times when investors price assets away from their objectively measured intrinsic worth. The educated and experienced professional money manager is best able to discern when those times are prevalent.

Judgment

Let's revisit Peter L. Bernstein: "being wrong on occasion is inescapable." Professional money managers accept this as true about all investors, including themselves. Accepting this heightens self-awareness and adds a healthy sense of skepticism about various "expert" opinions. For example:

1. How can asset allocation decisions account for ninety percent of a portfolio's performance?
2. What real evidence is there that markets are efficient or inefficient?
3. Does or doesn't historical data reveal anything about future performance?
4. Do all values really revert to a mean?
5. What are the real degrees of co-variance among different assets?
6. How did someone come to his or her investment assumptions?

Please note that this is a healthy level of skepticism, not cynicism. Skepticism is a natural ingredient of judgment, deliberation, verification, and empathy with investor desires.

Trained, experienced, and judicious money managers are as

necessary to your fiscal health as a trained, experienced, and judicious physician is to your physical health.

WHAT YOU THINK YOU KNOW *CAN* HURT YOU

How do I know individual investors shouldn't attempt to go it alone with respect to their money? Investors consistently react with emotion when it comes to their own money, especially during volatile markets. I've met more people than I can count during my career with stories of how they chased stocks in up markets and jumped ship during downturns, all the while losing their money while trying to time the next market move. As a financial professional, I'll let you in on a little trade secret. Some of us actually like down markets. That's because it's during downtimes that professional money managers seek and find some of the best opportunities.

THREE INVESTMENT TRAPS

Superlatives can't adequately describe the dramatic appreciation in stock prices over the past two decades, even during periods of volatility and uncertainty. Yet, while the market environment has proved its worth as a tool for achieving financial goals, it still amazes me how many investors fall short. Picking the wrong investments is the easy explanation for underperformance. In my experience, though, it's the method of choosing these investments that's more to blame.

Three primary pitfalls catch investors unawares and rob them of untold billions of dollars in returns each year. The bait is the false promise of big returns, and the appeal is strong.

Chasing the "Hot" Stock or Fund

Past performance is a highly unreliable way of measuring the future return of stocks and/or funds. Even so, past performance is typically the number one criterion that people look for in an investment. Thousands of investors base their entire investment strategy on finding the stock or mutual fund with the highest returns. These are the investments that get the most press attention. But by the time investors learn about these investments and actually put their money down, these hot performers are yesterday's news.

Unfortunately, almost every investment is marketed, at least partially, on the way it has performed in the past. So what can you learn from these statistics?

Past performance is increasingly relevant as a measure of value over the long term. In other words, a trend playing out over the past thirty years is credible. Information covering only the past five years isn't statistically valid for making inferences. As might be expected, however, less reliable, short-term information is often used to pique an investor's interest in a particular security. Remember that future performance cannot be predicted from short-term, past performance.

There is another consequence of investors pouring into a "hot" mutual fund after it has posted great returns over a recent short term. The manager of that fund suddenly finds himself confronted with more cash than he can invest within his style or within sectors that he has analyzed in depth. He finds himself forced to invest with less prudence. An inevitable result is that he accumulates stocks that will not perform as well as those he previously bought. The weight of these underperforming stocks diminish the fund's overall return, hence driving down the fund's net asset value.

Market Timing

"Buy low and sell high" is one of the most infamous gems of advice for how to make money on the stock market. After all, anybody can understand that, and many people try to do just that, but don't forget that adage about some things being easier said than done. Market timers attempt to identify a proven analytical process with which to make money through a continual process of short-term gains. They stake their money on an economic or company indicator that tells them when to buy or sell. Acting on these indicators results in numerous transactions, which generate proportionately high trading costs. These transactions can also create significant tax complexities and liabilities. Almost invariably, investors who try to time the market end up trapped in a reverse cycle of selling after big slides and buying when stocks are at their most expensive.

Market timers are more likely to miss or misjudge their cues than to get them right. We've all heard stories about the extraordinary success of a day-trader who made millions and then lost it all in less than a year's time. Of course, there's no explanation as to how the trader's process could have both worked and failed. Most likely, the cue or clue was based on a market anomaly, which didn't prove out over even an intermediate term, let lone the long term.

As I discussed earlier, there's been a phenomenal increase of newsletters, websites, and investment advisory firms that specialize in day-trading. During my two decades in the financial industry, I've yet to meet a day-trader who over a five-year period has outperformed any professional money manager. Investors who trade frequently typically underperform their benchmarks by an average of twelve percent per year. Another fundamental concept I hope you take away from this book is this simple tenet: *If you try to time the market, it will always tell you it's time to get out.*

What do I mean by this? Just look at the past twenty years

of market history. Joe Granville, one of the most respected and well-known investment gurus of his time, said in 1982 that the Dow Jones Industrial Average would experience a dramatic decline and would retreat back to a level of 100 points. His opinion caused one of the biggest one-day drop in history, based solely on emotional reaction to his expert opinion. The next day, the Dow commenced a two-decade climb, passing 1,000 points in 1982 and continuing to average 13.6 percent per year in real returns (after inflation) through the year 2000.

Why can't market timers succeed beyond the short-term? In short, because the market is not composed of merely a few people trading a limited number of securities in one country. The market is the sum total of every good and bad idea, every currency move and earnings report, every hiring and firing, every political development and natural occurrence. Every publicly traded security around the world is affected differently by random events. For example, a drop in the price of oil will move the prices of oil stocks down while boosting the price of airline stocks.

What can you conclude about predicting the direction of the market? Simply this: If you try to predict the market, you'll fail to make the most of your money. The professional money manager recognizes that the ultimate financial folly is to attempt to time the market. There is only one market prediction I've found to be always correct all of the time: *Trying to time transactions based on a system of market timing will cost you any lasting gains you could make with your assets. Guaranteed.*

If you won't take my guarantee, look at Figure 8.1 which shows what could have happened to a market timer during the five-year period ending December 31, 2001. If he had invested a hypothetical $1 million in the Standard & Poor's (S&P) 500 on December 31, 1996, and *kept it invested,* that $1 million would have grown to $1,627,500, a mean annual return of 10.23 percent. But what would have happened during that five-year period if he had decided to pull out of the market for a while, and then get back in. As a result of doing that, he could have missed the market's ten best single-day performances. If that was the case, his mean annual return would have been 1.12 percent. Figure 8.1 shows what a disaster he could have brought down on himself if he had missed the twenty, thirty, or forty best single-day performances.

Faulty Asset Allocation

Again, diversification is crucial to any prudent investment plan. You'll be hard pressed to find a financial professional who will debate this point. As discussed in Chapter 7, diversification is achieved with asset allocation, a strategy intended to reduce exposure to market volatility by composing a portfolio of different types of securities appropriate to an investor's time horizon and level of risk tolerance.

    I am going to repeat myself, to reinforce the point I made

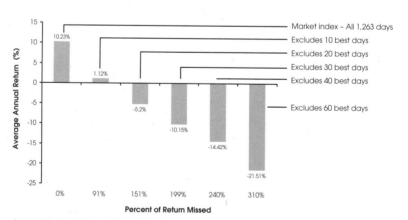

S & P 500 Index: 5 Years Ending Dec. 31, 2001

Source: Harris Bretall Sullivan and Smith, L.L.C.

Figure 8.1   The cost of market timing.

earlier. The trouble with asset allocation lies not in the theory, but in the application. Many financial consultants use the concept of asset allocation as an expedient sales tactic, supported by computer programs that generate "appropriately optimized" asset mixes for the customer. There is a high degree of risk that this cookie cutter strategy will reduce returns. Typical asset allocation programs lean toward conservative portfolios, *regardless of an investor's time horizon or level of risk tolerance.*

James Owens, a long-time friend and business associate whose career spans both the financial consultant and professional money management sides of the investment business, gave me a memorable anecdote of the downside of faulty asset allocation:

> I once met a consultant who had invested personal assets for a group of 1,000 doctors. We spent a lot of time discussing Modern Portfolio Theory and I could sense he was becoming increasingly uncomfortable. Eventually, I questioned him about his unease and he told me that while the market had been climbing an average of 15% per year, his portfolio had only been growing at 7%. He stressed that he had applied the classic allocation models outlined by Modern Portfolio Theory, though they had proved ineffective for managing his clients' money. He never understood that one cannot apply asset allocation across the board and expect to succeed. The secret to effective asset allocation is creating the ideal plan for each individual investor.

You need to have your investments diversified based on your goals, risk tolerance, tax situation, and age. However, I believe you can afford to be less conservative with your stock allocation—by as much as twenty percent. The only investors who can't afford to be less conservative are those who have a very short time horizon, a horizon usually shortened by some concern about their life expectancy. Stocks are subject to short-term volatility. But when one examines the long-term record, a consistent pattern of steady growth is apparent, even throughout the Great Depression of the 1930s and periods of correction and volatility that followed. The steady rise and fall pattern blends into a consistent long-term climb.

Frightened Away

That almost all investors sell during downturns has always fascinated me. Professional money managers know that those are the times to shop for bargains. When your favorite quality retailers hold sales and mark quality merchandise down by twenty-five percent or more, you rush to buy, right? You take advantage of the opportunity to buy quality items, made by well-known manufacturers, at bargain prices. Yet, when prices drop twenty-five percent on the stocks of sound companies with positive earnings, you're tempted to rush out of the securities markets, and you're not alone.

Remember the older investors from Chapter seven? They're going to have a hard time maintaining their objectivity when markets are volatile. It will always be frightening for them to see their stocks fall by as much as ten to twenty-five percent in value over a short period. If they're doing their own investing, they are statistically most likely to sell before they lose too much. When markets drop, investors viscerally feel their net worth falling and tend to sell out after the bad news. But by the time the bad news has arrived, it's too late. The market has flattened or is nearing bottom. This is absolutely the worst time to sell. In fact, if you were to find yourself in a like position and have available cash, I'd recommend this as the best time to buy. Get what you want while there's a markdown.

The same holds for market upturns. By the time the good news arrives, everyone knows about it already and you'll have to buy at a higher price. Investors who are still stinging from a previous decline may be hesitant to reenter the market upswing and miss out on even more good buying opportunities.

You can be sure the professional money manager is maintaining the holdings he's managing throughout a downturn, if not outright buying more securities at bargain rates. When the market rallies, these positions are already in the portfolio and increase in overall value. It's important to remember that a market downturn is important only if you're liquidating your portfolio on that particular day. Training, experience, and judgment have conditioned the professional to objectively analyze company fundamentals and assess market conditions. Some might argue that money managers aren't dealing with their own money, so that's why they are unemotional about their decision-making. But remember, fee-based professional money managers are compensated based on how well your portfolio is doing. So your best interests are also their best interests (see Figure 8.2).

Trusting in the Theories

With investing, as with all other disciplines, a little bit of knowledge can be a dangerous thing. Early in this chapter, I made the point that neither training, nor experience, nor judgment is suf-

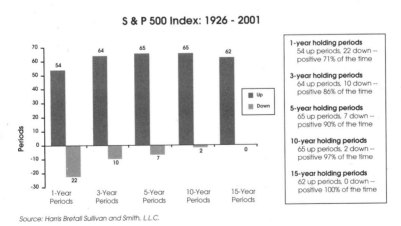

S & P 500 Index: 1926 - 2001

1-year holding periods
54 up periods, 22 down --
positive 71% of the time

3-year holding periods
64 up periods, 10 down --
positive 86% of the time

5-year holding periods
65 up periods, 7 down --
positive 90% of the time

10-year holding periods
65 up periods, 2 down --
positive 97% of the time

15-year holding periods
62 up periods, 0 down --
positive 100% of the time

Source: Harris Bretall Sullivan and Smith, L.L.C.

Figure 8.2 Historical benefits: the benefit of time.

ficient for successful investing. Perhaps you've taken some financial courses or have attended seminars conducted by credentialed professionals. Do those experiences qualify you to manage your own investment program? Only if you're already a financial professional. Otherwise, I say most emphatically, no!

The educational aspect of training is not only insufficient by itself, it can prove detrimental to successful investing. Remember again Peter L. Bernstein: "The overarching reality, the launching pad from which investment theory takes off, is that being wrong on occasion is inescapable, even for people who are very smart."

Recent investment theories and studies have provided firm foundations for further study into market behavior, structure, and costs. But to apply only the observations and deductions from these studies and theories to developing a successful long-term asset-enhancing program is fanciful at best. Recall our discussion of the highly respected Brinson and Beerbower studies from Chapter 7. Implementing an asset allocation program for an individual based on the results of those studies alone could be considered malfeasance.

Is the market so efficient that we should accept presently prevailing price-to-earnings ratios and other fundamental measures as infallible guides to managing portfolios? Please. Can education and training satisfactorily address the issues raised by the six questions posed earlier in this chapter without the added calculus of experience and judgment? Of course not (see Figure 8.3).

CONCLUSION

To put things bluntly, you haven't the time, background, or temperament to successfully manage your own investments. And you know by now that the pitfalls of commission-based investments,

1926	Joseph Stalin ruled as dictator of USSR
1927	German economy collapsed
1928	"Roaring Twenties" pushed stock market to new highs
1929	"Black Tuesday" – stock market crashed
1930	Hawley-Smoot Tariff Act
1931	Unemployment rate soared; U.S. banks collapsed
1932	Dow hit Depression-era low
1933	Hitler named German chancellor – Nazi terror began
1934	Depression continued
1935	Labor Union strikes
1936	Spanish Civil War began
1937	Recession
1938	Hitler annexed Austria
1939	World War II began
1940	Fall of France
1941	Japanese attacked Pearl Harbor
1942	Price controls initiated – shortage of consumer goods
1943	Detroit race riots
1944	D-Day – Allied forces invaded Normandy
1945	Post-war recession predicted
1946	Cold War began
1947	"Red Scare" revisited
1948	Berlin blockade
1949	USSR detonated atomic bomb
1950	Korean War began
1951	Excess income and profits tax
1952	Steel labor dispute – U.S. seized mills
1953	USSR detonated hydrogen bomb
1954	Stock market reached new highs
1955	President Eisenhower suffered heart attack
1956	Suez Canal crisis
1957	USSR launched Sputnik satellite
1958	Recession
1959	Castro became dictator of Cuba
1960	USSR shot down U-2 spy plane
1961	Berlin Wall built
1962	Cuban missile crisis
1963	President Kennedy assassination
1964	Gulf of Tonkin resolution
1965	Civil rights demonstration
1966	Vietnam War escalated
1967	Six-Day War in Middle East
1968	Martin Luther King, Jr. assassination
1969	Money tightened – stock market declined
1970	U.S. invaded Cambodia
1971	Wage-price freeze
1972	Watergate scandal began
1973	Arab oil embargo – oil prices tripled
1974	President Nixon resigned from office
1975	Fall of Saigon
1976	Economy still struggled
1977	Stock market slumped
1978	Interest rates rose
1979	Iran hostage crisis – oil prices skyrocketed
1980	Hunt brothers silver market crisis
1981	Interest rates remain elevated
1982	Worst recession in 40 years
1983	U.S. invaded Grenada
1984	AIDS virus identified
1985	Economic growth slowed
1986	U.S. bombed Libya; Iran-Contra affair broke
1987	"Black Monday" – stock market crashed
1988	U.S. Savings & Loan crisis peaked
1989	U.S. invaded Panama
1990	Persian Gulf War
1991	Global recession
1992	ERM U.K. currency crisis
1993	Great Midwest floods in U.S.
1994	Mexican Peso collapsed
1995	Oklahoma City bombing
1996	Fed Chairman Greenspan warned of "irrational exuberance"
1997	Asian financial crisis
1998	Russian default/LTCM crisis; White House sex scandal
1999	Y2K fears; Dow reached 11,000 for first time
2000	Money tightened – Dot-com bubble burst
2001	World Trade Center / Pentagon terrorist attacks
2002	Accounting scandals

Meanwhile, the S&P 500 Index had an annual compounded return of 10.6% (through 9/30/2001).
A hypothetical $10,000 investment made in 1/1/1926 would have been worth $22,559,775 on 9/30/2001.

Figure 8.3 77 reasons investors avoided the stock market.

Source: Harris Bretall Sullivan and Smith, L.L.C.

such as mutual funds, will prevent you from maximizing your tax efficiency, thereby helping you make and keep the most of your money. The professionally managed IMA is clearly the most effective tool for protecting and enhancing your wealth.

In the chapters that follow, I will address the structures, policies, and practices of some of the most respected and accomplished professional money managers in the financial industry. But first I will give you some insights as to how real investors have used IMAs to improve their overall portfolios.

IN THE NEXT CHAPTER

In the next chapter, I apply what we have discussed in Chapters 5 through 8 to a discussion of working with your investment advisor in selecting and monitoring investment managers. The point of departure for this discussion is the development of your *investment policy statement*. Chapter 9 is the most prescriptive chapter in the book. The descriptions, policies, practices, and procedures prescribed in Chapter 9 are based on my twenty years of experience as an investment consultant, and as a certified investment management consultant.

Managing Your Investment Managers: The Process of Investment Management Consulting

Alone we can do so little, together we can do so much.
—Helen Keller

Now that we've discussed how money managers work, different types and styles, and how to evaluate their risk versus return quotients, we will now turn to what you do once you engage the services of one or more managers for your family or business. Many investors presume all the work is behind them once they have laid out their guidelines, interviewed some managers, and engaged their services. But this is when the real work begins. And I do mean work! Ideally, after you've read this chapter, you'll have a thorough appreciation of all the different elements involved in monitoring a portfolio of asset managers, and you'll begin to understand my emphasis on using the services of an investment advisor who specializes in working with money management firms over trying to do everything yourself.

FIRST THINGS FIRST: THE INVESTMENT POLICY STATEMENT

A sensible man never embarks on an enterprise until he can see his way clear to the end of it.

—Aesop

An investment policy statement (IPS) is a written document that sets forth the overall plan for your investment portfolio. The IPS is written to cover not just your managed accounts or mutual funds, it incorporates all of your liquid investment assets, and in many cases your illiquid investments such as real estate. The IPS is important for any family or its trust, and becomes a requirement when we are dealing with any kind of retirement plan, such as a pension plan or profit sharing plan [Employee Retirement Insurance and Security Act of 1974 (ERISA) type plan].

In the world of professional asset management, it is generally viewed that if you do not have an IPS for your portfolio, then you don't have a "plan for your investments." Putting it another way, *if you fail to plan, you plan to fail.*

Even if your portfolio at this particular time is relatively small, it is important for you to develop an IPS. Otherwise, your investments become a loose aggregation of incohesive ideas that may cause your portfolio to suffer.

If you've been investing for many years and have never developed an IPS, don't panic. Over fifteen years of consulting, among literally hundreds of portfolios, many of which were substantial retirement plans, I found as a general rule that fewer than ten percent had an effective IPS in place before I was engaged as the consultant. An IPS is easy to develop once you have a blueprint (see Appendix C) and any competent investment advisor can help you develop one specifically suited to your financial objectives.

Let's discuss some of the key components that we generally like to see in a well-developed IPS:

1. *Performance objectives for your portfolio.* What is the overall investment return you are seeking over a full market cycle? Are you trying to earn an absolute return of ten percent annually or are you interested in relative performance of inflation plus five percent annually? (Note: A full market cycle is typically a minimum of five years, but can be measured for as long as seven to ten years, depending on how the money will be used.)
2. *Cash flow requirements.* Do you need your portfolio to produce income immediately or in the near future for retirement? If so, how much income do you need and how often?
3. *How much risk or volatility are you willing to accept?* Are you willing to accept market risk [generally viewed as tracking the same volatility as being 100 percent invested in the U.S. stock market as represented by the Standard & Poor's (S&P) 500]? Do you wish for your investments to have twenty-five percent less risk than the market or maybe fifty percent less risk than the market? (Note: This is probably the most important question to answer when you are developing your IPS. How you answer this question and define your comfort with risk and volatility will ultimately define your asset allocation and overall selection of IMA money managers.)
4. *Statement of responsibilities* (your role, your advisor's role, the role of your custodian or trustee, the role of your manager or managers, and so forth). We often call this area the identification of fiduciaries or responsible parties.
5. *Investment classes to be used* (equities, bonds, cash, real estate, I-shares, hedge funds, and so forth).
6. *What type of investments will not be included?* Generally there are restrictions for short selling, precious metals, private placements, and so forth.
7. *What specific qualifications must IMA managers or funds*

have in order to qualify to manage money in your port-folio?

- Size: Do they need to be managing a minimum of $500 million in assets?
- Track record: I recommend a minimum of three years, but five years or longer is best.
- Process: What is the manager's process for selecting securities?

8. *Communications.* How often should your advisor and/or money manager communicate with you? Quarterly is the minimum. Each client is different.

9. *Should you meet with your advisor quarterly in person (ideal for larger portfolios) or is semiannually enough?* Should you be able to speak to or meet with your IMA manager (usually only available when accounts are over $5 million)?

10. *Diversification.* How diversified should your portfolio be between equities, bonds, and cash? How about between investment styles, such as large growth, large value, inter-national, small cap growth, and so forth? What are the percentage allocations for each investment class and each investment style? (Note: Often a range may be used here, such as that equities shall be maintained between seventy and eighty percent, or that large value stocks shall account for no less than twenty-five percent and no more than forty percent for the life of the portfolio.)

11. *Performance measurement.* Which relative benchmarks will be utilized for each manager (e.g., Russell 1000 Growth Index for your large-cap growth manager). What is the benchmark blend that will be used for the entire portfolio (e.g., thirty percent Russell 1000 Growth/thirty percent Russell 2000 Small Value/twenty percent Global Value/ten percent Lehman Government Bond Index/ten percent money market)? (Note: These benchmarks are easily

tracked for each manager or fund and for your entire portfolio, not only since inception, but quarterly and year-to-date, and are generally available on-line.)

12. *Guidelines for manager termination.* Define very specifically what the managers need to know in regard to why and in what time frame they might be terminated. Can a manager be terminated for falling outside the stated investment style? For example, a manager who has agreed to a small-cap growth strategy investing in large-cap value securities for your portfolio. How about if a manager invests more than forty percent in one industry sector, such as health care, even though he or she has clearly agreed to never invest more than twenty percent within one industry? What if a manager buys twenty-five percent of a single security, even though he or she clearly committed to remaining fully diversified with never more than ten percent held in a single security? Should you fire a manager for missing the investment benchmark by five percent for a quarter, a year, or annualized over three years? How about volatility? If you engaged an investment manager because you thought he was risk adverse and you discovered that the manager was taking risk twice that of the S&P 500, should you fire him?

13. *General administration issues.* Where will assets be held? Is a trustee required? Is there an investment committee of one or many? Who will vote stock proxies (generally the manager performs this duty)? What are the annual fees for the manager, the advisor, the custodian, and others?

A well-defined IPS helps you to assess your financial, business, and personal investment characteristics, enabling you to take stock of what you are trying to accomplish with your funds over a set period. You will also help yourself tremendously by creating objective guidelines to help you at critical times when perhaps your emotions may tempt you to react against your best interests during a market decline. The IPS helps your advisor and your manager understand exactly how their respective performances will be evaluated, and how communication should occur between all parties.

An IPS is a dynamic document. As your life changes, so will your goals. Your goals could change due to receiving an inheritance. Perhaps you'll have to make a large distribution from your retirement plan. Whatever the reason may be, your IPS should be reviewed with your financial advisor at least annually. Any significant changes should be communicated to your portfolio managers in writing so they may make any revisions as necessary.

I realize this section may seem a little complicated if you've never undergone this procedure before, but I cannot emphasize strongly enough how crucial a well-planned IPS is to your overall financial success in terms of attaining your retirement goals, paying for college educations, or generating funds for a vacation home. Developing an effective IPS will help you attain your long-term financial freedom (see Figure 9.1).

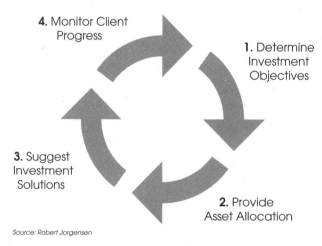

Source: Robert Jorgensen

Figure 9.1   Investment management process.

> *RJ's Investment Insight:* After all is said and done, the best way to develop an effective IPS is to work with a good investment advisor who has the background and experience to help you create a customized plan that fits your overall objectives. I would not rely on my own expertise to draw up my own will or trust—I would hire an attorney. The same applies to an IPS. Unless you are a professional investment advisor yourself, you need to hire a professional to help you draft your plan.

THE NEXT STEP: DEVELOPING AN INVESTMENT PHILOSOPHY

Philosophy goes no further than probabilities, and in every assertion keeps doubt in reserve.

—Froude

An IPS is not a contract, but a document that articulates an investment philosophy providing guidance for you, your investment advisor, and your money manager as to how your assets should be managed. Since it is not a contract, it is typically reviewed only by the client and the investment advisor. The IPS reflects your current status and philosophy regarding how your portfolio should be invested. Numerous elements comprise an effective IPS:

1. *Asset allocation.* How is this very important decision derived? As discussed in Chapter 6, modern portfolio theory has changed the investment landscape across all investments, not just IMAs. Deciding whether to utilize Modern Portfolio Theory (MPT) software, prepackaged asset allocation models, or develop your own strategy may all get the job done, although you must remember that this deci-

sion will effect your returns far more than any other decision you make. Make sure you are comfortable with your overall allocation plan at all times.

2. *What percentage of your assets will go into equities versus bonds?* What percentage will go into international versus domestic securities? Is this an investment philosophy question? You bet it is. Equities offer higher long-term investment returns than fixed-income securities, but they are also more volatile. You need to develop a positive outlook about investing, particularly when it comes to equities, because financial markets can be unforgiving over the short term. As an investor, you need to be willing to weather market cycles that may be generating poor results.

3. *You should generally develop an investment philosophy that keeps you fully invested either completely in equities or in equities and bonds.* Does it pay to attempt to time the market? Many investors and some newsletters and investment advisory firms think so. The problem is that there is little empirical evidence that market timers have been more successful than strategies that keep investors fully invested. My experience of studying the historical evidence is that there have been times that market timers or timing services have helped investors avoid market downturns, but most, if not all, miss on the rebound. That is, they may have gotten out successfully on a few occasions, but failed to recognize a rally at its start and thus missed strong moves to upside, in effect underperforming traditional fully invested portfolios. Rather than attempt to time the market, the best strategy I have found for long-term returns is creation of a globally diverse portfolio of investment styles (international, small-cap, large-cap, and so forth) using occasional rebalancing as certain styles decline and others surge ahead.

4. *Make sure you are comfortable with your time horizon.*
Ideally you should plan on a minimum ten-year holding
period. Studies show that the longer the holding period,
the lower the chances of a loss of principal and the greater
chance you will succeed.

Developing an overall investment philosophy includes these
points as well as numerous others. Your investment philosophy
will change over time due both to market conditions and changes
in your financial profile. The key is to create a plan and stick to
it. Don't jump around and buy the newest investments that Wall
Street creates. Remain consistent with small incremental adjustments and you'll be successful in the long run (see Figure 9.2).

WHY WORK WITH AN INVESTMENT ADVISOR?

You've already noticed my advocacy of using a professional investment advisor to assist in developing your IPS and managing
your wealth. In my twenty-plus years in the financial services
industry, I have yet to find a single individual investor who has
invested 100 percent of his own money over full market cycles
and been able to outperform the professional money managers
with whom I have had the pleasure of working.

Do successful "do-it-yourself" investors exist? Sure. But investing a fifty-stock portfolio in today's volatile markets is no
part-time job. It is a full-time disciplined focus on professional
money management, with some firms having a staff of as many
as 150 professionals dedicated to the daily handling of trades,
research, administration, asset allocation decisions, and portfolio
construction. I believe we may not see another decade of sustained growth, such as the 1980s and 1990s (17.55 percent and
18.20 percent respective average annual returns for the S&P 500)

Service / Consulting Process:	Quarterly performance reports and monitoring
Written Investment Policy:	A money manager will read and comply with a client's investment policy
Individual Portfolios:	You can create a better match between a client's objectives and risk tolerance and a manager's style
Manager Due Diligence:	Ongoing due diligence is conducted on all managers. Portfolio manager stability is critical to long-term performance
Fund Mislabeling:	So many funds tout one style of investing but practice another; it is easy for investors to be misled
Market Timing:	In a mutual fund, the investor makes the timing decisions not the manager
ERISA Liability:	A mutual fund cannot act as a fiduciary; a money manager and brokerage consulting divisions can act in this capacity
Tax Planning:	To minimize tax liability
Tax Liability:	When you buy a mutual fund you buy into the existing tax liability of the fund. If they have sold stocks for a gain, your pro rata share is allocated to you at year end
Fee Structure:	Essentially the same. You pay for the same services: management custody, trading, and reporting

Figure 9.1 Consulting process.

Source: Robert Jorgensen

for some time, which makes solid professional advice all the more critical to your success. Finding the right advisor to help you select the professional money managers best suited to meeting your goals is crucial to that success.

Scott MacKillop, CEO of Trivium who is a recognized industry consultant to the Individually Managed Account industry, has said

> Today Individually Managed Accounts are sold primarily through fee-based investment advisors at major Wall Street firms such as Smith Barney, Merrill Lynch, UBS Warburg, etc. A strong new distribution channel is emerging which is the 90,000+ independent investment advisors across the country.
>
> I believe the best way to find a good money manager is to find an advisor through a referral who specializes in money manager selection.

HOW DO YOU FIND A COMPETENT INVESTMENT ADVISOR?

This is a great question and one not easily answered. There are approximately 800,000 bankers, life insurance agents, annuity agents, trust officers, CPAs, attorneys, discount brokers, fee-only planners, stock brokers, financial consultants, registered investment advisors, real estate agents, and financial advisors in this country eager to sell you some sort of financial advice or product. So how do you, as an individual investor or corporate trustee, find the right firm or individual to help you? What about licenses to sell or offer securities? What sort of credentials are important? Should you work with an advisor at a major Wall Street firm or with an independent advisor? What about experience, objectivity, fees, and what I like to call the success quotient? These are just a few of the components that you need to consider when selecting an investment advisor to help you develop an IPS and assist you with manager selection.

There is really no simple answer to finding the right investment advisor. I'd like to direct you to one simple directory in the yellow pages such as the listings for CPAs, attorneys, or physicians, but no such directory exists. Even for those professions offering a listing, there is still no measure of qualifications or abilities, and the same holds true for financial professionals. However, there are a few guidelines on how to identify a good investment advisor who can help you develop a solid IMA portfolio.

The Investment Management Consultant Association (IMCA)

The IMCA was founded in 1985 in Denver, Colorado, by a small group of investment advisors and IMA managers, and has grown to become the single largest voice in the fee-based advisory industry today. With over 4,000 members, the IMCA has developed a highly respected educational certification program for the certified investment management analyst (CIMA) designation. The CIMA is awarded to those professionals who have completed a rigorous financial education program administered by the Wharton Executive Education School. Following training, advisors have mastered risk management, asset allocation, capital asset pricing models, and components of fixed income analysis. To illustrate mastery of the subjects studied and to receive the CIMA certification, advisors must take a four-hour examination and pass with an above-average grade.

> The Mission at IMCA is to ensure quality service to the public by developing and encouraging high standards in the investment consulting profession. As an organization, its role has been to broaden the public's understanding of investment management consulting and to promote and protect the interests of the profession.

Investment advisors today must keep up with a complex and constantly changing marketplace. They are continually challenged to meet the needs of investors who are facing uncertainty in a changing global investment environment. The level of competency and knowledge needed to help clients attain their financial goals is "greater than any time in the past" (IMCA).

In addition, CIMA holders must participate in continued education conferences and forums. You can identify a CIMA certified advisor within your community by contacting IMCA directly via phone, fax, or e-mail (see Appendix B).

The Financial Planning Association (FPA)

The FPA is the primary membership organization for the financial planning community. This is one of the largest independent financial organizations in the world, with membership currently over 35,000. The principal membership is composed of financial professionals "who champion the financial planning process" (FPA).

> FPA members are dedicated to supporting the financial planning process in order to help people achieve their goals and dreams. The FPA believes that everyone needs objective advice to make smart financial decisions.

The FPA has developed a highly regarded certification program that confers a certified financial planner (CFP) designation. Applicants must complete five educational components and sit for five proctored examinations and a final examination before being eligible to receive a CFP designation. Although not dedicated solely to IMAs and the managed account industry, as is IMCA, the FPA boasts highly competent professionals trained to integrate asset management strategies into their overall financial planning strategies.

Financial Services Firms

In 1986, E.F. Hutton & Co. introduced the concept of including the money manager, custodianship, and trading along with the firm's financial consultants together as a package for a three percent annual all-inclusive wrap fee, and the real growth of the IMA industry began in earnest.

Today, there are more firms offering IMAs than there were managers willing to accept accounts just fifteen years ago. Every notable Wall Street firm offers IMAs at one level or another, and those that don't are working to add IMAs to their offerings. In addition, banks, insurance firms, independent broker dealers, national CPA firms, retirement plan administrators, and independent turnkey asset management providers are now distributing IMAs (see a partial list of firms in Appendix B).

Can you get a reliable referral from these organizations for an advisor or a list of qualified money managers? The answer is yes. Most, if not all, have a service desk or a location on their home websites that can provide you with information on their IMA platforms. You can also typically request a brochure and even have a financial consultant or registered investment advisor contact you directly to set up an appointment.

REFERRALS AS YOUR ULTIMATE SOLUTION TO FINDING A FINANCIAL ADVISOR

> *Success of Financial Advisors is built on confidence—providing personal, customized service so that the client is comfortable is key. Having the best interest of the client at heart is the true test of a successful Advisor working within the IMA Industry.*
> —Steve DeAngelis, President of Persimmon Research Partners

In addition to these resources for finding additional information on the managed account industry, one of the most effective means for finding a financial advisor is by referral. Whether through a friend, a neighbor, a business associate, or another professional advisor, there are some important issues of which you should be aware before you entrust all of your assets to a single advisor.

Credentials

The financial services industry today is actually a great deal more complicated than it needs to be. We have multiple stock exchanges around the world, literally hundreds of thousands of financial professionals, hundreds of products from which to choose, and over 40,000 equity securities available for purchase in the United States alone. With all these product options, the Securities and Exchange Commission and National Association of Securities Dealers (NASD) has established some specific licensing requirements necessary for a financial professional to offer IMAs: the NASD license Series 65, NASD license Series 66, and NASD license Series 7.

Experience

Experience is the single most important factor in choosing the right financial consultant or investment advisor to help you through the process of selecting a portfolio of IMA managers. You might ask then what is the best way to evaluate success and experience of a money manager in the fee-based investment industry? Examine their track records. Every IMA is individually monitored from inception, year-to-date, and for each quarter. Advisors can demonstrate their experience by showing you the history and track record of the managers they use along with actual accounts, keeping client names and information confidential, of course. They should be able to show you annualized performance, asset allocation recommendations, strategic decisions based on market shifts or changes in client objectives, and how particular client issues are handled.

Finding the correct investment advisor is an important procedure. Do not select one based merely on referral or firm. Investors must find an advisor who understands their financial objectives and places the clients' interests ahead of his own.

IN THE NEXT CHAPTER

In order to illustrate how the prescriptions in this chapter can greatly enhance your wealth-planning strategy, I want to share some actual cases from my practice as an investment consultant. Some readers will enjoy Chapter 10 more than any of the other chapters in this book. I hope all readers find that this chapter reinforces my messages about the benefits of using IMAs.

The Secrets of Success: Money Managers and Clients Revealed— Interviews with some of America's Best Money Management Firms

Real Life Stories from the Field

Men are wise in proportion, not to their experience, but to their capacity for experience.
　　　　　—James Boswell, on the life of Samuel Johnson, 1791

This book grew out of the desire to introduce investors to the rewarding realm of IMAs. Thus far, I've defined IMAs and reviewed their history, discussed the advantages of professional money managers, and outlined their techniques and strategies for highly effective portfolio management.

In this chapter, I provide some profiles of investors with whom I am privileged to enjoy personal relationships. These are stories about ordinary people who should invest in IMAs along with the reasons why. In addition, I share insights into what I believe is necessary to be successful at making the most of your money.

THE RELUCTANT BUSINESS OWNER

Early in my career, I developed a great deal of business setting up retirement plans for small business owners. I often found small business owners were so busy trying to make money and stay ahead of personnel issues and the day-to-day management of their companies that they'd end up neglecting their own personal financial well-beings. Truth is, they just didn't have the time to do everything.

I remember particularly one fellow who was a very successful owner of a small chain of gas stations. Each station had a mini-mart and repair shop. The owner had been in the business more than twenty years and he had never looked into a retirement plan. He was already fifty-five years old and really hadn't saved anything for retirement. Of course, until we met, no one had ever talked to him about a retirement plan, either. He was earning roughly $200,000 annually and was paying, on average, thirty-five percent in federal taxes and an additional seven percent in state taxes.

I was diligent in recommending he invest with professional money managers each time we talked, but he told me he wasn't saving much after taxes and had only a small amount of money in savings, certainly not enough to hire a money manager at a $100,000 minimum investment.

I showed him how at his age (then 55) he could contribute up to $80,000 annually in a defined benefit pension plan while at the same time reducing his tax bill from over $85,000 a year to about $35,000. He'd then have the balance to save for his retirement. He followed my advice for seven years and then retired.

He still thanks me to this day for showing him how to create a retirement plan using IMAs that ultimately allowed him to retire with $800,000. He retired early and has been touring the American southwest with his wife by motor home—one of his lifelong wishes. His kids now operate the business and have invested in the same manner to work toward their own retirement plans.

RJ's Investment Insight: Individual investors and business owners frequently ask me what investments I recommend. Instead of telling them what to invest in, I tell them first how to invest. I always offer the same answer: retirement plans. When you're young, your paycheck is used to pay for a lot of things as you establish yourself. My advice is you should also pay yourself and do it first. Make it your highest priority. This is the last true 1:1 tax deduction, the money invested compounds tax-deferred, and you only pay taxes when you're ready to spend the money. Investors can contribute anywhere from $11,000 in a 401(k) to as much as $100,000 annually with a defined-benefit pension plan, within the confines of age and funding time limit. Most Americans will need 50 to 100 percent more money in their retirement than they might think they'll need. Don't cut yourself short. You might live a lot longer than you think you will.

THE DIVORCEE

A lifetime career as a financial advisor brings you in close contact with many wealthy families. And while intentions are always for the best, things don't always work out for every family. That's just reality of our society.

I started working with a particular family in the midst of a very tough divorce. The husband was a very successful dentist who had expanded his practice to several offices and was enjoying a thriving business through referrals, a good many of whom attended social and philanthropic functions that his wife helped sponsor in addition to running the household and raising two children.

The divorce settlement allotted that she would receive monthly alimony for twelve years and one half of her ex-husband's profit-sharing plan, which amounted to $300,000 at the time.

I worked with her to determine how to maximize her retirement plan over those twelve years until she reached age 59½ so she could then use the plan throughout her retirement. This was very important because she hadn't worked since her ex-husband had finished dental school over twenty years previously. Reentering the job market at that stage of life wasn't a viable possibility.

The real challenge was her fear of the stock market or investments of any kind. This isn't uncommon for people who remember the Great Depression of the 1930s. Her family had lost everything in the stock market and had to sell their home for next to nothing and live with other relatives just to get by. In short, she didn't trust any method of investing other than a federally insured interest-bearing savings account.

I tactfully gave her the bad news right up front. I told her if she didn't invest her $300,000 settlement in equity investments, she would not be able to keep pace with inflation and would have insufficient funds on which to live comfortably in retirement. If she were ready and eager to reenter the workforce at age 60, a regular bank savings account would be adequate. Now I had her attention.

I walked her through market history and the benefits of owning equities, which have averaged over 10.6 percent growth per year since 1926 (including through the Great Depression) versus investments such as Treasury bills, which have earned four percent over the same period. I recommended a large-cap growth and value manager and explained how each would actively manage her money for her every day. She brightened considerably when she learned about how an IMA would enable her to know how her money was being invested and how it was performing all the time. Still she retained her skepticism.

Gradually, as her account grew, so did the number of IMA managers she hired as her confidence grew in the process with measurable results. I'm happy to say this client today has just over $1.2 million in her portfolio and she's quite comfortable and secure living on $84,000/year (seven percent), which she draws from her plan. Incidentally, she's come full circle on the stock market. She loves it. She even watches Nightly Business Report, with particular attention to her money managers and the stock she owns whenever they are featured.

RJ's Investment Insight: It's rewarding for me personally to look back on this client's performance over a 10-year basis. She's experienced some of the best compounded returns of the literally hundreds I've tracked. That's because once the Investment Policy was set up she stayed with the plan and did not waiver. She started off relatively naïve about investing, but trusted her well-being to the professional money managers we hired and their expertise at optimizing her portfolio. As time passed and favorable progress was made, she entrusted all of her money to IMAs. Early on, she was nervous about the fluctuation of value in her portfolio. That's understandable. Everyone is a little uneasy about market fluctuations at first. Investors who watch the market constantly often get panicky, especially during volatile markets. Changing investments and managers based on day-to-day performance hurts in the long run. For the lay investor, the stock market is eighty percent emotion and twenty percent reality. My goal is to gradually and subtly reverse this perception over time with education and performance.

MUTUAL FUND MAN

Every few years or so throughout my career, I've enjoyed meeting some exceptionally bright and successful investors. A few years ago, I had the pleasure of meeting a young executive who had proved very successful at building a small computer technology company, which he in turn sold for over $8 million.

When we met, he explained how he had been investing all of his assets in no-load mutual funds, some of which were passive investments matched to specific indices. He had been applying this investing method for about three years, and since the market had been performing well over this period, he believed he was already using "professional management" and did not see the need to work with individual money managers. I explained the advantages of IMAs, particularly their tax advantages for someone like himself who had a great deal of tax liability on his assets, but he determined he was going to stick with his mutual funds.

As mentioned, this fellow is a very bright individual, entrepreneurial and very independent. He knew a great deal about the financial markets because after he sold his business, he made investing his full-time job. He read *The Wall Street Journal, Forbes, and Business Week*, and watched CNBC daily. Additionally, he applied his extensive experience in the computer technology arena to hours of researching mutual funds and securities on the Internet. He would typically make very substantial purchases, sometimes investing as much as a $1 million in a single mutual fund. One of these single large mutual fund purchases eventually changed his whole investment perspective.

Recall my discussion in Chapter 4 of how a mutual fund is like a community swimming pool. With a single portfolio or investment pool, you must accept what's in the pool at that time you enter. You are a part owner in the community and share in any upside or downside or any capital gains declarations a pooled fund makes at the time you are an owner.

This investor made a colossal misjudgment when he invested over $1.1 million dollars in November in what was at the time a very successful growth mutual fund. What he didn't know then and has since learned is how mutual fund companies make year-end capital gains distributions in either November or December of each year. The fund that he had just purchased had enjoyed a highly successful year and distributed a short-term capital gain of eighteen percent and a long-term capital gain of six percent. Since he bought into the fund just prior to the distributions, he inherited the fund's tax liability and therefore received a 1099 for what for him was "unearned" income capital gains of over $210,000! Adding insult to injury, the fund ended the year off approximately five percent, so he not only had to pay taxes on gains he did not receive, but his fund was down $55,000.

Having learned the very hard way, this investor still buys mutual funds today, but nowhere near as many. He also knows never to buy at the end of the year until he determines whether there will be a large embedded capital gain at the time of purchase. Most of his assets are now in IMAs, where, as a taxable investor, he now enjoys the benefits of "tax-efficient" investing.

> *Where an IMA can really deliver value for an investor is in their taxable accounts. In today's marketplace investors are seeing a literal explosion in tax-aware, tax-efficient products such as Index Funds, ETFs, Tax-Managed Funds, etc. The absolute bottom line is that it's indisputable that a Tax-Aware IMA that may deliver the same performance pre-tax as a similar mutual fund can deliver anywhere from 2% to 5% additional return than the fund on an after-tax basis.*
> —Donald E. Cody, President of Tax-Efficient Investor

THE DOCTOR WHO KNEW TOO MUCH

I've met literally thousands of investors during my twenty years in business and had a unique opportunity few people in the financial industry have: a chance to work with the ultimate successful investor.

Since I made the decision early in my career to focus only on premier professional money managers, I was always fascinated when meeting people who had developed their own systems for managing money and therefore believed they had no need to hire a professional money manager to oversee their money. I won't argue in this book or elsewhere that you shouldn't own and look after some stocks on your own. But when it comes to handling significant liquid assets in a diversified portfolio, you're going to need expert help unless you happen to be a professional money manager.

A highly accomplished physician was introduced, through his practice, to a group of top biotechnology executives. As a doctor, he has the professional expertise to understand the complexities of new gene therapy treatments, pharmaceuticals, and medical breakthroughs that would not only have major impact on patients but also on the publicly traded firms that produced these modern miracles.

His vocational relationships with the chief executives of these same firms provided him with key information on these firms, offering an insight unavailable to even the savviest Wall Street analyst, let alone the average investor. He had accumulated a substantial retirement plan with more than $1.5 million dollars in a relatively short time. That's a significant retirement plan, considering he was just forty-five.

I first met him in early 1991. His accounts had been averaging over thirty-five percent growth per year for about 7 years running. I certainly couldn't criticize his portfolio as I saw he was diversified among forty-plus biotechnology firms. He possessed thorough knowledge of his holdings, his turnover was low, and he obviously was experiencing great success. I could only identify one issue to raise with him, which was the concentration of his entire portfolio in small growth style pharmaceutical and biotechnology firms. He agreed with my diagnosis and decided to invest fifteen percent of his portfolio with a large-cap value manager I recommended.

As things turned out, it's a good thing he did so. You might remember how the Clinton Administration proposed sweeping health-care reform following the 1992 election. The Clinton proposal called for government price controls of HMOs, health-care facilities, and what was perceived as a key culprit of health-care inflation: pharmaceutical research, development, and manufacturing.

While having little effect on the quality of health care in the United States, the proposed regulatory changes literally crushed stock prices for the entire health-care industry, particularly the pharmaceutical and biotechnology sectors. These sectors plummeted approximately forty percent over the next twelve months, and my client lost more than fifty percent of the value of his individual stock portfolio.

His investment in a large-cap value stock IMA helped ease the pain, as this market sector was appreciating while the growth sector was getting hammered. In retrospect, he wished he'd made a greater allotment to his value IMA.

This doctor and I are still close friends today and he still enjoys trading stocks, though they now represent about five percent of his overall portfolio, with the rest of his money invested in IMAs.

RJ's Investment Insight: There's never been a better example of how doing everything right can go terribly wrong. This doctor is one of the smartest people I've ever had the privilege to know. He knew not only the companies in which he wanted to invest, he knew how to make his money grow. His character is such that he didn't let pride get in the way of my recommended diversification strategy, even at the height of his success. I knew he was overweighted within the pharmaceu-

(continued)

tical and biotechnology industries. One thing you learn over two decades of professional investment experience is that you never know what event will affect a sector of the market. Just as pharmaceuticals and biotechnology were riding high, they were hobbled by market reaction to proposed government legislation that never even came to fruition.

Investment professionals will never stop preaching to you about asset allocation and diversification for stabilizing your returns and lowering your overall volatility. This investor needed to be invested in stocks apart from those securities he literally knew too much about. Remember, every market sector is subject to both good and bad performance. Odds are heavily against your success if you stick with only one sector over the long run.

THE MARGIN TRADER

This is one of the most fascinating experiences I have ever known in twenty-plus years working in the U.S. stock market. In fact, it's so unusual it's almost hard to believe, but everything told here really happened.

A good acquaintance I've known for years has always had a strong fascination with the market. He's a very bright, hardworking family man with an Ivy League degree and an MBA. He's a sales and marketing guru with one of the top firms in the country, and over the past twenty years he's honed his skills to the point that he can accomplish in twenty hours what takes his colleagues more than forty.

He loves to trade the market. As I've said already, this is great. I encourage everyone to own one or two stocks to trade on their own, if for no other reason than the hands-on education that comes with the experience.

Even though we'd known each other for years, my friend rarely took my advice. Like a lot of other accomplished high-net-worth investors, he has the tools, talent, and hunger to make all his own investment decisions, never seeking my advice or that of any other industry professionals. Until recently.

He's always loved being a trader and he made his first real money in 1983, right about the time of the great bull market which began its run in 1982, with the Dow climbing roughly from 750 to over 2500 by 1987. He would follow the market daily, reading *The Wall Street Journal, Forbes, and Investor's Business Daily,* and watching CNBC and other financial broadcasts, and he traded individual stocks almost daily, focusing primarily on communications and technology. However, he never really made any serious money until 1998.

With about $20,000 in cash in February 1998, he had a hunch that stocks such as JDs Uniphase, Broadvision, and Iomega were ready to take off. In fact, he was so confident in his intuition he didn't buy just $20,000 worth of stocks, he bought $40,000 on margin. Margin is that dirty little six-letter word that can either help you or crush you—there's no middle ground. At the time, his decision was rewarded handsomely. The "new economy" was kicking in and nearly every stock in the technology sector was taking off like a rocket.

My friend and his wife had a great run. She's a stay-at-home mom with a decade of Wall Street experience of her own and she would handle trades, too. By March 2000 they had amassed a $3.2 million portfolio with over fifty technology stocks on margin and had net equity of about $1.6 million, since they were still using about 2:1 margin.

They were just about the happiest couple of investors you could meet. Then again, so were a lot of people about that time. Those of us in the financial industry were a little wary of how fast and high the Nasdaq had risen and how many new "investment experts" had appeared along with the run up. I remember nightly news reports about how everyone on the street from the guy that shined shoes to the checker at my grocery store was in the stock market. No one needed a professional money manager because it was incredibly easy to make money on Wall Street. You already know what happened.

My friend certainly had learned how to run his portfolio up, but he didn't possess the objectivity and discipline to know when to sell certain positions. You might think it's not that complicated, but honestly, how do you feel about selling anything that continues to rise in value? It's the kind of discipline any financial professional recognizes with a quiet smile. The discipline that comes with specialized education and experience. The kind that let's you know when it's time to sell. I tactfully tried to advise my friend who saw himself as a long-term holder of his stocks that you can't be a long term holder if you're on margin. Since his method had worked so well in the bull market, why mess with success? Well, the story ends pretty quickly. In short, he took a big loss like a lot of other people. In fact, he didn't lose most of it; he lost all of it as Nasdaq experienced a correction exceeding seventy-five percent of value.

My friend will now grudgingly admit, from time to time, that this was a good lesson, even though a bitter one. Today, he's given up on the get-rich-quick method and is thinking smart and looking forward to retiring in twelve to fifteen years with a realistic retirement plan and a more conservative investment strategy. Since March 2000, when the Nasdaq began its roller coaster dive, he's become a firm believer in IMAs. He started small with just one global IMA, but he's confident in the process and appreciates the discipline it takes to run a forty- or fifty-stock portfolio. Successful investing doesn't happen overnight. It happens by identifying and following a strategy, applying a focused investment plan, and hiring a top-notch professional money manager to run your portfolio on a day-to-day basis in both up markets and down markets.

> *RJ's Investment Insight:* There's a well known old adage on Wall Street that says, "Never confuse brains with a bull market." I'd add for margin investors, "Investment leverage is a double-edged sword but it cuts much deeper when the markets are going down."

NEWSLETTER MAN

There isn't an industry in the world today that sells more magazines, newsletters, investment programs, on-line tips, or books as the financial services industry. And why not? There's a ton of money in it! When one pauses to reflect that the total capitalization of all financial service investments in the United States alone is more than $13 trillion it's easy to understand why so many individuals and firms make a living by selling their "expert advice" to you. On the other hand, all this information, regardless of quality or accuracy, makes it more than a little confusing to determine a reliable source of investment advice.

Believe it or not, there are more than 500 investment newsletters available in the United States today. Imagine trying to navigate through this maze of investing strategies, from going long, to short, to market timing, to stock buys of the moment. It's a daunting task to say the least, even if you're a full-time financial professional, and it's next to impossible for the individual investor.

I have a client who used to love newsletters. He's a professional scientist with a PhD who'd been investing for over thirty years, during which time he'd accumulated over $3.5 million in liquid securities. He was open to new investing ideas, and when he first became my client he agreed to put fifteen percent of his portfolio into IMAs. This didn't interfere with his investing or pursuing the opinions of numerous investment experts. More than anything else, he loved reading financial newsletters, and he'd contact me at least once a week with trades and strategy changes that he'd learned about. As his advisor, I'd tactfully discourage this as not being in his best interests, but he would insist that the customer is always right. Even so, his newsletters began to cost him more than the subscription fees.

Selecting a newsletter is a little like picking a novel to read. Since you're going to end up reading the investment newsletter every week, it needs to fit with your investment philosophy, and that's their underlying drawback. My client was sold on precious metals and precious metal stocks. He loved gold, silver, and platinum. He'd made considerable money trading gold stocks on the advice of one of his newsletters, especially when gold rose from $35 an ounce in 1971 to over $850 an ounce nine years later. Also, being a bit of an economic pessimist, a common characteristic among precious metal investors, he'd gravitate toward newsletters that told him what he wanted to hear.

The early part of the 1980s was characterized by double-digit interest rates, hyper-inflation, and seventeen percent money market rates. Naturally, these conditions drove the price of gold, silver, and platinum to their highest historical levels.

Even after precious metal investing sank into a fourteen-year slump beginning in 1988, my client still kept subscribing to newsletters that specialized in what he loved, precious metals. Now imagine owning a newsletter, magazine, or research report that publishes information on only one subject, such as new issues, Internet stocks, health-care stocks, or, as in my client's case, precious metals. Do you think publishers and editors are going to tell you there's no need to buy their publications or subscribe to their websites for the next few years because their sectors of the market are down? Of course not. At least general financial publications, which offer an overall financial perspective, will provide you with other news that may be of value to you. The specialized financial newsletter is more akin to a hobby magazine than a source of financial information.

Bottom line: this client was continually influenced by his most recent and favorite publications and that's what cost him. Without saying "I told you so," I've gradually helped him realize the critical difference between investing seriously and as a hobby. Hobbies are great. Everybody should have one. But you shouldn't stake you financial future on them. This client now realizes that he should leave sector selection and management to the expertise of the professional money managers who run his IMAs, and you know what, he does.

> *RJ's Investment Insight:* It's a good idea to use financial news-letters or other sources to increase your understanding of market trends. But don't let them cloud your judgment or objectivity. It takes a lot more than a convincing essay crafted in time to meet the latest deadline to predict market sentiment, economic developments, and which sectors are the best avenues for making the most of your money. You need the expertise of professional money managers to maximize your success.

IN THE NEXT CHAPTER

The next three chapters are composed of interviews that I personally conducted with leading independent money managers throughout the United States. I have selected these money managers from across different investment styles. Chapter 11 is composed of interviews that focus on tax efficiency and growth investing.

CHAPTER 11

Meeting Top-Tier Money Managers: Tax-Efficient and Growth Managers

Placing all of your investible assets in an index fund is basically un-American.

—Louis Navellier

Investment wisdom isn't found in financial charts or mathematical models. Nor is it available in the finance section of your local library or bookstore. You can't learn it from financial broadcasts or by subscribing to newsletters, magazines, or websites. While all of these are creditable sources of information, they do not impart the wisdom and discernment you need to make the most of your money.

As you learned in Chapter 8, successful investment management is the result of years of formal education and industry experience. I've had the privilege to meet with some of the top professional money managers in the industry. I didn't talk with them in an attempt to learn what the next hot stock will be. Instead, I went with the desire to explore their styles, their methodology, their philosophies and the quality of their thinking, their talent, and the integrity of the money management firms they represent.

Of course, this is just the tip of the iceberg. There are many more firms with comparable reputations and records of achievement. The following managers are among the best and they can give you a glimpse of some of the intangibles that should be considered in forming a long-term investment relationship. After reading this, you may even want to hire one of these managers to run your money.

We'll start off with two of the most important styles of professional money management: tax efficiency and growth. These managers and their respective firms have built reputations spanning decades of successful investing for institutions and individuals.

TAX EFFICIENT DISCIPLINE: JOHN SPRINGROSE, OF 1838 INVESTMENT ADVISORS

As I've discussed the benefits of IMAs versus other forms of investing in the previous chapters, two themes have cropped up again and again: individual professional focus and taxes. Of all the styles of money management available, nowhere are these two advantages more readily apparent than in a tax-efficient account.

Tax-efficient money managers represent every category of investment style, although they have one consistent thing in common, which is a mandate to maximize after-tax returns. Since tax considerations vary by investor from year to year, tax-efficient accounts require a high degree of detail-oriented management.

I had the opportunity recently to discuss this style of management with John Springrose of 1838 Investment Advisors. 1838 represents the core investment style, encompassing both value and growth strategies. Tax-efficient management requires a greater level of expertise than that of conventional money managers. This discipline requires that each investment decision be evaluated on the basis of capital gains taxes, which are incurred for each specific trade. Tax-efficient managers must know the holding period and the cost basis for each security in each account. It's a phenomenal level of detail, but that, of course, is the most distinctive factor between IMAs and mutual funds.

Jorgensen: The name of your firm arouses my curiosity. How did you get started?

Springrose: 1838 is the year Francis Drexel started the money management business in Philadelphia. A group comprising the Drexel Burnham investment management department bought the operation in 1988. We traced our roots back to 1838, so we became 1838 Investment Advisors. It has a lot of benefits, not the least of which is we always end up first on consultant databases. We were an independent partnership for the first ten years, during which our assets grew from approximately $1 billion to about $5 billion. In August of 1998, we sold our firm to NBIA, a municipal bond insurance company. We did that with the hope of tapping into their very large customer base. Today we have about eighty people and manage approximately $11 billion, primarily in large-cap equities.

Jorgensen: Can you guide us through your tax-efficient portfolio? I'm very interested in how tax efficiency affects your stock selection.

Springrose: The first thing we to do is create a model portfolio. That's our large-cap core model. By *core,* I mean we're sector neutral. We don't take sector bets and we don't make any market timing bets. We come up with a well-diversified forty-stock portfolio. All the modern portfolio theories make the false assumption that there are no taxes and no transaction costs; however, the biggest transaction costs are taxes.

We then customize our model portfolio for the individual. Every individual's situation is different, so we compare the individual's portfolio to our model to see how close it is. When we want to make a trade—for example, move out of Intel and

into Cisco—your position in Intel will be different from my
position. It's the same security, but it really isn't the same security
because we probably have a different cost basis and a different
holding period. You have to worry about short-term and long-
term capital gains, of course. You have to make a determination
as to whether the trade is going to have a higher after-tax rate
return. Of course you think that Cisco's going to have a higher
pretax rate of return, but how long is it going to take you with
Cisco to make up the taxes you're going to have to pay on Intel?
That's going to depend on whether it's a short-term or long-term
gain and how many different tax lots you have in Intel.

I have tax lots in Intel with a cost of $5. It's going to be very
difficult for me to blow out that tax lot on Intel unless Intel is
really in trouble. If you manage tax-efficient portfolios, you have
to look at each individual portfolio and each individual security
right down to the tax lot level. You have to make individual
judgments based on these factors. You can't do that in a mutual
fund. You can't separate your tax lot on Intel from my tax lot on
Intel.

We're looking after three things. In the past, money managers
have only had to worry about two things. Return maximization
and diversification. The third ingredient is tax minimization, which
varies by individual and tax lot. We endeavor to get the individual
as close to our model portfolio as we can to minimize the taxes.

Jorgensen: Is the tax-efficient portfolio a recent development,
or is it something that you've been doing for some time?

Springrose: We've been focused on tax efficiency for about
seven years, and we keep enhancing it continuously. We apply
optimizer technology to handle large numbers of accounts. When
you think about it, it's pretty difficult to manage individual portfolios for a large number of accounts. It's really easy to say, "Just
don't buy any tobacco stocks," but it's really hard to say, "I
own Chevron and have a really low-cost position, but the client
likes Exxon Mobil better." It's difficult to find good reasons why

Exxon Mobil would be better than Chevron, so we might as well hold Chevron. What we're talking about is individual account management.

Jorgensen: What kind of communication takes place between the client, the financial advisor, and your firm to determine the individual needs of a client?

Springrose: We do a profile for every client. The financial advisor has the ability to say, "Here's my client; here's the securities that he now owns. Tell me what you're going to do for that client before you do it." There's a setting that comes back with the profile called return amortization, and this can be done with an existing account as well, which is a judgment as to a client's tax sensitivity. The financial advisor works with the client like a screw that needs to be tightened down. In a year during which he's not terribly worried about taxes, or he has other losses to offset the gains, we can loosen that screw a little bit. If he has other circumstances in which it needs to be tightened, then we do that. It's all part of our optimization process.

Jorgensen: What about returns? How does an investor compare what you do with other money managers?

Springrose: We report both pre- and after-tax returns. How much it costs really depends on the year. In 1999, our after-tax returns were higher than our pretax returns. That's unusual, but what we're looking for is a tax efficiency ratio. That's after-tax returns divided by pretax returns. We would like that to be in the 95 to 100 percent range. There were some very unique opportunities in 1999 to take that over 100 percent, but that doesn't happen often.

Jorgensen: Suppose I work for WalMart and have $10,000 in my checking account and $2 million in WalMart stock, with all kinds of cost bases. What can 1838 do for me?

Springrose: One-stock portfolios are difficult, especially with someone from WalMart, because those people are probably very wealthy. But the first thing to do is look at the tax lots. The next thing to do is determine the degree of diversification desired. Our company is developing new ways to get rid of one-stock positions on a very tax-efficient basis. But right now, if you have $2 million and you want to diversify, you just have to do it and take $200,000 a year over the next ten years, preferably with the high-cost stock. Once that's done, as time passes, other opportunities, such as a negative month, avail themselves. Losses can start eating away at those WalMart gains. But you have to get started. If you don't start, you'll never get where you need to be.

Jorgensen: What would you say to an individual in the top tax bracket with a fairly significant net worth about the benefits of an IMA versus a mutual fund?

Springrose: I'd ask to see his year-end mutual fund statements so I could take a look at the substantial capital gains that were taken. There are many horror stories about the fund business. There's one about a certain fund which decided that it wasn't getting new business because it had too many embedded capital gains, so it just sold everything one day and bought it back the next. So it just realized all the gains and now it's back to zero.

Without beating up mutual funds too much, because there is a place for them for some investors, it doesn't make any sense to be in a mutual fund when you have the net worth for an IMA in which a professional manager looks after your unique needs and circumstances.

Jorgensen: Do you think a mutual fund can be tax efficient? Some people talk about the tax efficiency of index funds. Do you think that's possible in a volatile stock market?

Springrose: You don't get much diversification with index funds. The only mutual funds that make sense to me as being remotely tax efficient are Putnam's. They open a mutual fund and when it gets to a certain amount of embedded gain, they close it and start a new one. So investors are in mutual fund 1, 2, or 3. They all hold the same stocks, but at least they have a chance to be tax efficient. That's the only method that makes any sense to me at all in terms of tax efficiency.

Jorgensen: John, can you give us some details on what kind of effort it takes to create your forty-stock portfolio?

Springrose: We divide the world into eight economic sectors, including technology, health care, consumer cyclicals, consumer staples, etc. We have one analyst responsible for each sector. The tech analyst does only technology, and it's his job to come up with a strategy for his sector and identify stocks that fit that strategy. One of the keys to our success is keeping our analysts intensely focused. They've been focused on their respective sectors for a long time and know which Wall Street analysts are worth considering. We believe that the world is so complex that you have to specialize. We have eight primary people who do this, and, of course, each has a back up.

Jorgensen: How do you reduce the universe of large-cap equities to a manageable size that permits you to take a close look at individual stocks?

Springrose: We do everything on a sector-by-sector basis. The common denominator in each sector, and this is a broad generalization, is the ranking of stocks in each sector by order of relative attractiveness. That means ranking stocks on a relative price-to-earnings ratio to sector and peers. For example, in pharmaceuticals if Upjohn normally sells at a certain sector multiple and it's now selling way below that sector multiple, then from a statistical standpoint, that's attractive. So we rank the stocks and then go on to the fundamental work.

Jorgensen: I've always known your firm as a core manager, though if I look back, I can see some growth stocks in your portfolio. How would you characterize core in terms of the investment style spectrum?

Springrose: We're absolutely core, and for us, that means we have a mix of value and growth stocks. It means that we don't take sector bets. If you're value oriented, that means you're going to be more into financial stocks than technology. We don't take that bet on behalf of our clients. If you look at the value and growth indices, the average difference over the past ten years has been ten percent. So the most important decision an individual makes is choosing value or growth. However, our clients don't want to take that risk. I'm sitting here looking at a piece of paper listing all of our stocks. It's color coded. We have approximately twenty-two stocks in the Russell 1000 growth index and eighteen stocks in the value index.

Jorgensen: How do you control risk? Is it mostly diversification?

Springrose: That's certainly one way. I'll start at the top, though, and say that I think the biggest risk right now is not being in the market. If you're our client, we presume you want us to manage equities, so we seldom hold more than one percent in cash. When we sell something, we want something else to add.

The next biggest risk is trying to guess which sectors are going to outperform others. It would be really easy to sit here today and say that technology's going to outperform. But there are plenty of other times when another sector is the leader. So for us, sector neutrality is really important.

We want to make our stand in stocks. As important as the stocks you own are the stocks that you don't own.

Jorgensen: So you're trying to mirror the S&P, principally?

Springrose: That's correct.

Jorgensen: How long does it take you to establish a full position in a relatively liquid stock like the large-caps in your portfolio?

Springrose: A full position is about $300 million. How long it takes to establish really depends on the stock. If you're going in to buy something like General Electric, you can get there very quickly. If you buy Esteé Lauder, it could take up to a week or a week and a half.

Before we ever buy a stock, we write a thesis. We try to come up with no more than 10 points on what we believe will make the stock go up. We write these points down when we buy it, and you'd be surprised what a marvelous tool it proves to be when a stock doesn't meet expectations and time comes to sell.

People talk a lot about changing fundamentals, but nobody really knows what that means. We learned a long time ago that if we put down the fundamentals of why we're buying a stock, we can always go back and put some teeth into the words, changing fundamentals. Take McDonald's, for example. You'd never hear us say that we're going to buy McDonald's because they sell more hamburgers than anyone else. You might hear us say that we're buying McDonald's because we expect them to triple their number of stores in the Far East. In fact, we did buy McDonald's, and that's one of the things we said. And we sold McDonald's because they didn't do that. We expected them to triple their Far East operations if our scenario was going to come to fruition.

Jorgensen: Can you look over the market during the coming ten years and tell me what you see?

Springrose: I've been at this since 1976, and I'm confident that the risk and reward system pays off. If you take the risk of being in the equity market, I'm confident the reward will be there. Are we going to have bumps along the road or are we expensive right now? Sure. Some stocks are very expensive. Others are bargains.

You have to work hard at it. Part of the reason people say it's expensive is because day-traders have driven prices up. Look at the stocks that get all the press: AOL, Dell, and Microsoft. All the rapid growers and all the tiny tech companies. Of course I wish I had been in the start-up tech companies over the past year, but as a professional investor, I want to make sure that I know the risks I'm taking and I want my reward to be steady. I think over the next 10 years, with our style of investing, you'll be compensated for the risk you're willing to take.

Comment

The adage holds true that the only certain things about life are death and taxes. This is especially true of investing. For a high-net-worth investor, taxes are the single biggest draw on returns. But in a variable stock market, taxes are the one thing that can be positively controlled. Tax-efficient management, as practiced by 1838, perfectly illustrates why I believe IMAs are the ideal vehicle for high-net-worth investors.

THE BIG PICTURE ON GROWTH: JACK SULLIVAN, OF HARRIS BRETALL, SULLIVAN & SMITH

Large-growth stocks get lots of attention these days, and for good reason. They both outperformed and then underperformed in back-to-back markets.

Many investors admit they'd like to own some of these stocks, which represent many of the most dynamic, best run companies in the United States. This sector is the specialty of Harris Bretall, Sullivan & Smith, not a large firm by industry standards, but one I have long admired because of the quality of their process and their people.

Harris Bretall, Sullivan & Smith uses a bottom-up approach to selecting stocks and points with pride to its dedicated research team. What sets this firm apart is an investment philosophy that looks at big-picture forces that transform the economy in addition to individual company performance.

I met with Jack Sullivan, one of the partners, to discuss the company's unique perspective on the market and what drives it.

Jorgensen: Tell me how you got started.

Sullivan: Back in 1962, I graduated with an accounting degree near the top of my class. I came out of school and learned that accountants made about $200 a month working 16-hour days.

And I remember writing to my father saying, "Dad I've made a terrible mistake."

It was a fairly dynamic market at the time and I started applying some accounting techniques to buying stocks while in the Army. When I was discharged, I joined Dean Witter at a very exciting time in the investment business. I moved up the ranks to become sales manager of the San Jose office, working with trust companies such as San Jose National Bank Trust Company. These guys liked the way I picked stocks and asked me to become a portfolio manager.

Instead, I went to Bank of America in 1970, going from the sell side of the business to the buy side. I had nine years of background and had been a principal at Dean Witter. I started at the bottom again at Bank of America, though was quickly exposed to big money and more or less stepped into managing $100 million.

Bank trust departments had that kind of money in those days. After three years, I left to lead the Western Asset office and hired my partner, Harry Smith. We ran that office for a while and I then had an opportunity to join Harris Bretall.

Jorgensen: Was it a large-cap growth firm at the time?

Sullivan: Yes, but it was a little different. At that time you had the beginnings of professional money management for individuals. Harris Bretall was an institutional firm with a minimum account requirement of $10 million. We once got a call from a guy who said he'd like us to do accounts of $100,000. We told him we had no interest. If only we'd known then what we know now.

My partner, Dave Harris, started buying successful companies, reasoning that the performance of a universe of successful firms can help with future projections. That was his specialty. When I joined Harris Bretall, they had the philosophy that sticking with high-quality companies was in the best interests of the client.

Then came the relatively severe market correction of 1973–1974. It was a rough time, and Dave couldn't find value companies in which to invest because the earnings streams didn't justify the valuations. We ended up with a big cash position, which earned us a reputation of being market timers. It's taken us twenty years to get rid of it.

Jorgensen: You had great performance numbers, though.

Sullivan: The numbers attracted a lot of money. In those days, $50 million was a big account. I joined in 1981 and was very comfortable with my partners. It was sort of an investment counseling business. We did research and we talked to clients, but there was never any real marketing effort. We had a good reputation on the street and it was sort of a gentleman's firm. In 1984, my old firm Western Asset bought sixty percent of Harris Bretall and gave us $1 billion, essentially all of the equity money, to manage. We hired some of their people and this was the driver that put us into the technology arena. Harry Smith joined as a partner and changed the scope of the firm. Western Asset also wanted us to help develop its client base. By the end of 1986, Western Asset decided to focus on fixed income and sold out to an East Coast company. We bought back the sixty percent that they owned, and from that became the firm we are today.

We were also lucky. By the end of the first quarter of 1987, we decided to raise cash since we thought the market looked high. We kept raising cash until we had an eighty percent cash position and ended 1987 with a return of twenty-one percent, which I believe made us the number one company in the country. That was the good news. The bad news was that guys like you, the consultants, said we were market timers with unrepeatable results.

Jorgensen: Tell me a little about the research effort. What sort of effort is dedicated to research and how does it come to you?

Sullivan: Before 1987, we thought we were pretty good analysts. Our primary job as money managers was to know the best people in the business and what they are thinking about technical analysis. We determined that if we were really going to be substantial, we had to develop our own internal research staff. In 1991, we hired David Post as a dedicated researcher, which was something unique for a small firm. David was extraordinarily good at asking research questions. He came to us with a fantastic depth of knowledge. So, as our assets grew, we asked him to build a research team.

We had forty to forty-five names in the portfolio and were putting $450 million into each position. We really had to know what was going on in those companies and had to have somebody calling those companies bimonthly to determine whether our models were correct. Those calls are still important. We buy companies with the idea that we're going to own them for at least three to five years. These companies keep succeeding quarter after quarter. You can't do this blind. You have to have somebody who knows the CFO, the investor relations person, and, depending on the size of the company, the CEO.

It was our perception in the early 1990s that the quality of Wall Street research was diminishing as the really good guys went off to form their own firms. We decided we needed to get these people; so we did.

Jorgensen: How big is that universe?

Sullivan: It's about 250 names, screened from a database. We have certain criteria as to size. Our screens have grown along with market capitalizations. Those positions give us pretty good clout with the companies. We want to be good long-term holders, and the companies have complimented us on two things. One, we try for face-to-face meetings with management. We've also been complimented on the quality of the questions we ask and the depth of understanding we have of their operations, including how they make their money, how they keep their profit margins, where they get their revenue growth, and the nature of their particular problems and how they address them.

Jorgensen: Value investing came back into style between 1992 and 1994. What are such periods like for a growth manager? What do you do when other investment styles outperform yours?

Sullivan: We stay true to our discipline. We had a number of consultants point out that of large-cap, high-quality growth managers, Harris Bretall didn't go out and buy Caterpillar under the guise that it was a growth stock, and didn't go into foreign markets under the guise that they were growth areas.

A lot of our competitors did that. We held our clients' hands and asked them to stay the course. It was actually a positive time for us because it seasoned our client base. Some of the hot money left, but a large portion stayed and learned what we're about and got comfortable with us. The bulk of our current clients were with us during that period.

We also developed a very compelling macro outlook. We calculated how we would get to Dow 5,000 based on something we called the three Ds: disinflation, demographics, and the death of Communism. Subsequently, these themes have broadened into globalization, demographics, and technology.

Jorgensen: You guys write some great industry pieces to help your investors understand topics including health care and technology. How have these pieces helped your firm?

Sullivan: These are basically think pieces. We started with the idea of writing a quarterly piece to send to our clients addressing the previous quarter. Each quarter, one of us compiles this piece.

Our commentary is usually macro oriented, advising clients to stay the course.

Jorgensen: Many of these macro views sound like a top-down market perspective. Your research, though, is bottom up. How do you mesh the two?

Sullivan: Macro is a framework. You can't think about investing in finance or insurance companies unless you have some idea about what's happening with interest rates. You can't invest in technology unless you have some idea of what's happening with the overall economy. You can't invest in health care without some sense of what's happening in Washington. So we set up an economic framework. We decided that we have to have an attitude toward the way the economy is developing now and nine months from now, because that's reflected in the market. What's the outlook for inflation? Modest inflation and a strong economy make for great earnings.

Other things we examine include earnings and interest rate outlooks. What is the market's supply/demand characteristic? There's a huge amount of supply coming. We feel we measured the available amount of cash for investment, and that's even bigger. There's approximately $4 trillion out there in cash. That's $4 trillion out of a $13 trillion equity market. That's a lot of money on the sidelines.

We also make judgments on the international scene. We make a judgment on the President's popularity and the political atmosphere. There was a correlation that showed that markets loosely track the President's popularity. Federal Reserve policy is also something we look at.

We have a fixed-income guy who's an economist. He's a member of our strategy committee. We ask him what's happening in the bond world every month because bonds are much more sensitive to what's happening on a macro level. He gives us a run down. That's the background music for our bottom-up stock selection. It's a framework for how we view the world.

Jorgensen: If you were going to pick industry groups for the next ten years, what would they be?

Sullivan: Well, we're still feeling the effects of a nasty correction that started in 2000. We review everything to make sure we really have a good handle on what's happening. We review our macro themes such as globalization. We asked ourselves if that's still in place. Is there trouble in Asia? Yes, but we think we can get through it. We talk about demographics. You know the story on the baby boom. Every seven seconds, someone turns fifty. Half the baby boomers are still under forty, so there's still a lot to play out.

Now, let me ask you: what was the year in which the fewest number of people were born relative to the population? 1933. 1998 represented the lowest number of people turning sixty-five. We did a plot of what happens between now and 2020. If you want to see a vertical climb chart, this is it. If you want to be successful, do something for 65-year-olds. Why? Because they buy 2.4 times more prescriptions than people between fifty-four and sixty-four. The big pharmaceutical companies are going to do very well and at a time when their pipelines are kicking in. The negative aspect is that, politically, pricing can be a tough thing. So we have to evaluate that. But if you want to make money, companies like Pfizer, Johnson & Johnson, Abbot Labs, and Merck are going to grow annually at sixteen percent or more. That's one cornerstone of the portfolio. The demographics demand it.

We understand the dynamic and how rapidly change occurs. But our research approach keeps pace with these changes. We just require good earnings for our clients. We hold companies that have a very clear concept of branding. We want companies that are going to be the leaders ten years down the road.

Another area is finance. It's a mixture of a low P/E multi-ple, consolidation, globalization, and demographics all coming together.

I talked about technology recently at a couple of road shows, but my table pounder was Citigroup. Take a look at what they had. It was about 43 before it went up and split. Not only do they have Smith Barney, they are literally taking American finance to the rest of the world. I like to tell my audiences a little story about a trip I took to Ireland. They have a place by Shannon Airport called Lough Derg. It's like Lake Tahoe. The land is beautiful and cheap and I decided to buy a place on the lake. I went in to do the financing and I said I'd put down twenty percent. The banker proposed I put down eighty percent and the bank would finance the other twenty percent. That's the way things work around the world. One of the things that has moved the United States economy so dramatically is the kind of financing we do here.

Jorgensen: Why does your firm operate primarily in the IMA arena?

Sullivan: Remember, three guys financed our firm. We had limited resources. We addressed the mutual fund concept and it was always a $2–5 million project. We started with this over ten years ago. It was always a lot of money at a time when we were concerned with getting high-quality people. This is the challenge for firms like ours. Do you hire a top-tier guy like Dave Post, or do you open a mutual fund? Do you build a research team, or do you open a mutual fund? We're happy with the way we've spent our money because we have a distribution channel, research team, and portfolio managers that we think are the best in the business.

Jorgensen: How do you see the future of the business, in which more and more people will be able to hire individual account managers?

Sullivan: We were very early into the consulting business with Prudential, and we moved on to get Paine Webber and E.F. Hutton, each of which validated our process. We love working with individuals because it's a wonderful, stable business, perhaps even more so than institutional clients. Once you gain someone's confidence, he stays with you. People look at our portfolio and say, "That's the list of stocks I want to own."

When our results started to get really good, individual business took off. I think that's where the future of our business lies. We made the decision that the nature of the business had changed. Consultants, like yourself, were going to make the asset allocation decision, and we were going to be hired for our ability to pick stocks.

Jorgensen: There's been considerable growth of index funds. What do you think about them?

Sullivan: Index funds are good for some people, for the cost. I found myself answering this question for a client about six months ago. I told him that we were going to beat the index over the next five years by a wide margin. Index funds have had tremendous growth because they are politically sensitive. They were market weighted at a time when market weighting was very hard to beat. The earnings growth at the lower end of the index funds was also faster than most people anticipated.

We saw this in 1992–1993 when our stocks were still making respectable earnings gains, but the market wasn't interested because it was focused on smaller companies coming out of a recessionary environment with earnings growth of thirty-five to forty percent. The S&P went through a period in which its earnings went up about thirty-five percent a year. It's virtually impossible for anybody to compete against an index when the market and a manager have equal weighting. I think that's changing dramatically. It takes intensive high-quality research, but you can beat the S&P 500 pretty regularly. Active managers are going to have to beat it by four to six percent in order to justify their fees.

Jorgensen: Jack, you have a lot of experience in the market. We're sitting here a couple of years into the new century and valuations are as high as they've been since 1929, even though the market has come down. How does an individual investor plan for the next ten years?

Sullivan: I've been in the business since 1962, and I've never seen the ducks lined up as positively as they are now. The three macro themes of globalization, technology, and demographics all come into play. I think that for the first time, we can see our way through the next ten years as a better period than the past ten.

I'll give you two examples that have impacted me personally. When I came into the business in 1962, my final interview was with Dean Witter himself and I asked him how solid his company was. He told me that Dean Witter handled six percent of the business done on the New York Stock Exchange, and as long as the company continued a level of 2.5 million shares a day, we would be fine. That was the volume in 1962—2.5 million shares a day. Just compare that with what we do today.

The other story involves my father, who married late in life. He was a taciturn man and never offered me much advice. When I got out of the Army with a wife and three kids and decided to work in San Jose with Dean Witter, my dad said to me, "I've got some advice to give you." I was shocked, of course, because he never did this. He said, "Never, never pay more than $13,000 for a house." A fixer just sold in Atherton for $6 million to some 29-year-old kid, all cash. The point is that the world has changed, and for the better. Things look positive going forward. Sitting here, we can't imagine how good things will be and how long these things will take to play out.

Comment

We've spent a lot of time reviewing all the advantages of a long-term investment strategy, but sometimes the perspective of an industry veteran like Jack Sullivan is even more illuminating. His experiences are impressive. His outlook and particularly his optimism are infectious, and I left our meeting with my own market perspective enhanced. With the many forces coming together the way Jack Sullivan sees them, in spite of recent market volatility, it's an exciting time to be an investor.

GROWTH BY THE NUMBERS: LOUIS NAVELLIER, OF NAVELLIER AND ASSO.

Despite established methods of value- and growth-oriented investing, every manager hones specific processes and criteria defining their individual styles. In my mind, no manager exemplifies this more than Louis Navellier. Louis is what's known in the industry

as a "quant." And while textbooks might define his style as small-
to mid-cap growth, it's his amazing aptitude with statistics and
quantitative analysis that has made his reputation. His style is
based solely on numbers. Abstract concepts, such as company
fundamentals, are transformed into numbers for crunching in his
always-evolving, computer-driven system. His performance record
certainly backs his approach.

The Navellier style stems from modern portfolio theory (MPT),
an academic approach to mixing risk and return. Navellier bridges
the gap between theory and the real market with his thorough,
computer-based analysis. Portfolios comprise high-alpha stocks
that exhibit a consistently higher rate of return than the market.
These stocks are scientifically picked and are later cycled out of
the portfolio as their positive qualities deteriorate. It's a little like
momentum investing, but is based on a highly sophisticated screening system.

If you watch the financial shows on TV, chances are you've
seen Louis Navellier. He's frequently consulted for his views on
market developments. His relentless and regular analysis of nearly
every stock on the market gives him an unmatched perspective.
He also publishes a highly successful newsletter, *MPT Review.*

Despite the number cruncher stereotype, Louis is affable and
easy going. I caught up with Louis before one of his many road
show presentations, of which he does more than eighty a year.

Jorgensen: How did your style evolve?

Navellier: When I was in college, I was fortunate to have two
bright teachers named Bob and Steve. This took place over twenty-
four years ago at Wells Fargo Bank, back when you had to
keypunch mainframe computers. Bob and Steve took the liberty
of having students like me do a lot of the work for them, and we
would write and run programs. Bob and Steve were working on
index funds, trying to mirror the market with 332 stocks. We did
the industry groups perfectly. We got all the betas at 1.0 so it

should have tracked the market perfectly, but we messed up. We beat the S&P 500 and the folks at Wells Fargo were furious. With everything corresponding as it did, we should have tracked the market perfectly. It turns out that there were some annoying high-alpha stocks that always beat the market. Back then, finance textbooks said that the markets were efficient and beta explained everything, including anomalies. We figured that the return that wasn't correlated to the market was the mysterious alpha factor.

Wells Fargo's problem became my opportunity and I set out to document high-alpha stocks and started publishing *MPT Review*. High alphas are much more prevalent among small- and mid-cap stocks. Once you get into larger stocks, you can beat the market, but sometimes you have to take more risk. My big break came when Hulbert, who ranks newsletters, gave me the highest cumulative rating of any of the newsletters they tracked. Setting up IMAs and running portfolios evolved out of the rankings.

We started working primarily with E.F. Hutton consultants. The managed account business for retail investors at the time was dominated by E.F. Hutton & Company. We grew from there. In the old days, we'd sit up in the hills at Lake Tahoe with the phones ringing and the money flowing in. Now the business has changed. We have to be priced and packaged for distribution. We like to be sold properly. We like to be allocated properly, because when managers are properly mixed, there's less risk in equities. There's nothing scary about the stock market when styles are mixed together the right way.

Jorgensen: How do you explain your style to someone who isn't familiar with your track record?

Navellier: It's a three-step process that runs stocks through three separate filters. We start with over 10,000 of the most liquid stocks and use every piece of data we can get our hands on. The first is a quant filter (quantitative analysis), which is a reward/risk filter that measures alphas, betas, and standard deviations. The second is a series of various fundamental filters run on a one- and three-year basis. Today, these include strong earnings momentum, strong operating growth, earnings surprises, and others. Finally we take the best thirty stocks from each portfolio product. These are optimized to create less portfolio volatility and less risk. In other words, we choose stocks that zig when other stocks in the portfolio zag. It also allows us to have our cake and eat it, too. I get a high rate of return for a reasonable amount of risk. The nice thing about the system is that it also forces us to sell when stocks don't balance each other or one increases in risk. It's a very disciplined process that we run every weekend. The reason it's done on weekends is that both the fundamental and quantitative analysis is run on VAX computers. It's an incredible task, and although computers have gotten faster, we're still on the weekly research cycle because of the amount of work. The risk/reward is done on Friday night, and the fundamental stuff takes all day Saturday. Every Sunday morning, when I have no distractions, I sit down and pick the best thirty stocks. It's a labor of love, but it also gives me a jump on the competition Monday morning.

Jorgensen: You've mentioned the intensity of the research. How many people are involved?

Navellier: Besides myself and senior portfolio manager Alan Alpers, who comanages most of the products, there are four people supporting us in research and one consultant. The research is very expensive, and most of the cost comes from leasing time on the VAX computers as well as purchasing and cleaning up databases. Wall Street is a kind of marketing machine, and research people like me are rare. Other people do it, but many aren't as serious. They'll compare a small stock to the S&P 500, which is like comparing a Chihuahua to an elephant. They both have four legs and a tail, but that's about it.

Jorgensen: You have portfolios covering nearly all market sectors. Do you ever adapt your style to suit market conditions?

Navellier: No. In order to work with the investment consulting industry, I have to stay within a certain box. I may change my systems to suit market developments, but I'll always stay within that style box. I apply my systems to all market sectors. One thing that can mess up the model is quick style shifts, for example, growth one quarter and value the next. Another thing that can mess up the model is massive liquidity problems.

Jorgensen: Do you have to reinvest in technology to stay ahead of your competitors?

Navellier: We've always been state of the art. As more data become available, we slice and dice the system to make it more precise. Now that we make our models dynamic, we always stay on the cutting edge. We test what works on Wall Street quarterly, because that's when data are refreshed, and we tweak our models quarterly. If data came out continuously, we'd tweak them continuously.

A few years ago, I remember visiting a very large pension fund. If you manage a billion dollars, you can talk to these guys. I told them that I'd stopped using earnings momentum because it stopped working in 1996. They said, "Are you nuts? You can't change your system." I said, "I have to. It doesn't work."

There are some very famous momentum managers looking for jobs right now because they followed it blindly. They didn't realize that things only work on Wall Street until everybody does it. Cash flow worked when Michael Milken was doing leveraged buyouts. Momentum worked until everybody did it. We had something called consistent growth that worked really well, then fell out of favor. You have to change your models, because the leading academics, some of whom have tried money management themselves, realize that static models don't work. Finally the consulting industry is coming around. We have to be nimble. We use dynamic models and we see no one currently who's approaching what we do.

Jorgensen: You've been associated with modern portfolio theory, and your newsletter is called *MPT Review*. Can you tell me how your style works in association with modern portfolio theory?

Navellier: Modern portfolio theory is the standard measurement of risk and return. That's all it is. We knew some people who would do this kind of analysis over a five-year basis and say, "Hey, everything looks the same," meaning the markets were efficient. So they decided to create an index fund. But what happened five years ago is irrelevant to what happens today or over the next five years. Some smart people at Wells Fargo operated on a three-year basis, and guess what? Some patterns began to emerge, leading them to think that indexing wasn't the answer after all. Some people went to three-year exponential analyses, which more heavily weights recent data. I myself went to twelve-month linear analysis because I think markets are seasonal.

Basically, I came to a different conclusion using modern portfolio theory than other people. I believe there are inefficiencies and anomalies that can be documented, and that's what I do. I know statistics inside and out, and I know that what I've done is statistically relevant. All sorts of quants have emerged now. Richard Bernstein is very credible. So is Melissa Brown. We're a new school on Wall Street and we all feed off one another's successes.

Jorgensen: Index funds gained in popularity. How do you feel about active versus passive investing?

Navellier: I started a newsletter to prove that you can beat the S&P 500. Our large-cap portfolio has beaten it consistently, and on a risk-adjusted basis as well. It's a tough index to beat, mostly because of the small composite problem. The S&P's performance is based mostly on that of a few big stocks. Late in 1998, earnings went negative on the S&P and there are still record high P/E ratios with all the money that continues to pour into that sector, much of it from large index funds. Wall Street thinks it's crazy because all these index fund investors have no idea that earnings are flat. They're chasing past performance. The reason mid-caps took off is because large-cap stocks cracked and all that institutional money had to go somewhere.

Jorgensen: Louis, you manage private accounts and you run a few mutual funds as well. Why should an investor consider an IMA as a better alternative?

Navellier: The reason IMAs are better than mutual funds is simple. In the past few years, every asset class except for large growth and growth indices has lost money. An advisor could have put some money in a tax-efficient value fund, and that fund could have lost assets because the manager was out of style. If the mutual fund goes from, say, $1 billion to $500 million, you have a tax time bomb going off at the end of the year because the people in the fund have to pay taxes for shareholders who sold out.

Over the years, a lot of the advisors who were using mutual funds have found out that you can't manage taxes with funds. Rapidly growing mutual funds are more tax efficient. Shrinking funds are tax time bombs. So IMAs are taking off because people realize they are tax efficient. People also want service, and you get a far higher level of personal service with IMAs.

Jorgensen: Is the mutual fund customer different?

Navellier: I think because of market style shifts that mutual fund investors are hot-dot chasers. A lot of people coming into IMAs are people coming off the rebound from mutual funds that are just not as strong as they used to be. They may not be in the top ten percent anymore. It bothers me. I have to have mutual funds because of large institutional clients, 401(k)s, etc. If I don't have funds, I'll lose accounts. There's good mutual fund business in pension funds, but there are also a lot of dot chasers out there.

Jorgensen: When you look at market sectors, how do you know when there's going to be opportunity?

Navellier: First of all, I can't see ahead any better than anyone else on Wall Street. Quant is a little like driving while looking through the rear view mirror. It shows me the conditions under which a sector will perform. Fundamentally, small-cap is better than large-cap, but large-cap is liquid and safer. Small-cap is like real estate on the edge of town. When real estate does well, its value grows. But when real estate isn't moving, it shrinks. The key to small-cap is volume, and if you told me that Nasdaq was going to move 600 million shares a day, I'd tell you that's not enough, so let's buy mid-cap. If that was going to be a billion shares a day, I'd say let's buy small-cap.

Comment

Louis Navellier's approach breaks away from that of a lot of academics. He values recent data over long-term data. He finds anomalies in the market where other MPT adherents see only efficient markets. His performance certainly backs him up. And his techniques are enlightening. Can the average investor compete with Louis Navellier's weekly employment of supercomputers and stock analysis? The answer, of course, is no, and that makes me, for one, glad he's available for hire as a money manager.

A TWELVE-POINT FOCUS: JIM HUGUET, OF GREAT COMPANIES

I have always found it fascinating how many different approaches money managers have developed for building successful firms. There are about 15,000 money management firms in the United States. Only about 400 are accepting new clients. I have personal contacts with 300 of these firms, and am comfortable placing long-term money with about 30 of them.

My comfort with these firms is based on my evaluation and measurement of investment performance over a twenty-year career. Soon after I begin a due diligence review of a money manager operation, I form my opinion on whether or not that firm will be successful over the long term, when they may encounter any number of market cycles.

When I first met Great Companies cofounders Jim Huguet and Jack Kenney early in 2001, they had approximately $150 million under management. Today they have over $350 million and growing. I knew that this firm had all the requisite elements for success.

Jorgensen: I think the story of how your firm was founded is almost as interesting as the Great Companies process. Why don't we start this interview there?

Huguet: I love telling the story. You see, I spent the bulk of my professional career as a consultant to Fortune 500 firms. I was fortunate to gain insight as to what really made these multinational firms so successful. After I sold my consulting practice, I found myself with more money than I had ever had. I had absolutely no idea how to invest the proceeds. I began a search for the right investment strategy. I read books such as *The Intelligent Investor* by Benjamin Graham and the books by Peter Lynch. I attended seminars, read *Barron's*, and watched CNBC. I learned one thing from all this work and effort: that over long periods of time, stocks were a better investment than bonds. That was all I learned.

Jorgensen: Were you discouraged or disillusioned?

Huguet: No, I wasn't really discouraged. I just knew I needed to get more of the facts. I knew from my consulting experience that once I had enough of the facts the answers would jump out to me. So, I started thinking about companies that I had consulted with over some thirty-plus years. Firms such as Proctor & Gamble, Bristol-Myers Squibb, Coca-Cola, Gillette, and Johnson & Johnson, to name a few. I began to ask myself, what characteristics did these world class companies possess? What were the common characteristics that you could find in "great companies"? Many of which had been around for over 100 years. What would happen if you invested in some of these great companies? Would you beat the market over time?

Jorgensen: So really, the beginnings of Great Companies as an investment firm was a consulting project for yourself as the client instead of a Fortune 500 corporation as a client?

Huguet: Yes, not only was it a consulting project, it turned into a book, *Great Companies, Great Returns* (Broadway Books: New York). Through in-depth research, analysis, and interviews with some of the top executives of these "great companies," I was able to identify twelve common traits that not only appeared in the book, but are the basis for our investment process today:

1. The company is highly regarded by management experts and by knowledgeable executives.
2. The company is publicly traded.
3. The company is headquartered in the United States.
4. The company has been in business for at least fifty years, and has survived the founder.
5. The company has a market capitalization in excess of $15 billion.
6. The company does business globally, and has at least forty percent of revenues and profits from international operations.
7. The company has outstanding shareholder returns.
8. The company is in a "terrific" business.
9. The company is protected by strong barriers.
10. The company is aware that people are its most valuable asset.
11. The company's management team keeps the company in "prime," that is, a state in which the company will not get old.
12. The company has an innovation mind-set that turns change into opportunity.

Jorgensen: Your process sounds so simple. Why hire a money management firm? Couldn't you just apply these principles and invest your money on your own with a discount broker?

Huguet: That's a very good question. Truth is, you can. In fact, the book was really written for individual investors. I even give insights not only on how to select great companies in which to invest, but how to manage the portfolio week in and week out. The problem is most investors don't have the time, discipline, or overall knowledge to manage their own portfolios. They need to develop extreme objectivity in managing their own portfolios. That is very difficult when we enter down market cycles. We started Great Companies registered investment advisors so that we could handle portfolios for people.

Jorgensen: Would you say that any of the twelve traits is of greater importance that the others when it comes to trying to generate long-term returns?

Huguet: Yes. There are really two critical traits that invariably impact the success of a company more than anything else. First, they need to be in a "terrific business." They need to be in a business with low labor costs and high returns, such as consumer product companies like Coca-Cola and Gillette. These companies invest in research, develop new products, expand distribution, and increase market share through brand awareness. Conversely, retailers like Nordstrom's or commodity businesses like IBP (the meat packers) are cyclical and are dependent on retail economic cycles or something like the price of grain.

Jorgensen: You often speak of beating the S&P 500 over time in your firm's literature and in your book. Over time, is this achievable?

Huguet: Well, Robert, as you know, it is very difficult to beat the broad market over long periods of time. It is well documented that only about twenty-five percent of all fund managers outperform the S & P 500 over time.

Although we are a relatively new money management firm,

we have back tested our stock selection process over many different market cycles for a fifteen-year period and found only a specific number of truly great companies that had all twelve traits with which we could have easily beaten the broad market. Remember, within the S&P 500, only about twenty-five firms actually outperform the aggregate index on an equal-weighted basis. The key is finding which ones, and that is what we are attempting to do.

Jorgensen: Speaking of narrowing the field, you typically only hold fewer than twenty-five stocks in your portfolio. Isn't that risky?

Huguet: I may go against the academic investment community on this point, but I believe that diversification is a sign of ignorance. We believe that to maximize returns and minimize taxes, we need to invest in a concentrated portfolio of good stocks, that are in good businesses, and we must act like an investor in those businesses. Not like a speculator who is after a quick profit.

Jorgensen: I am guessing that you are talking about market timers, right?

Huguet: Well, remember when I was doing my research for the book, I verified what I already knew. That is that I couldn't successfully time the market in general or concentrate too heavily in one sector. Eventually the market will catch up to you and what was hot today will go down tomorrow. As informed and as successful as we are at Great Companies, we have no idea which way the market is going to go at any particular time. We just invest in great businesses, and let the market recognize the success of those businesses, and translate those successes into equity appreciation.

Jorgensen: Thanks, Jim. You have made a believer out of me. I wish you and Great Companies good luck and great fortune.

IN THE NEXT CHAPTER

Readers will find the interviews in the following chapter as interesting and as insightful as those they have just read. Chapter 12 focuses on the strategies of a value investing manager and the strategy of a core investment manager.

CHAPTER 12

Meeting Top-Tier Money Managers: Value and Core Managers

Not by age but by capacity wisdom is acquired.
—Titus Maccius Plautus (254 B.C. to 184 B.C.)

Now that you've had a chance to learn about the philosophies and methods of four leaders among tax-efficient and growth professional money management, this chapter will reveal what lies behind the successes of managers and their firms known for their achievements within their respective styles. Again, what's apparent in common among each of the professional money managers profiled here and in the previous chapter is their high degree of education and professional experience. In addition, you can't help noticing the intensive discipline and passion for achievement each of these managers brings to his practice.

THOROUGHLY MODERN VALUE: JAMES HESSER, OF RORER ASSET MANAGEMENT

Many investors have misconceptions about value investing, which prevents them from taking advantage of the opportunities offered by the prudent value manager. One false impression is that value managers invest only in stocks of depressed companies, which leaves their investors sitting on the sidelines during periods of rapid appreciation. This is simply not true.

This chapter will acquaint investors with Rorer Asset Management. Rorer portfolios have been fully invested throughout periods of bull markets and have performed impressively regardless of growth booms.

How does Rorer do it? Rorer's take on the value discipline includes a concept of "relative valuation," which, thanks to an exhaustive quantitative process, enables managers to identify value no matter how high the market climbs. I asked company president James Hesser to explain how Rorer Asset Management has become one of the premier value players in the business.

Jorgensen: Most value managers state that they buy out of favor stocks that trade at a discount to their inherent value. How does the Rorer process differ?

Hesser: Ted Rorer quantified value. Traditionally, firms took a top-down approach. I know that many of them today, at least for presentation purposes, have modeled the bottom-up process. But Ted developed a very special valuation model. He back tested and made sure it worked, regardless of universes and market conditions. He would always be able to identify stocks of value.

He used the term *relative valuation,* or relative out-of-favored-ness, if you will. We look at a company's five-year historic norm relative to the market. And therefore, we're always looking for companies that are attractive in terms of valuation relative to the rest of the market. If we take our 1,000-company universe, half of those companies are always going to be more attractive than the other half. By that definition, we'll never find ourselves in a period during which everything's too overpriced to buy.

Jorgensen: A lot of managers have been adding value by sector weightings, buying areas of the market that they feel are due for appreciation. That's essentially a top-down approach, but your firm has stayed with the bottom-up process. Do you think that's still effective?

Hesser: The bottom-up process does two things. One, it keeps you disciplined. It's very important to stay disciplined within your process and style. Secondly, it helps us spot the next market leader or group of leaders.

In the case of Rorer, I mentioned the 1,000-company universe. The first model is relative valuation. We look at a company's P/E ratio, price-to-book, price-to-cash-flow, price-to-sales, and dividend yield. We compare those five measures of valuation to the company's five-year historic norm relative to the market. Every company gets a raw score, and those points are equally weighted. That score is then ranked relative to each of the 1,000 companies. We then push 500 companies off the table because by our definition, they're overvalued. We look for a catalyst to cause these companies to return to favor. Without the catalyst, investing in these companies would be like trying to catch a falling knife. Identifying this catalyst is the real challenge of value investing.

We also apply an earnings momentum model. We define earnings momentum as occurring when a company experiences upward earnings estimate revisions from analysts tracking that company. An earnings surprise weighs very nicely in that formula. A company receives a more favorable score if analysts are moving estimates up than if earnings stay flat or are downgraded. So we wind up with 75 to 100 companies that have attractive valuations and upward estimate revisions. Oftentimes, this method leads us toward the next sector of the economy that will do well in terms of price performance on the market.

Jorgensen: That sounds like a very effective method of finding hot sectors. Can you give me an example?

Hesser: The banking group is a very good past example. In fact, some people say right now, based on rising interest rates, that banks are trading at a very attractive multiple range. And when we screen them based on earnings, if we were to see all the banks receiving upward estimate revisions, that would prompt us to take a look at that group and ask what's happening there. We did that during a rate rise in 1994 and started to purchase banks in the latter half of that year. As rates trailed down the following year, we did quite well due to the banking component we had purchased. Energy is no different. Neither is telecommunications or technology. The process directs us to the right sector.

Jorgensen: You mentioned five measures for valuation: P/E, price-to-book, dividend yield, etc. Which one do you consider to be the most important gauge of valuation?

Hesser: Generally, I'd have to pick P/E. But you get the extraordinary surprises with a company like Time/Warner, where you have to evaluate cash flow. There are other companies where it's the same. That's why we have to go in and define value using broad measurements and that's why we use all five.

Jorgensen: Sometimes a value stock can look even more attractive as it drops lower. Can you tell me more about your sell discipline and how it protects your clients from the undervalued stocks that keep going down?

Hesser: A stock like that would be one like the Bank of New England, which went down all the way to zero. Some very fine money managers bought it and kept buying it all the way down. What happens with some firms is a kind of negative vortex in the decision-making, which can happen especially when the decisions are made by committee.

Ted Rorer felt he had to have a nonemotional check to eliminate this kind of potential for disaster from the portfolio. With the Rorer process, we buy a company right at the point where expectations change. Consider Scott Paper Company. You could have bought it for $35 a share back in 1989, and many people did. It was a value stock back then because it had numerous problems to overcome. You could still have bought it for $35 a share in 1993.

Scott Paper was an even greater value in 1993, and Al Dunlop was rumored to be a candidate for CEO. Based on Chainsaw Al's reputation, the analysts started to revise their estimates upward. This was purely on the assumption that if Dunlop did the things he had done at other companies, earnings would return in force to Scott Paper. We know what happened to Al later at Sunbeam. He couldn't turn it around. But expectations are what drives a stock in the initial weeks and months. Scott went from $35 all the way to $80 and Rorer owned that stock because it passed our screens.

Had these events not transpired, had the expectations not come to fruition, then there would have been a precipitous drop in the stock. That's where the stop-loss is critical. That's a fifteen percent relative stop-loss to the S&P 500. We're not interested in being run into cash in a market correction. We prefer to remain fully invested. The stop-loss is calculated off the average cost to all our investors of a full position of three percent of the total portfolio. That's important because sometimes we take half a position, so we have the ability to do a dollar average.

Sometimes it's caused us to miss a few opportunities, but it also makes sure we're able get out before experiencing a precipitous drop. It significantly decreases volatility, and one of the most important components of a value manager is the ability to control volatility. Our stop-loss got us out of banks in 1990 and also led us during the correction of 1998 to get out of a few stocks and raise cash so we were able to do some buying at the height of the correction.

Jorgensen: Does market capitalization affect your portfolio?

Hesser: Sure. As our asset base grows, we have to be concerned about liquidity and the ability to move effectively. We're fortunate that our universe is the medium- to large-capitalization companies. The size of our firm is approximately $12 billion, and the good news is we've always been in the most liquid part of the market. Sometimes, as cycles run, when small-caps take off, we might be able to sprinkle the portfolio with a name or two, but we'll never be able to move down into that world. Size prevents us from doing that. But most of our clients already have a small-cap manager in place. When we buy a position, we buy it for all our clients, and we don't like it to be more than fifteen of the daily trading volume for a particular issue.

Jorgensen: Can you give me a picture of the way your firm is organized and the way your research is done?

Hesser: Rorer has approximately 100 employees. We're evenly split between marketing, client service, and operations, which includes trading and support. There's also the investment side, comprising analysts and portfolio managers. When you look at the analyst side, we've tried to hire what I term industry-experienced analysts. We've been able to attract them by offering ownership in the firm. Rorer has been a beneficiary of numerous mergers, which have brought some of the industry's top analysts to our team.

When an analyst comes aboard, we try to make him a generalist. When a company makes it to our short list, we assign it to an analyst to establish a relationship with its senior management. Once Rorer has taken a position, if news breaks that's not good for the company, we have to decide how to move, and we need answers very quickly. The analyst also verifies the data that brought the company to our attention in the first place. Finally, the analyst is often visiting the company, confirming why other analysts are raising the estimates. It's a continuous procedure.

Jorgensen: What's your average turnover?

Hesser: Between forty and forty-five percent.

Jorgensen: One of the biggest differences between growth and value investing is volatility. Can you tell me why growth stocks are more volatile?

Hesser: It's clearly associated with their valuation and the high multiple they command. In the case of value stocks, the reason for the low multiple relates to their specific industry, or the valuation has been knocked down by bad news. When the news isn't favorable, but the earnings are there, it's just a matter of waiting for sentiment to change. The flip side is where you have all price and no earnings. Any type of disappointment at that level is going to have a cascading effect.

Jorgensen: What's your outlook on the market over the next ten years?

Hesser: I think it will be a very exciting time. I look at the glass as being half full, not half empty, and I see some great things happening globally. The world economies are coming on strong. I have nothing that leads me to believe that the United States will be considered anything but a good place to have one's assets. I see more money coming into the market via retirement funds, and perhaps Congress will be willing to do something proactive with Social Security. This will only benefit the stocks we hold. Technology will take on a greater role. Productivity is extraordinary, and despite what Alan Greenspan says, I don't think it's slowing down, only improving in a world environment where inflation is very much under control.

Jorgensen: Many people think about the economy as a growth story. Where does value fit into that, and can you anticipate the next style shift to value?

Hesser: Everything moves in and out of favor. One minute you're the darling, and the next minute you're the wallflower. Maybe those cycles are becoming more compressed and a manager of our style, using relative valuation, will be able to capture the best opportunities at the right times. We don't want to go in off the high dive when we buy companies. We'd much rather take some of the risk off the table and buy these stocks at the moment of "out-of-favored-ness."

Comment

In an era of hot money and an explosively rising market, many investors forego the balanced and diversified approach that will make them money no matter which stocks are the current Wall Street darlings. Value is an equal partner to growth and should be part of any portfolio built on a prudent long-term strategy. Rorer Asset Management's approach to value is highly effective even in a hot growth market, making it palatable to investors who might otherwise assume that their money is lying dormant until the next style shift.

It is virtually impossible for anyone other than a trained professional to safely and efficiently make money using the value approach. Rorer's disciplined, quantitative process removes much of the unpredictability from value stock selection. It creates a smooth pattern of return, which, when examined over the long term, achieves results every bit as attractive as those of the growth managers currently in the limelight.

CORE STRATEGIES: JOHN WATERMAN, OF RITTENHOUSE NUVEEN

Investors have a large selection of money managers from which to choose, especially when it comes to large-cap growth. However, unlike mutual funds, which focus primarily on performance, it is the subtle style differences professional money managers use in exercising their disciplines on which prosperous, long-lasting relationships are built with clients.

In this section, we will focus on a core manager with a slight growth bias, Rittenhouse Nuveen. Rittenhouse has earned its well-respected reputation as a core manager by focusing on process, stability, and discipline. Rittenhouse portfolios have long-term horizons, which offer significant tax advantages to investors. While Rittenhouse may forsake the popular appeal of being an aggressive growth manager, the company possesses an impressive rate of return through long-term market cycles.

Jorgensen: Rittenhouse has a portfolio defined as core equity. Where does that fall in the growth/value spectrum?

Waterman: There are two primary definitions of core. One way people look at core is as a blend of growth and value. We see ourselves as being on the growth side of the spectrum and believe the stocks we buy are core holdings. These stocks are the cornerstone for any core portfolio. We buy global market leaders. If you want equities, you should employ different investment styles to be diversified.

Jorgensen: How large is your firm? Is it all equity?

Waterman: We have approximately $15 billion under management, all comprising large-cap growth-style investing. We run all-equity accounts and balanced accounts in that style. So, you can have an account that's ninety-eight percent–plus invested in equities. We don't time the market so we keep low cash positions. You could also have a balanced account that's approximately seventy percent weighted in equities and thirty percent weighted in cash and bonds. That account owns the exact same stocks, but on a proportionate basis to the equity account. We believe we're taking some risk with the stock, but we also believe we're going to help investors grow their money. The bonds dampen volatility. We actively manage the bonds, both in terms of average maturity and shifting spreads between high-quality corporate and treasuries. Our bond strategy is very conservative because we believe stocks are where the risk lies.

We have approximately 130 people, including 20-plus portfolio managers and 4 full-time research analysts. We stay on top of the companies in which we're invested. It's a dynamic world. Just when you think you know a company, there's a lot more you suddenly need to learn, so you really need to pay attention to all the daily developments, which takes a big team.

Jorgensen: I know your equity selection focuses on companies that meet certain criteria, including an A rating, large capitalization, consistent dividend growth, and predictable earnings growth as well as a ten-year history. Would you elaborate on these?

Waterman: At last count, there were over 10,000 ticker symbols. If you apply a $5 billion market cap screen, that takes you down to about 600 stocks. If you then apply the A rating criteria, that takes you down to about 200 stocks, those on which we focus. We look at either Standard & Poor's common stock ranking as a measure of a company's earnings growth, or Valueline's financial strength rating, which is available for all companies. We screen companies for the A rating, a $5 billion market cap, and until earlier this year we had a dividend requirement. We now consider non–dividend-paying stocks. Dividends, the ten-year history, and predictable earnings growth are all factors we look for in determining which companies we want to own.

What we're trying to ultimately do with our screen is buy stable, proven growth companies. There are growth managers who focus on aggressive growth, which are the really fast-growing stocks that haven't been around so long, such as Internet stocks. There are growth managers out there looking for earnings acceleration. There are the GARP (growth at a reasonable price) managers who are seeking growth at a reasonable price. We place ourselves in a fourth group, which looks for proven, established companies that consistently grow their earnings. Our portfolio might include stocks that have been around for 100 years or more, such as General Electric, Proctor & Gamble, and other companies of that caliber. They've been through world wars. They've been through depressions and recessions. They've proven themselves and they're going to be around and continue to grow, whatever happens in the world.

Our rating screen and market cap requirement help us zero in on companies. It takes some time, at least it used to, for a company to grow to $5 billion. Companies also have to be around for a while to earn that A ranking. That's why there are only about 200 companies that meet our criteria. The ten-year history is a similar factor. We want to look back and know a company's been in business at least ten years and perhaps tested in a downturn economy.

We now make some exceptions to the dividend rule because some of the most proven and stable tech companies don't pay them. Companies that pay dividends typically have experienced a rapid growth phase and have moved into a more stable, sustainable growth period. Their growth has slowed down a little and they're starting to throw off some excess cash.

Our basic premise holds that over the long term, stock prices track earnings growth. In theory, if you buy a company with a thirty-percent growth rate and it delivers, that should translate into a thirty percent appreciation of the stock price. I have to stress the phrase "in theory," because a lot of people want to buy the thirty percent grower. Our whole philosophy is based on the belief that the thirty-percent growers can't sustain that growth. Their earnings aren't that predictable. High growth has to slow down eventually. We think the job of trying to figure out when it will slow and sell before that happens is pretty tough to pull off. The recent market declines have proven this discipline. We prefer to buy a steady fifteen percent grower with highly predictable earnings such as a Johnson & Johnson, in which we feel it can grow in the thirteen, fourteen, or fifteen percent range and sustain it. We can make more money over time with less risk that way. The fifteen percent growers tend to deliver, whereas the thirty percent growers often don't.

I like to tell people that we're buying the Volvos of growth stocks, but we're going to drive faster than the speed limit. Over our twenty-two year history, we've gotten our clients where they want to go and we've had returns consistently in the top twenty-five percent of growth managers. Noncore growth managers buy race cars that go 150 miles per hour. Some will beat us, but others will break down and not finish the race.

Jorgensen: There are some very good companies out there, especially in the technology sector, that don't pay dividends. I'm interested in how that affects your screening process. Is this just a peculiarity of technology stocks or is there something larger going on here?

Waterman: The dividend has been a criterion of ours for many years. This business was founded before personal computers, and in the late 1970s, if you wanted a simple way to identify stable proven growth companies, you looked at their dividends. If companies paid dividends, they had probably moved into a stable period of growth.

We continue to view dividends as a tool from the perspective that companies that consistently increase their dividends at a high rate are sending us a signal that management is confident that future earnings will pay those dividends. Companies try to avoid cutting their dividends at all costs, so often if companies start to have less confidence in future earnings growth, they'll slow the rate of dividend increases. Another tactic, and a lot of individual investors don't realize this, is to increase dividends every five quarters instead of every four. These companies still claim in their annual report that the dividend has gone up every year, but the interval between increases is longer. We view behavior like this not as an automatic sell, but as a sign that we need to take a harder look at the earnings outlook.

A lot of companies in the consumer staples area such as Colgate, Walgreen's, or Proctor & Gamble continue to increase their dividends. The same holds true for health care. Merck, Johnson & Johnson, and Pfizer have great cash flows and grow their dividends. General Electric is another example. The CEO of G.E. has enough cash to invest in all the attractive opportunities GE has, and after it's done that, it can still grow thirteen to fifteen percent a year. If GE spent more money, it would start to go into less attractive projects which wouldn't add a lot to earnings growth. The management team is disciplined enough so that they will still grow the dividend at a healthy rate and still work to engage in share repurchases.

There's a trend in technology in recent years to not pay dividends. Looking at the late 1970s, we can find only one technology stock that didn't pay a dividend, and that was Digital Equipment. Last January, there were fifty-six technology stocks in the S&P 500. Thirty-one didn't pay a dividend. Because growth potential is so great, the management of tech companies believe they're going to make their money on stock price appreciation, and there is clearly a trend to not pay dividends.

Jorgensen: Your firm uses a bottom-up equity selection process. What kind of research do you do, and do you have any top-down processes that affect your investment strategy?

Waterman: We believe the companies in which we invest are widely followed by Wall Street and we have the benefit of getting research on, say, Coca-Cola or Intel from virtually all the Wall Street firms, large and small. The challenge we have with a stock like Coca-Cola is not lack of information. It's making sure we're on top of all the information that's out there, and acting on it. We rely on outside research, though we have analysts internally who are responsible for not just following that research but keeping on top of what's important. There are several things we do. We sit in on company quarterly earnings conference calls, which we consider a valuable process. For example, when Dell announces its earnings, our tech analyst is on that call and he gets not only the benefit of hearing a first-hand description of earnings for the quarter, but often management will make a forecast about the coming year. We also have the benefit of the Q&A period, during which we ask questions and hear the questions of all the other analysts. We talk to these companies. We visit them and many of them visit us.

Pfizer, which we own, recently had a half-day analyst meeting in New York and we had the benefit not only of attending that meeting, but also a lunch afterwards with the CEO, COO, and CFO. Only half a dozen firms were invited. We were able to talk to them first hand about their business and their outlook.

When an analyst comes to our five-member investment committee, we ask him to take all the information we've acquired about a stock and boil it down to two pages or less, focusing on three areas. The first is to identify where earnings growth will come from over the next three to five years. If the company is projected to grow an average of fifteen percent over the next five years, we want the analyst to precisely and confidently identify how the company will achieve that growth. The second part covers risk. The third part is a rationale for why we should own the stock, why we own it if we do already, or why we should sell it. Analysts have to be pretty articulate within two pages or less. We continually refer to this template while we own the stock and continually reexamine the results.

I've already mentioned the screens we use. We typically own between twenty-five and thirty stocks, so we're fairly concentrated. If you want to do better than the market over time, you have to own enough of a stock to make a difference. We question whether other large-cap managers can do as well owning fifty to sixty stocks. Obviously, with small-cap managers, there are liquidity issues that make a difference. Typically we don't try to swing for the fences with our stocks, but we want to hit a lot of singles and doubles. We don't put more than five percent of our portfolio in any one stock or more that fifteen percent in any one industry and no more than two times the market in any one sector. You won't see us with ten or fifteen percent of the portfolio in one company, no matter how much we love it. If a position grows to over five percent, we'll let it run to maybe six percent before we pull money out to keep the portfolio diversified. We don't make big sector bets. This business is based on futures, and no matter how confident we are in our ability, we know we can be wrong. So the most important thing we can do for our clients is to keep their portfolios diversified.

When we get to the actual stocks, we examine both bottom-up and top-down aspects. If I had to weight one more than another, number one would be buying companies with solid earnings, which is clearly a bottom-up process. I've already talked about how we spend time sorting our 200-stock universe using all different types of financial criteria, including internal and external earning consistency, predictability measurements, earnings growth rates, historical revenue growth rates, historical projected earnings growth rates, and valuation measures. We sort this database by these criteria over and over again to see what names come to the surface. This isn't a quantitative black box. By using different screens on our stock universe, we'll see a certain stock appearing near the top of the list based on a number of different criteria. That's a signal that we ought to take a closer look and do some fundamental analysis of that company to determine if it really fits in the portfolio. We also do the screens by the eleven economic sectors as defined by S&P. That's very much a bottom-up process.

We are top-down from the perspective that if we were purely bottom-up, we wouldn't even look at the sectors we buy. We would just buy the companies we like best. If they were all in technology, we'd end up with a portfolio that was all technology. Clearly, because we have sector constraints, it's top down. We also consider, at the margin, where we are in the economic cycle. One of the members of our investment committee is an economist, and every week he gives us an update. We may identify a stock in the retail area, which is a consumer cyclical sector. If that stock is attractive on a bottom-up fundamental basis but our economist tells us that we're late in the cycle when the economy is expected to slow, we don't want to be adding to our retail exposure. We would describe that as a subtle top-down process. And the reason I say subtle is that it will only affect the portfolio at the margin.

We would consider a classic top-down approach to be that of a manager looking where we are in the cycle and making a decision to rotate a significant percentage of the portfolio into certain sectors based on a top-down view of which sectors were due to perform.

We don't do that. We're low-turnover managers. We believe that you will do best in this business by being patient over time, so we make relatively few changes. When we make a change, we consider where we are in the cycle. By the way, because of our A rating criteria, we don't buy deep cyclicals. A classic top-down manager might rotate into an auto stock or an aluminum stock or a chemical stock at a certain point in the cycle. Those stocks don't meet our quality criteria. A retail stock, a high-quality energy stock, or something in financial services might fit our criteria at the right time.

Jorgensen: You mentioned low turnover as one of the characteristics for which you strive in your portfolio. Tax efficiency is a big advantage IMAs have over other forms of investment. What is your turnover, and do you consider yourself a tax-efficient manager?

Waterman: Our turnover is approximately twenty percent. I've read that the average equity mutual fund has a turnover of around eighty percent. We aim to be low turnover, and for the past three years the average has been approximately twenty percent. I think that puts us on the low end for professional money managers. Our belief is that with the high-quality stocks we buy, more often than not we're going to do better for clients by being patient and giving them time to work, rather than making a lot of changes to the portfolio. That translates into an investment philosophy we like to describe as naturally tax efficient. It's not a tax-managed product in the sense that taxes don't drive our decisions. We're making the best investment decision and the best pretax returns we can for our clients. Our approach of buying these proven growth companies, of being low-turnover, patient investors, has turned out to be very tax efficient. We let our winners run and we sell our losers, which happens to be one of the most tax-efficient ways to run money. If you were to look at our performance over the past three to five years, our tax efficiency is in the ninety-three to ninety-five percent range, which I think would put us up among the best tax managers.

Jorgensen: How should investors who are looking for just one manager to handle the bulk of their assets approach the selection process? Is your definition of a core portfolio appropriate?

Waterman: I think investors have several options. I'm assuming they're working with a consultant who's assessing risk tolerance and time horizon. The real benefit of diversification is smoothing the ride and lowering volatility for clients. They don't necessarily make any more money over time.

If you have a client with a high-risk tolerance or a long time horizon, perhaps the consultant puts him with an aggressive growth manager with a lot of technology holdings. The investor makes money and sleeps at night doing so.

In contrast, for clients who have shorter time horizons or lower risk tolerances, diversification makes a lot of sense because it smoothes out the swings in their portfolios. I certainly believe Rittenhouse is one of their best options because our high-quality, blue chip, stable, growth stocks are relatively low-risk performers. These are companies that aren't going out of business. They hold up well during corrections. They go down in value, but not as much as smaller companies. They often recover faster because after a correction, there's typically a flight to quality. If I could have my money in only one group of stocks, these are the ones I'd choose. Another approach would be using a manager who applies more of a growth/value blend.

Jorgensen: What is your benchmark for performance?

Waterman: Depending on the consultant, we use either the S&P 500 or the Russell 1000 Growth, which is more aggressive because of the technology weighting. Internally we use the S&P 500.

Jorgensen: What is your perspective on index funds?

Waterman: I think there are three general points to consider. First is the assumption the media puts forward to the effect that indexing works. However, if you study all the indices, the only one that has done consistently well is the S&P 500. If you look at the Russell 2000, the EAFE (Europe and Far East Stock Index), or any other index, active managers have beaten the pants off them, so there's only one out there that is a concern.

Secondly, a lot of people think that the S&P 500 represents the market or the 500 largest companies. That's not true. It's 500 companies picked by an eight-member investment committee at Standard & Poor's. In other words, the S&P is an actively managed portfolio that happens to have worked very well in the market environment over the past couple of years. It isn't passive investing. It happens to be a benchmark that firms can license, so they can passively copy it, but the S&P itself is actively managed. The stocks S&P has added have been in the technology area to boost performance. They've been weeding out the traditional smokestack industries, so the S&P is not representative of the broader market.

If somebody truly wanted to match what the market did long-term, they'd buy the Wilshire 5000, which tracks 7,500 market-cap weighted stocks.

The third point about the S&P is that it's done so well because it's market-cap weighted, meaning that the returns are weighted based on the size of a company. In the past three or four years, returns have been skewed by a few very large technology companies that have delivered dramatic returns. Take a company like Microsoft that already has a $240 billion market cap that goes up 100 percent in one year. There's never been any company so large that's gone up so much in percentage terms in any one-year period of time. When that happens, given the market-cap weighted nature of the benchmark, that really pushes up the S&P return. You have to wonder whether that's sustainable over the long term.

The next question you have to ask is whether these benchmarks, particularly the S&P, are becoming overly dominated by technology and the performance of a few very large tech stocks. If clients are asking Rittenhouse to run diversified portfolios to keep risks down, can they have it both ways? Or will they want us to run a technology portfolio to keep pace with the S&P 500 and recognize that they are going to have to take more risk in doing so?

Increasingly, consultants are going to have to educate their clients about how dominated these benchmarks have become by technology. We think this is going to increase even more over the next three to five years and consultants need to make sure clients understand the trade-off of risk versus reward if they want their managers to keep up with these benchmarks.

Comment

Not long after our interview, I saw John Waterman on the news, where he is often consulted for his experience and his inside track on some of the most highly regarded companies in the country. I find his take on index funds both compelling and fascinating. I'm most impressed by Rittenhouse's long-term focus. As with Dr. Jeremy Siegel, whose scholarly work the company embraces, Rittenhouse knows there is less risk in holding quality stocks over a long period than with other supposedly safer alternatives. For many investors whose objective is comfortable retirement, the Rittenhouse Volvo is a much smarter choice than the hot rod funds of the moment.

IN THE NEXT CHAPTER

Diversification among styles and major asset classes is a necessary tactic for protecting and enhancing your wealth. From Chapter 13 you will glean some valuable insights from a manager who invests in foreign securities and from one of the country's leading fixed-income investors.

CHAPTER **13**

Meeting Top-Tier Money Managers: International and Fixed Income Managers

There are few, if any, jobs in which ability alone is sufficient.
Needed, also, are loyalty, sincerity, enthusiasm and team play.
—William B. Given, Jr.

VALUE WITH A GLOBAL TOUCH: ROBERT GALLAGHER, OF BRANDES INVESTMENT PARTNERS

Value investing is a highly developed and successful style that hasn't attracted a lot of public attention of late because of the focus on large-cap growth at the beginning of the new century. For many investors, especially those leery of ultra-high valuations now seen on Wall Street, value investing and its long-term perspective is appealing. Brandes Investment Partners is a firm known for its application of value investing in foreign markets.

Founder Charles Brandes learned the principles of value investing directly from Benjamin Graham, considered one of the primary originators of the discipline. Brandes continues to be known for its global value approach, providing investors with a core value portfolio in domestic markets and the added diversification of global opportunities.

Indeed, for someone seeking to add an international component to his investment strategy, there is no safer way to participate in emerging markets than with a value approach. When I first encountered Brandes in the late 1980s, it was a small, $120 million shop. Today, Brandes manages over $40 billion in assets.

I recently sat down with Bob Gallagher, one of the seven voting members of the company investment committee, who explained what value investing means to Brandes Investment Partners and its clients.

Jorgensen: How much of your total business comprises individually managed accounts?

Gallagher: We have $40 billion in assets, virtually all of which are in individually managed accounts. Of that, institutional accounts represent some $20 billion while private clients account for the other half. We subadvise mutual funds within the institutional group, though don't offer them directly. Our purpose is to manage money, not market mutual funds.

Jorgensen: Can you elaborate on how your firm's value style evolved?

Gallagher: When Charles Brandes was a broker, he had the great fortune to meet Benjamin Graham, who was an educator and mentor to numerous well-known value investors. Charles was lucky enough to be one of them. He realized that this was a chance to build a foundation for his investment philosophy, and in 1974 decided to break out on his own.

Think about it. This was 1974, the depth of stock market woes. The oil crisis had driven the market down for two consecutive years, down fourteen percent in 1973 and twenty-six percent in 1974. That period was truly a perfect time for value investing. Some of the first accounts Charles took over had foreign securities in them. This was before the rise of American Depository Receipts

[ADRs are issues listed on U.S. exchanges that represent the valuations of important foreign stocks]. Most practitioners of value investing focused on the United States, but Charles decided to utilize the value discipline on foreign stocks as well.

Value, purchased on an absolute basis, is inexpensive. There are many different ways of exploring and determining value besides the classic barometers of low price-to-book, low price-to-earnings, and low price-to-cash flow. It could be comparison with investment alternatives, performance history, and competitors on a local, regional, or worldwide basis.

Jorgensen: How do you go about picking stocks?

Gallagher: We are a pure bottom-up organization. We start with a large number of analysts with industry responsibilities. In order to be a good, solid value investor, you've got to understand what a company does. For example, do you know what Nike does? Nike doesn't make anything. It subcontracts everything. And yet most people think Nike makes shoes and sports clothing. It doesn't make anything except images. If you have that understanding of what Nike does, you can look at its financial statements and understand how the company makes money. It's the manufacture and resale of shoes and advertising. We take a similar approach to many different industries. We seek to understand what businesses do and how they make money. This is key to determining whether a company is a good value investment.

We also consider the international marketplace and different accounting standards. You have to know if companies are comparable on an apples-to-apples basis and have to make gross adjustments to financial statements in order to do this. If it's a situation of great complexity, one way to deal with it is to move up the income statement and eliminate some of the noncash charges that can be more discretionary, depending on accounting standards. You must be able to understand revenue recognition. That's huge in the international arena. You see a lot of restatements in this country. Waste management, for example, is revenue recognition. What it comes down to is fundamentals. How companies make money and how they report it. You can also use the big stick value parameters of price-to-earnings, price-to-cash flow, and price-to-book. We look at things as a multiple of earnings or cash flow, book value, net asset value, and enterprise value as a determination on value. For example, we may say that a bank is worth eighteen times earnings. We will only purchase that bank if it's trading at a significant discount. That's how we approach value.

Jorgensen: How does the value process work within your company?

Gallagher: This is a big organization. On the investment committee, we have seven voting members and fifteen members total that are participants in the investment process. The implementation of this process is a team function. It starts with the investment committee and incorporates a huge effort from operations, trading, and the whole portfolio management group.

The process includes a great deal of communication. With individually managed accounts, clients are constantly informed about what's happening with their accounts and about all specific transactions because they own those securities. It's not as though you're buying into a mutual fund and you don't own the stocks. If you open an account with us, you could theoretically fire us and keep the securities.

Value investing relies on communication because we buy into market areas perceived negatively. It's a challenging endeavor, especially when the media tells people to get out of emerging markets. And there are always some very high profile investors who attract attention when they pull their money out. The popular sentiment is usually telling you the exact opposite of what we advise. Just what are you going to think if you're not an investment professional?

Jorgensen: How do you decide whether a particular market is developed enough for investment?

Gallagher: We have a fundamental need, not just a desire, for accurate historical data going back over a definable period. We also need a country with an established rule of law and method of dispute resolution. The marketplace must be organized so that trading is reliable and understandable. It's more difficult for a value investor to operate within these perimeters in underdeveloped markets, though they are the fundamental safety factors.

Jorgensen: How do you decide on allocations by country? How do you decide when to commit a large percentage of your assets to one attractive area?

Gallagher: We have no minimums and do not have to be in any market. If something does not represent value, we will not invest. We were not in Japan from 1986 to 1994. We simply didn't have a weighting in the second largest world market. We hold a maximum of five percent per security at cost. We can allow it to appreciate, but at cost it's five percent. Our maximum investment in any one industry or country, at cost, is the greater of 20 percent of our total portfolio or 150 percent of that country's allocation in a benchmark such as the EAFE index. That provides the discipline to prevent us from becoming over-allocated and provides us with greater opportunity to find value wherever it is, and that may be in markets that are extremely out of favor or small. We don't follow the allocations of any benchmark.

Jorgensen: Suppose an investor commits funds to a value manager. Should he be looking for a domestic manager as well as an international manager? Is your global portfolio designed to take proper advantage of both opportunities?

Gallagher: Our approach means that we take advantage of value wherever it occurs. Our portfolio is designed so that one particular area isn't over-weighted, but our bottom-up, issue-by-issue approach lets us look at each individual opportunity versus the whole portfolio. If we look at a stock in Brazil, we ask ourselves if that stock is any better than the ones we already have in the portfolio. If it's significantly better, we make the switch.

That individual, security-by-security process lets us constantly examine the portfolio and makes it stand up to the available value opportunities. If we look at something in a market that's a screaming bargain, maybe fifty percent undervalued compared to something that's only ten percent undervalued, we may make that switch. We have the confidence to be a single-value manager domestically, internationally, and globally.

Jorgensen: How do you advise a value investor to stick to his discipline in periods dominated by growth?

Gallagher: For Brandes, patience is the key. Our average time horizon for a hold is three to five years. If someone is interested in short-term profits, we feel that's more akin to speculation on price movement rather than investment in the value of a company. Now a growth firm would probably tell you that a short time horizon is still investing, because you're looking at growth in earnings over this short period, but it's Brandes' view that disciplined investing takes longer.

We try to align our thought process with that of the management of the companies in which we invest. They have long-term outlooks because they're looking at capital expenditure budgets. What sort of return are they looking at? It's not a six-month return. Large capital budgets require a multiple-year return. You have to align yourself with management if you're going to be pure investors in that way. The only thing we sell is our process. If there's no confidence that our process is sound, we have nothing.

Comment

Even if you embrace a different investment philosophy, it's hard not to admire the focus and discipline apparent at Brandes. Committed value investors believe that history bears out their strategy. While growth comes into fashion periodically, so does value, and over the long term, both types of portfolios have comparable performances.

The international arena makes a value practice, such as Brandes, attractive. Investors can take confidence in the client focus that has driven the Brandes process, even at the expense of potentially larger profits. That's not something you'll find everyday on Wall Street. There's little wonder the small shop I found years ago has seen such success.

THE WORLD OF BONDS: STEVE WLODARSKI, OF MCDONNELL INVESTMENT MANAGEMENT

It's no secret that stocks get all the attention from the investing public when the markets are going up. When they are going down, investors looking for safety invest in bonds. They've been touted, and for good reason, as the most effective long-term investment. But for many investors, the attraction of bonds remains undiminished. Those who want steady income or added security need a commitment to bonds, plain and simple. The tax-free income of municipal bonds is certainly a prime attraction for many high-net-worth investors.

But while many people believe that bonds are simply purchased and held to maturity, fixed-income securities is actually an area where an investor stands to get a high level of added value from a separately managed account. The complexities and the nuances of the bond market are such that it is virtually impossible for the individual to pursue the same strategies as the professionals. To get a full explanation of what goes into managing a modern fixed-income portfolio, I recently had a conversations with Steve Wlodarski, CFA, Vice-President, and Senior Municipal Portfolio Manager at McDonnell Investment Management, one of the largest fixed-income specialists in the business. To be sure, he has his work cut out for him. While stocks continue to soar, the slowly creeping rise in interest rates have made the past few years difficult for bonds. But like many of the other professionals we've met, Steve will explain how his firm's discipline and strategy work today and down the road.

Jorgensen: Since 1926 stocks have averaged over ten percent per year and bonds less than four percent. As a bond manager, how do you help clients understand the importance of bonds in their portfolio?

Wlodarski: One of my bosses who was an equity guy once made the comment that most people with a long-term time horizon should probably never own any bonds. And that might be part of the answer. I view it as a diversification question, depending on client objective and time horizon. Even in the last twenty years, we've had periods when equities just haven't gone straight up like recently. From a diversification standpoint, you don't want to put all your eggs into one basket, so to speak. You want to have diversification across several different asset classes. Bonds meet a different need of a client's portfolio; they provide a continuous stream of income. They don't have the volatility, good or bad, that stocks necessarily do.

We did a study of equity versus bond returns during the great bull market from 1982 to 2000, and one thing we looked at was municipal bonds on an after-tax basis for clients that are in maximum tax brackets. We found that once you adjusted for taxes, and we used some very conservative adjustments, the differential historically over the past eighteen years on a pretax basis between municipals and equities was about eight percent. On an after-tax basis that narrows to about five percent a year. So your returns on an after-tax basis start to narrow a bit. There are periods, like the early 1990s where you have seen some volatility in stocks. Bonds tend to cushion that volatility in the returns and pride a steady stream of income. It depends on client objectives—how much tolerance they have for risk. I have one client who says to me, "I really don't care about growth in my portfolio, I just want my $300,000 a year in tax-free income."

Jorgensen: What sorts of time horizons make bonds an appropriate choice for investors?

Wlodarski: I wouldn't start with age as a qualifier, because there are some very conservative thirty- and forty-year-olds out there. The qualifying statement from a client who says, "I don't want the volatility; I just want to keep what I've got." Those are the people who should be weighted more heavily toward bonds, definitely a person who needs a stable income stream. When you do see that one- or two-year downturn in the stock market, he's going to still want to draw income.

Jorgensen: Oftentimes as advisors, in helping clients with bond decisions, we go through the various options: governments and government/corporates. We basically throw in the term "higher quality" in describing them. Is that how you would differentiate the two categories?

Wlodarski: Perhaps we ought to start out with some definitions. Government bonds are issued by the U.S. government, which is considered the safest entity. A step below that are agencies of the U.S. government, and it's believed that the government would back those agencies up in a financial crisis of some type. There are a whole range of corporate bonds based on their credit worthiness that can also be considered. The way we look at these different securities is based on their credit quality and the market environment, the economic environment, and how much more income and yield you might get from a government bond versus an agency bond versus a corporate bond?

Secondly, what has that historical trend been? This is something, as bond managers, we can examine and make some determinations going forward. If we look at what happened, say a year ago, when we had a financial crisis, government/corporate bonds were yielding .25 percent more than government bonds. There's a trade-off. For the safety of the U.S. government you're giving up .25 percent in interest versus buying a corporate bond. In many cases these were lower tier corporate bonds—BBB rated—still investment grade, but the lowest level. Today, the yield on these lower tier corporate bonds is 1 percent or 1.5 percent over government securities. Had you been an investor at the point when the yield spreads were very narrow, you would have lost principal value when the yields widened out, back up to about 1 percent. In some cases, depending on the maturity of the bond, the principal could have deteriorated 3, 4, or 5 percent. You miss opportunities if you're not monitoring these trends on an ongoing basis.

Sometimes clients dismiss the idea of yield spreads by saying that they don't lose any money if they just hold the bond to maturity. In fact they do, because they lose the opportunity to get more income. If in this environment the client is buying high-quality securities, when the yield spreads widen again, he has the opportunity to get a whole lot more income, and he's preserved his capital. A bond manager looks at all these trends in the market and hopefully selects and makes some judgment when to avoid risk and when the market is paying him a premium for extra risk. In that way he can generate higher income and higher returns on the portfolio at safer points in time. To answer simply, sometimes the safety of governments has a higher relative valuation and there are other times when you are compensated for marginal incremental risk on the corporate bonds.

Jorgensen: Following up on that, Steve, during times when we have increases in interest rates, no matter how good a bond manager is, when you're holding bonds in a rising interest rate environment, you're going to lose capital. What do you say to a client during periods like this about the advantages of having somebody manage the bond portfolio versus just holding on to the bonds and paying no fee?

Wlodarski: The client has lost money, and I often use the example of just holding bonds to maturity. What you do lose is opportunity in those types of situation. If interest rates rise one percent, you can sell the bonds that you held, and hopefully as a professional manager you've been positioned and own a bond that has done a little better than the market. Then you can go out and buy a bond that has a much higher rate of interest in the new environment. You may take a loss on selling that bond, but with bonds, that higher rate of interest and income that you're getting for, say, the next five years is going to compensate you for the loss that you take. You're converting that loss today into a higher income stream in the future. If you're in a taxable portfolio, the loss that you take today can be used to write off gains that you're realizing perhaps in a stock portfolio. The loss isn't really a loss because the higher income means that it will be recouped.

Jorgensen: On the same lines, if you were talking to an investor and they were trying to determine the benefits of having $300,000 to $400,000 in a separately managed bond account versus a pooled fund, what would you say to them? I know your firm offers both.

Wlodarski: They have three different alternatives, really. They can do it themselves, put their money into a number of mutual funds, or they could hire a bond manager to do it. I don't really find that many people with that amount of assets who are moving into mutual funds. The average deposit in mutual funds like ours is somewhere in the area of $15,000. Most people with that size of assets are looking to buy the bonds directly on their own or hiring a bond manager to do it for them.

When buying bonds on your own, you limit your ability to access the opportunities of the market, to trade, and the opportunities a bond manager can see on a day-to-day basis that the individual can't see. You're also missing some of the discipline. People don't want to take losses, necessarily, because they don't see the benefit in doing that. We can do that and improve the portfolio significantly in the future. A rising rate environment is a real test of a manager's ability to add value down the road for the client and improve the income on the portfolio. This is probably one of our busiest years of the last three. When rates are falling and returns are wonderful and everything's going well, a bond manager may not do all that much work! But in a year when rates are rising, we are extremely busy.

Jorgensen: In buying municipal bonds for my clients in a specific state, I've felt as though I could never get the same pricing as a firm like yours might get on the same issue. There are so many funds and so many managers buying up the issues in large lots, I've told clients that it's imperative, particularly on the municipal side, to hire a manager just for pricing alone. Can you comment?

Wlodarski: I think that ability to access the market is one of the things I alluded to previously. It helps if you're with a firm that's recognized as a large institutional buyer. When there are deals that are priced, we get notice of them weeks in advance. We are solicited for our interest days in advance. They're coming to us, asking at what level we would care to purchase so they can price the deal accordingly. When everything comes down, we have a lot more leverage as a large buyer. In many of the deals, we get into fights over the bonds, because there are five institutional orders for an entire maturity on a bond issue. We may have situations where the bonds are divided between us and five other large institutional buyers and we're even cut back. I don't see how an individual in this type of environment could stand a chance unless the deal doesn't do well. One trend is that when bonds are offered to retail investors first, typically what we see is that the bonds are marked up ten to fifteen basis points in yield (0.10 to 0.15 percent). For institutional investors, they lower the price because they know that the retail investor has less information, less access to the market, and is less sophisticated generally.

Jorgensen: At what point should an investor consider municipal bonds?

Wlodarski: Generally the twenty-eight percent tax bracket, but two years ago we saw situations where municipals were attractive for clients even in the lowest tax bracket. Many people use municipals in accounts that weren't taxable, because when they yield 100 percent of taxable bonds and the yield spread starts to revert back to normal, you're going to get outperformance. Other times, the yield spreads on municipals vary and one of the things we do on larger accounts ($5 million-plus) is move between municipals and taxables. Sometimes it's not attractive for a client in a twenty-eight or thirty percent rate. The tax bracket is really the key in the value on municipals in the market but generally twenty-eight percent is the tax bracket.

Jorgensen: Let's briefly go through the strategy your team uses for buying municipals and government/corporates in portfolios.

Wlodarski: The team concept is really the key because my specialty is buying municipals and I manage the municipal team here. We have two people that focus on corporate bonds. We have one that focuses on mortgage-backed securities and asset-backed securities. We have another person that focuses on federal agencies and short-term. We have team specialists and we all work together in coordination. We look at relative valuations in different sectors. The team specialists have input into the decision as to where they see the value in their specific area of responsibility. Then the portfolio managers in conjunction with the eighteen specialists are responsible for certain groups of accounts, and they're familiar with the objectives of those programs and accounts and clients and make a determination as to what the allocation should be. Most of the time for clients in the higher tax brackets, our decision is that we're going to be 100 percent in municipals. Based on the input, we may make decisions that now is the time to lower those municipal allocations because the municipal valuations are very high and for clients in the twenty-eight percent tax bracket we should have a U.S. Treasury or agency allocation.

Once we come up with these numbers, which are kind of intuitive, we then run a number of statistical tests on the portfolios. We run them through scenarios. What if, instead of the yield spreads on municipals and corporates going from 100 basis points to 50 basis points (1 to 0.50 percent), they go from 100 to 125 (1 to 1.25 percent)? What happens to our portfolios? What is the total return? So we test our expectations constantly and we try to establish break-even points where we know that this is a low-risk opportunity, because even if the yield spreads go against us, we come out even. These are the types of opportunities that we look for—they have protection.

Jorgensen: In recent years some people have suggested that you can capture eighty percent of the return of the bond market by staying in intermediate maturities, seven to eight years or less without all the associated volatility. Would you agree with that?

Wlodarski: We agree with that wholeheartedly. Our program is designed for capital preservation. For a conservative client we think a five-year average maturity target is appropriate. You have about eighty percent of the yield with about thirty percent of the downside. In 1999, that's pretty much the way it worked out. Even our more aggressive clients that are in ten-year maturity bonds were down 1.25 percent. When you see a lot of funds that were down 2, 3, 4, or 6 percent last year, those numbers look really good, although I hate to say negative numbers look good.

Jorgensen: Oftentimes with a state-specific client, let's take California, because they have a fairly high tax rate, a firm like yours will buy municipal bonds in a state like Illinois. Why would you buy an out-of-state municipal bond knowing that the income is taxable in California where the client resides?

Wlodarski: One reason is diversification of risk. It's tough to talk about this when we've had a good economy for the last seven or eight years, but it wasn't too long ago when California faced the Orange County crisis. That was an impediment to the way California bonds traded and yielded in the marketplace. You had defense closures in the state and there was risk associated with bonds in those days. We've had a strong economy and the municipalities are flush with cash balances, so nobody's worried about risk right now, but to put all your money in one state is just bad diversification. California's the largest state that issues bonds; it's fifteen percent of the market. You're limiting your opportunities if you stay in California. It's like buying only fifteen percent of the S&P 500. Many times the valuations on California bonds are very, very high. If a client starts a portfolio today and the valuations on California bonds are high, it's bound to underperform on a total return basis because valuations are bound to return to normal, and that may offset any tax benefit. In comparing a California bond with an out-of-state bond, we look at the yields on an after-tax basis and oftentimes the impact is that the tax penalty is justified by the yield.

Jorgensen: You've mentioned high-yield bonds. Would you say there are bonds that approach the risk of equities?

Wlodarski: I found a study by Ken French, one of the best financial writers, and he was saying that even the low-investment grade bonds have a beta of 1.0 and the beta of an equally weighted S&P is always higher than that, so bonds never approach equities.

Jorgensen: Tell us about the research effort that goes into your decisions.

Wlodarski: I think that one thing that research provides you is the ability to monitor your holdings on an ongoing basis. I think that the typical individual looks at a couple of things on bonds besides the credit rating. They look at the maturity and the yield, and many times the yield drives the decision because most people want to boost their income and get the highest yield possible and aren't really focusing on a lot of the details. We look at all kinds of things on bonds. We look at factors like call features. We actually ask questions about the purpose of the bonds and who pays the bond back. In the municipal market, there's a lot of AAA rated bonds with different purposes. All AAA rated bonds aren't created equal. All bond insurers aren't created equal and have different capabilities. We follow all the bond insurers and we've established a ranking system for all the major insurers, so we know which ones have the strongest capital ratios and which ones are competing aggressively for market share. Some will work with tax increment financing districts in which a developer will come in and creates a municipal entity that is going to develop a project, putting in the sewers, the lighting, the roads. The developer comes in to sell homes and businesses in the area. Those bonds are kind of speculative. When municipal bonds have gotten into trouble in the past, those are the kinds of areas that have been more afflicted and have tended to go into default. When times are good, of course they do very well, but at the top of the economy, people are going to be moving into these types of issues. Unless it's an established project where the revenue streams are solid, you may not be buying the right bond, and there's going to be risk there. So we research and ask questions about the bonds. How much of the project, for example, is developed? Many of these bonds are insured, they're all investment grade, but if there is ever an economic downturn, we'll know the first bonds that will start having trouble. It's an extremely in-depth process and extremely timely. A bond may be priced today, and I can go walk into an analysts office and have questions asked in an hour or two.

Jorgensen: The bond environment has been ideal lately, but looking forward, say ten years, what do you think people can expect out of the bond market?

Wlodarski: Since I'm buying bonds for customers, I always start with the assumption that I think bond yields are too low. That's where value can be created. We've been in a great economic environment and it's going to be very difficult to speculate as to when that changes. If there's an economic downturn, bonds are going to perform as they have historically. They're going to appreciate in value and the yields that we've been seeing over the past few years are relatively high in a real sense relative to inflation. Municipal bonds are attractive, of course because of the tax benefits. Relative to inflation, you're getting your two to three percent above inflation on an after-tax basis. That's generally what you'd expect from a taxable bond. From that sense you have the prospect for bonds to do well longer term. There are concerns. Mr. Greenspan's been appointed for another four years. I won't project his reappointment for 2004, but I think his goal is perhaps to slow a little of the speculation by raising rates. If he's successful, I think the trend for interest rates is extremely positive, and now is a good time to be investing in the bond market.

Unlike stocks, where investors may at least think they can perform adequately on their own, there's little question that the subtleties of rate spreads, and comparative credit ratings are beyond most individuals. I believe the questions of access and research alone make the case for hiring a skilled bond manager. Beyond the perceived security of the bonds themselves, it is the actual active management itself that provides the ultimate layer of safety from the fluctuations of the market.

IN THE LAST CHAPTER

I wouldn't have invested as much time and effort in writing this book if I didn't believe fervently in the future of this proven approach to wealth management. In the last chapter of this book, I share with you some of the reasons that I and some other IMA pioneers believe that the best is yet to come for investors who work with individual money managers.

CHAPTER 14

IMAs Today and Tomorrow

The future according to some scientists will be exactly like the past, only far more expensive.

—John Sladek

Investment is a word that can be used to sell just about anything from a stock portfolio to a questionable land deal. Just as one form of investment gains wide acceptance, another is rapidly developed and touted as the smart new way to invest your money.

Despite my enthusiasm, I do not wish to portray IMAs as "the next big thing in investing." IMAs have evolved over time and have been refined to meet the needs of specific investors. For these people, the advantages are distinct and compelling.

More high-net-worth Americans are investing in the stock market. Yet, for a variety of reasons, many of these people invest their assets in less efficient vehicles that are simply more heavily marketed, more in vogue, or simply more familiar.

Familiarity shouldn't be underestimated. After all, it's a source of confidence. Personally, I would never invest my hard-earned savings unless I had a high degree of comfort that the investment vehicle was proven and recommended by people in the know. This is precisely the level of confidence I want to share with you here.

FOUR INDUSTRY PERSPECTIVES

Rather than just imparting my personal experience, I want to provide you with perspectives on the managed account industry drawn from four pioneers who helped build it and continue to shape the way it evolves. Their names are well recognized on Wall Street for their contributions to the investment industry.

Len Reinhart is a true visionary who has probably done more than any other person to shape the IMA business. It was Len, along with Jim Lockwood, who first convinced money managers to lower fees and minimum account balance requirements. They did so, and IMAs became an option for individual investors.

Len Reinhart: What are now called IMAs began with institutional retirement funds. Prior to the 1970s, most companies offered fixed-return retirement plans. In other words, they had to pay a certain amount to retiring employees. There were few limits on what a company or institution could do with the money before distribution. In other words, a company could invest the retirement funds however it wished. The only obligation was to pay a certain amount as planned when someone retired.

When the Employee Retirement Insurance And Security Act was enacted in 1974, it changed the picture completely. The Employee Retirement Income Securities Act of 1974 enabled pension clients to sue companies for fiduciary irresponsibility. Suddenly companies had to be responsible with the way they handled money and invest it prudently. Few companies possessed the necessary expertise to effectively manage a retirement plan, and professional money management firms stepped in.

My involvement with the IMA business began with E.F. Hutton. Jim Lockwood and I saw an opportunity to bring some of the advantages of IMAs to high-net-worth individuals. We had technology in place that offered professional managers the ability to administer multiple smaller accounts. We convinced managers to lower their fees while we took on some of their paperwork and distribution through our financial advisors.

Today IMAs are currently approaching $400 billion in assets and that's up from what I estimate to be about $10 billion in 1987. There is a convergence of forces at work that will propel a great deal more money into the IMA industry. First, baby boomers are generating an enormous amount of wealth. At the same time, wealth is being passed on by previous generations. People are also receiving lump-sum distributions from things like 401(k) s and are in possession of significant amounts of money.

In years past, people would take a sum of this size to a broker. Many people are uneasy about making decisions of this kind themselves, and that's where a product like a mutual fund or an IMA comes in.

The big difference between mutual funds and IMAs is that mutual funds are measured on a total return basis (after taxes and after fees). In 1987, when we really got started with the all-inclusive IMA or *"Wrap Account"* the average mutual fund turnover was only 12%. Today with funds actively seeking higher returns the average turnover is closer to 100%. The fund that attracts the most money is the one that had the biggest gains the previous year. Individually managed accounts, on the other hand, are designed to be measured on an after-tax basis and this is what will drive the IMA industry in the next ten years.

Today most major financial service firms have created fee-based departments to offer both fee-advised mutual funds and IMAs. UBS Paine Webber is one such firm. I asked Bruce Bursey, Senior Vice-President of the Investment Consulting Services Division, to explain how professional money management fits under the UBS investment umbrella.

Bruce Bursey: Investment Consulting Services at UBS Paine Webber provides professional money management, asset allocation, and fee-based mutual fund programs. In addition, there are financial advisor programs, which run money on a discretionary basis, as well as financial planning and wealth management. We have an ability to access the specific type of expertise a client is seeking. I believe that's the future of the financial services business. Competitiveness is going to be based on the ability to specialize in specific areas and provide the respective expertise. When you look at investment consulting and professional money management, it includes the whole profiling process that goes along with financial planning and the specialized needs of high-net-worth clients, including tax and estate planning expertise.

AN INDUSTRY POISED FOR GROWTH

As I've mentioned in previous chapters, many of the larger financial services firms just now entering the IMA space also offer mutual funds. Up to now, most banks and large insurance firms just entering the fee-advised industry have started with fee-advised mutual funds and added IMAs over time as their advisors and planners get more comfortable with the process. The fact that these large financial institutions are just now entering the IMA industry, along with well-established mutual fund families creating new investment options, guarantees greater scale and lower fees for the industry, which is great for consumers.

ADVICE AND GUIDANCE

While this book primarily draws the distinction between IMAs and commission-based forms of investing, particularly mutual funds and variable annuities, the different vehicles can and do coexist with promising results in the same portfolio. Cerulli Associates is a customized consulting and research firm that has been reporting on global asset management trends since 1992, and has become one of the key publishers of data on the IMA industry. Kurt Cerulli speaks to the research his firm conducts on both mutual funds and IMAs.

Kurt Cerulli: We've always tracked mutual funds and IMAs together and found that while the IMA side was older, mutual funds had the higher growth characteristic. The mutual fund industry harnessed itself to the 401(k) explosion, and that had a huge impact on growth. We've seen signs of that changing and foresee the IMA side poised to grow dramatically over the next decade.

We see not only the continuing need for advice and guidance, but also an increasing investor desire to do things differently. Investors are looking for professional money management. They're increasingly concerned about taxes. In many cases, they're learning mutual funds aren't as tax efficient or flexible as they would like. Consumers are gravitating toward the kind of professional money management that provides a more sophisticated standard of service along with personalized investment options and maximum tax efficiency.

As Kurt points out, there appears to be a shift with investors causing them to take a closer look at IMAs, which is contributing to the new significant growth forecasts. His firm's research also points to significant growth in almost every type of fee-advised investment service as investors have become increasingly wary of commission-based products.

FINDING SUCCESS IS IN THE MATH

Although performance and risk analysis in this book receive brief attention, there is significant additional mathematical computations performed behind the scenes in order to evaluate professional money managers. Standard deviation, r-squared ratios, Sharpe ratios, upside-downside capture, and a host of other calculations come into play in successfully analyzing a professional money manager's ability to oversee client portfolios under all types of circumstances. Dr. Michael Eddeses, one of the foremost mathematicians in the financial services industry, explains his advocacy of IMAs over the past 20 years. He outlines the erosive effect that taxes have when it comes to creating and preserving wealth and adds a mathematical perspective to the effect taxes have on your portfolio.

Michael Eddeses: One thing you can predict with certainty is taxes. You can predict and control tax consequences on a portfolio by investing in an IMA, which sets your assets apart from other investors who could pull out of a pooled investment and severely affect your tax penalties.

Another predictable factor is fees. The average mutual fund charges 1.4 percent annually and you pay approximately 2.5 percent each year in taxes. That reduces your earnings power by four percent, which may not sound like much until you consider the phenomenal effect it has on compounded wealth accumulation. If your advisor tells you your assets will grow ten percent annually, when really, they're growing only six percent, you'll have just one fifth of what you would have had at ten percent over a twenty-year span. It's meaningless to make a projection without taking into account after-tax and -fee results. You can reduce the 2.5 percent annual tax rate on the average mutual fund to 0.5 percent with a tax-aware IMA.

As stated so clearly by Dr. Eddeses, for high-net-worth investors, an IMA is unquestionably the most efficient vehicle. Add to this ideal investment the ability to combine distinctive management styles, and you create a diversified portfolio combining growth with value, small-cap with large-cap, domestic with international, and other variations.

MANAGED ACCOUNTS FOR $50,000

I won't characterize an ideal IMA client, although an investor with at least $50,000 available in liquid assets is eligible. Current program sponsors report the average client has $500,000 in assets (Cerulli Associates). There are many profiles for such an investor. Some have inherited wealth. Some are self-made success stories and have acquired wealth through success in the corporate world. There are more millionaires in the world today than at any time in our history.

The person with between $50,000 and $500,000 of liquid assets can achieve the right level of diversification with one or two managers. Individual investors can rely on core managers to provide the right blend of value and growth. Exchange traded funds, for instance, permit the purchase of a single issue correlated to a specific index.

Wall Street is an industry in flux, as big firms rush to catch up with the explosion of online trading and the investor information revolution. At the same time, more new products and services are being introduced. The mutual fund explosion is fewer than twelve years in the making. IMAs are no exception, and it's a little astonishing to think that the industry as we know it has been around since 1987, when there was only about $10 billion invested in IMAs. Where it's heading is obviously an open question, although it appears to many financial experts to be the next investment product headed for explosive growth of the kind that fueled the mutual fund industry during the 1980s and 1990s. Some experts believe that a further lowering of fees and account minimums will attract more investors through increased accessibility. Others foresee a merger of services to the benefit of high-net-worth individuals. One innovative new product currently taking the industry by storm is the multidiscipline account (MDA).

MULTIDISCIPLINE ACCOUNTS: THE IMA OF THE FUTURE?

One of the latest and most promising IMA developments for investors is the option of diversifying assets among several professional money managers in what is termed a multidiscipline account. Numerous major investment advisory firms are arranging this new program with independent money managers. The direct benefit to the investor is the ability to invest an amount smaller than these money managers would accept from a single client.

MDAs offer all of the inherent advantages of IMAs, including direct portfolio ownership, manager selection, customization, and enhanced tax efficiency. In addition, MDAs provide investors with access to a vast array of investment options covering entire capitalization or style categories, whereas traditional IMAs are limited to a finite universe. For example, most MDAs are composed of at least three distinct subportfolios covering specific investment groups. So, an MDA permits involvement in large-cap growth, large-cap value, and large-cap blend investments, whereas traditional IMAs would typically limit you to one of these options. MDAs are currently structured with low investment minimums, offering the benefits of owning three or more IMAs with as little as $50,000 allocated to each subportfolio.

This flexibility enhances the significant benefits of IMAs discussed throughout this book, with the added ability for investors to create a single portfolio diversified among managers with different styles or asset class specialties. This is just another example of how the IMA business is growing from a process mode toward becoming a well-recognized investment product.

I foresee more centralization and consolidation occurring within the financial services industry. Investors generally want to deal with one person handling their finances. In the past, very wealthy families have had this convenience, going so far as to have a family office, if you will, in which a professional money manager worked to invest the family's money. I think the IMA industry can be considered the opportunity to create a family office for the increasing number of high-net-worth investors in this country. A financial advisor should be able to offer the right kinds of managers to meet a person's financial goals and be there so people can call to check up on progress toward attaining their objectives or to make adjustments to meet personal needs, for example, college tuition payments.

Steve Wallman, CEO of Foliofn believes his firm has already developed the next generation of MDA type accounts on his Folio (stock basket) platform:

> Folio investing has brought IMAs as close to the average individual investor as possible. Utilizing IMA-Folios for investing, the sometimes cumbersome money management process of trading individual stocks, reconciling the trades, recording cost basis, depositing securities, and providing meaningful performance measurement is virtually transparent and is all managed with the click of a mouse.

FINANCIAL TECHNOLOGY FOR THE MANAGED ACCOUNT INDUSTRY

Technology is obviously a dramatic catalyst for change in the financial services industry. On-line trading has proved that the computer is an acceptable interface for some investors, and every major firm is exploring this ramification as more and more business goes online, including professional money management.

Technology is clearly changing the way investment managers and financial advisors service their clients. Today we can essentially provide the entire consulting process online. Technology is also refining the ability to examine all the different investment scenarios and historical data for asset allocation recommendations for clients in a matter of minutes instead of hours. Time-weighted performance measurement has been traditionally paper based. Today, all of the reports are available in electronic format in real time.

Looking forward, I believe there will be more personalization of service with increased focus on each investor's special situations. I think that reporting is going to be far more goal based and realistic for clients. Investor ability to access account information and play an active role in the management process will increase, and investors will enjoy far more input with a direct line or on-line access to their financial advisors permitting the personalization of how money managers oversee their assets. The more you, as an investor, get involved, and the greater your understanding of what's going on with your investments, the more successful you will be and the better the investment industry will become for all involved.

CONCLUSION

It's important to me that I have conveyed throughout the course of this book the message that investing with a professional money manager in IMAs and my personal philosophy are closely related. It wouldn't be possible to continue this day-in and day-out commitment to my work if it didn't satisfy my personal as well as professional objectives.

As the financial services industry evolves over the coming decade, I believe, along with the professional opinions expressed in this book, that we'll witness IMAs capture market leadership as the investment of choice among high-net-worth individuals.

This is an endlessly fascinating and meaningful development in which I am privileged to play a role. I plan to spend the rest of my career studying and working to find the best means for my clients to make the most of their money. I hope that some of the enthusiasm of my financial experiences entices you to investigate this method of investing further as you work toward achieving your dreams.

Investors should first begin with a vision of what they want the money for. Once that vision is in place, their destination can be reached with a good plan, a good strategy, a set of principles to stay on course, and a competent professional money manager to deliver you.

—Robert Jorgensen

Investment Professional Certified Designations

CFP, Certified Financial Planner. Holders of the CFP must have passed a comprehensive ten-hour examination administered by the Certified Financial Planner Board of Standards in Denver. In addition to investing theories and principals, the examination covers insurance, real estate, alternative investment, budgeting, ethics, and estate planning. To remain holders of the CFP designation, these professionals must complete thirty hours of continuing education every two years.

CIMA, Certified Investment Management Analyst. Holders of the CIMA must successfully complete a one-year course of study covering portfolio management, risk measurement, performance measurement, investment policy, ethics, and investment manager selection. After successfully completing the one-year course, candidates for the designation attend the University of Pennsylvania's Wharton School for a week of fifty hours of instruction, at the end of which they must pass a comprehensive four-hour examination. This program is administered by the Investment Management Consultants Association (IMCA) in Denver. To remain holders of the CIMA designation, these professionals must complete thirty hours of continuing education every two years.

CFA, Chartered Financial Analyst. Holders of the CFA specialize in investment management and securities analysis. Many portfolio managers hold this designation. They must pass three comprehensive examinations administered by the Association of Investment Management and Research (AIMR) in Charlottesville, Virginia. Among the topics covered in the examinations are investment management, securities and portfolio analysis, corporate finance, accounting, securities regulation, and ethics. Holders of the CFA must meet continuing education requirements as dictated by AIMR.

ChFC, Chartered Financial Consultant. Holders of the ChFC must complete ten courses on financial planning topics, and then pass multiple examinations. The topics studied are similar in scope and content to those of the CFP curriculum. This program is conducted by the American College in Bryn Mawr, Pennsylvania. To remain a holder of the ChFC designation, these professionals must complete sixty hours of continuing education every two years.

PFA, Personal Financial Specialist. Only a certified public accountant (CPA) is permitted to earn this designation awarded by the American Institute of Certified Public Accountants (AICPA) in New York. CPAs who hold the PFA must have at least three years of experience in financial planning and pass a comprehensive examination. They are required to meet continuing education requirements and certain practice standards as dictated by the ACPA.

RIA, Registered Investment Advisor. The RIA is administered by the Securities and Exchange Commission (SEC). This designation is required for any investment manager who manages more than $10 million or who practices in more than one state. No formal course of study or examination is required; however, to receive the registration an investment manager must pay a one-time fee and file once a year the ADV form with the SEC. The form consists of two parts.

Part I details the manager's education and experience, the number of clients, the custodial arrangements for the securities owned, and disclosure of any disciplinary action taken against the investment manager by any local, state, or national law enforcement or regulatory agency. Part II discloses the investment manager's fee schedule, the services offered, and a description of the investment style used.

Industry Associations

Financial Planning Association (FPA)

The Financial Planning Association is the membership organization for the financial planning community, created when the Institute of Certified Financial Planners (ICFP) and the International Association for Financial Planning (IAFP) unified on January 1, 2000.
5775 Glenridge Drive, NE
Suite B-300
Atlanta, GA 30328
www.fpanet.org
(800) 322-4237

Investment Management Consultants Association (IMCA)

IMCA is a nonprofit association with more than 3,000 members in the United States and abroad, dedicated to ensuring quality service to the public by developing and encouraging high standards in the investment consulting profession.
9101 E. Kenyon Ave.
Suite 3000
Denver, CO 80237
www.imca.org
(303) 770-3377

Money Management Institute (MMI)

MMI is the national organization for the individually managed account industry, representing portfolio manager firms and sponsors of investment consulting programs.
1101 17th Street, NW
Suite 703
Washington, DC 20036-4726
www.moneyinstitute.com
(202) 347-3858

Investment Company Institute (ICI)

ICI is the national association of the American investment company industry, representing America's mutual funds, closed-end funds, and unit investment trusts.
1401 H Street, NW
Washington, DC 20005.
www.ici.org
(202)326-5800

REGULATING AGENCIES

National Association of Security Dealers (NASD)

The NASD is the largest securities industry self-regulatory organization in the United States.
1735 K Street, NW
Washington, DC 20006
www.nasd.com
(202) 728-8000

Securities and Exchange Commission (SEC)

The primary mission of the SEC is to protect investors and maintain the integrity of the securities markets.
450 Fifth Street, NW
Washington, DC 20549
www.sec.gov
(202) 942-7040

INVESTMENT LICENSES

Series 7 (General Securities Representative Examination). This registration qualifies a candidate for the solicitation, purchase, and/or sale of all securities products, including corporate securities, municipal securities, options, direct participation programs, investment company products, and variable contracts.

Series 63 (Uniform Securities Agent State Law Examination). The Series 63 examination is designed to qualify candidates as securities agents.

Series 65 (Uniform Investment Adviser Law Examination). The Series 65 examination is designed to qualify candidates as investment adviser representatives.

Series 66 (Uniform Combined State Law Examination). The Series 66 examination is designed to qualify candidates as both securities agents and investment adviser representatives.

IMA PLATFORM PROVIDERS

Brokerage Firms

A.G. Edwards
www.agedwards.com
(877) 835-7877

Ameritrade
www.ameritrade.com
(800) 669-3900

E*Trade
www.etrade.com
(888) TRADE88

Merrill Lynch
www.ml.com
(800) MERRILL

Morgan Stanley
www.morganstanley.com
(212) 761-4000

Pershing/PEAK,
www.pershing.com/man_acc.htm
(201) 413-2000

Prudential Securities
www.prudential.com
(800) THE-ROCK

Raymond James
www.raymondjames.com
(727) 567-1000

RBC Dain Rauscher
www.rbcdain.com

Russell Managed Portfolios/Russell Investment Services
(Alliance between Fidelity investments and the
Frank Russell Company)
www.russell.com/US/Investment_Products/Managed_Accounts
(800) 787-7354

Schwab Institutional
www.schwabinstitutional.com
(800) 648-6021

Smith Barney
www.smithbarney.com

TD Waterhouse Institutional Services
www.tdwaterhouseinst.com
(800) 934-6124

UBS Paine Webber
www.ubspainewebber.com

Wachovia Securities
www.wachoviasec.com
(877) 879-2495

Independent Turnkey Asset Management Providers (TAMPS)

Advisorport
www.advisorport.com
(800) 252-0569

AssetMark Investment Services, Inc.
www.assetmark.com
(800) 664-5345

Envestnet Portfolio Management Consultants
www.envestnet.com
(312) 827-2800

Lockwood Financial
www.lockwoodfinancial.com
(800) 200-3033

London Pacific Advisors
www.lpadvisors.com
(916) 564-1500

Net Asset Management
www.netassetmanagement.com
(310) 479-1009

Oberon Financial Technology
www.oberonft.com
(408) 524-8000

SEI Investments
www.seic.com
(800) DIALSEI

Vista Analytics
www.vistaanalytics.com
(888) 219-6502

West Hills
www.westhills.com
(312) 629-0303

INVESTOR RESOURCES

Financeware.com. Financeware's mission is to power the future of financial advice through cutting-edge probability analysis tools, coupled with a revolutionary goals-based advising system called Wealthcare.

Morningstar.com. Morningstar, Inc., is a global investment research firm offering an extensive line of products and services for individuals, financial advisors, institutions, and the media.

NelsonInformation.com. Nelson Information has been a leader in providing information and software to the global institutional investment community for over twenty-five years. Nelson's product line includes MarketPlaceWeb, proprietary databases, and a full line of comprehensive directories covering all facets of the institutional investment industry.

Personalfund.com. Personal Fund, Inc., was founded by leading financial and technology experts to empower individual investors and their advisers to invest conveniently and successfully.

TaxEfficientInvestor.com. Premier website identifying the most tax-efficient portfolio managers nationally for both the IMA and mutual fund industries.

Sample Investment Policy Statement

FOR: INDIVIDUAL OR FAMILY TRUST

The purpose of this Investment Policy Statement is to establish an attitude and/or investment philosophy between The Johnson Family Trust and the Sample Advisory Firm through the following investment objectives and policies:

A. Clearly define the services/nature of the relationship and encourage effective communication between the Sample Advisory Firm and The Johnson Family Trust.

B. Establish an understanding of The Johnson Family Trust for reasonable objectives, expectations, and guidelines of his/her/their investment portfolio.

C. Create the framework for a well-diversified asset investment mix that utilizes the permitted asset classes and normal allocations in order to generate acceptable long-term returns at a level of risk suitable to The Johnson Family Trust.

D. State the agreed upon basis for evaluation of the performance of the account's assets and the Sample Advisory Firm.

This statement is not a contract. It is intended to be a summary of an investment philosophy that provides guidance for The Johnson Family Trust and the Sample Advisory Firm.

THE PORTFOLIO

The portfolio will be invested exclusively in Individually Managed Accounts (IMAs) and monitored by the Sample Advisory Firm for its performance on the basis of the following criteria:

1. The mutual fund and/or the IMA manager's specification of and adherence to a clearly articulated and appropriate investment philosophy and process
2. Material changes in the manager's organization and personnel
3. Comparison of performance results to appropriate indices that takes into account asset class and investment style

Each mutual fund manager and/or IMA manager is responsible for managing the assets of their respective investment in accordance with the stated objectives and policies as set forth in their prospectus or the manager's portfolio characteristic summary provided by Lockwood Financial Services.

If applicable: The fixed income portion of the portfolio will be invested in *tax-free municipal bonds* with Security restriction instructions to Tobacco *Stocks* adhered to as defined by The Johnson Family Trust.

INVESTMENT OBJECTIVE

The portfolio seeks to provide an Investment Objective defined as Moderate Growth which will consist of a portfolio allocation of *60% stocks, 35% bonds,* and *5% cash*. Assets in this portfolio will be primarily used to provide *a steady stream of moderate income and growth.*

TIME HORIZON

The portfolio is suitable for investors with an investment horizon of *no less than ten years.* Capital values do fluctuate over shorter periods, and the investor should recognize that the possibility of capital loss does exist. However, historical asset class return data suggest that the risk of pricipal loss over a holding period of five years or longer can be minimized with the long-term investment mix employed by the Portfolio.

RISK TOLERANCES AND PERFORMANCE EXPECTATIONS

The Portfolio will be managed in a *diversified balanced portfolio of stocks, bonds, and cash* over the established horizon and is consistent with the stated objectives. Financial research has demonstrated that risk is best minimized through diversification of assets.

No guarantees can be given about future performance, and this Statement shall not be construed as offering such a guarantee. It should be recognized that the Portfolio is invested in actively managed mutual funds and professionally managed individual accounts and that the actual weightings of these investments can and will vary, resulting in higher or lower returns than those presented below.

ASSET ALLOCATION

Academic research suggests that the decision to allocate total account assets among various asset classes will far outweigh se-

Conservative Risk tolerance	Moderate (100% bonds)	Aggressive (40% bonds/ 60% stocks)	Aggressive (100% stocks)
3-year average return	+5.37	+9.39	+11.61
Low cumulative return	−1.22	−58.27	−80.89
High cumulative return	+65.99	+112.88	+194.58

Source: Ibbotson Associates. Based on three-year holding periods, returns are average annualized rolling returns. Fixed income represented by U.S. intermediate-term corporate bonds. Equities represented by Standard & Poor's 500 Index. Annual return period is 76 years: January 1926 to December 2001.

curity selection and other decisions in the impact on portfolio performance. After reviewing the long-term performance and risk characteristics of various asset classes and balancing the risks with regard to market behavior, the following asset classes were selected to achieve the objectives of the Portfolio. Target expected weightings and permissible ranges of exposure are also detailed.

The Sample Advisory Firm manages the allocation of assets in the Portfolio. From time to time, when market conditions warrant as deemed necessary by the advisor, the allocation of assets in the Portfolio may deviate from the "Target Allocation" within the "Permitted Range." Such deviations are minor modifications to

Asset class	Target allocation (%)	Permitted range (%)
Cash	5	5–15
Fixed income	35	30–50
Large value	20	15–25
Large growth	10	10–20
Mid-cap value	10	0–15
Mid-cap growth	5	0–15
Small-cap value	5	0–10
Small-cap growth	0	0–10
International	10	0–20

the strategic "Targeted" allocations and are not an attempt to "time the market." These periodic modifications are designed primarily to reduce overall investment risk in the long term.

To implement the recommended Asset Allocation, the Portfolio will invest in numerous mutual funds and/or IMAs that focus specifically on segments of each asset class.

REBALANCING PROCEDURES

From time to time market conditions may cause the Portfolio's investment to vary from the established asset allocation. To remain consistent with the asset allocation guidelines established by this statement, each asset class in which the Portfolio invests will be reviewed on a quarterly basis by Sample Advisory Firm and rebalanced back to the annual target allocation if the actual weighting varies by five percent or more from the recommended weighting.

DUTIES AND RESPONSIBILITIES

Investment Advisor

The Advisor, Sample Advisory Firm, is responsible for assisting the client, The Johnson Family Trust, in the following:

- Making an appropriate asset allocation decision based on particular needs, objectives, and risk profile for the client
- By being available on a regular basis to meet with the client
- Periodically reviewing the Portfolio for suitability based on the information provided by the client
- Providing the client with each current prospectus and/or manager portfolio characteristic summary selected in the Portfolio

The Client

The Client, The Johnson Family Trust, is responsible for the following:

- Providing the advisor with all relevant personal information regarding financial conditions, net worth, risk tolerance, and notification of any changes of this information.
- Reading and understanding the information contained in the prospectus of each mutual fund and/or the manager portfolio characteristic summary of each IMA manager.

ADOPTION OF THE INVESTMENT POLICY STATEMENT

I (we) have reviewed, approved, and adopted this Investment Policy Statement prepared with the assistance of _____
(Sample Advisory Firm).

_____   _____
Client's Signature   Date
The Johnson Family Trust, Trustee

_____   _____
Client's Signature   Date
(Spouse's full name)

_____   _____
Advisor's Signature   Date
Sample Advisory Firm

investment glossary

Active management An investment process designed to outperform a benchmark by actively buying and selling securities perceived to be incorrectly valued. Active managers typically have high turnover and costs.

ADR American Depositary Receipt Foreign companies trading on U.S. markets. Examples include Ericsson, Nokia, Royal Dutch Petroleum, Sony, and Toyota, to name a few.

ADV Independent fee Only advisors or money managers are required by the SEC to provide a copy of this document to each prospective client. The ADV is a disclosure document that outlines the business, the state where the firm is registered, the principals, and all fees and expenses.

Aggressive growth A method of stock investing focusing on low market capitalization stocks.

All-inclusive fee Expense to clients as a specified percentage of managed assets. Fee-only managers earn higher commissions only if portfolio values increase.

Alpha A measure of higher generated return relative to standard return model predictions.

Arbitrage A strategy or transaction attempting to profit from inefficiencies or imperfections in the pricing of similar or identical investments. Program trading is often referred to as index arbitrage.

Ask The lowest price of a stock or security. For example, with a quote of $45^{1}/_{4}$–$45^{3}/_{8}$, the ask price is $45^{3}/_{8}$. A lower offer may not be accepted. The ask price is also called the offer price. Brokers often describe a quote of $45^{1}/_{4}$–$45^{3}/_{8}$, as bid $45^{1}/_{4}$, offered at $45^{3}/_{8}$.

Asset allocation The method of investing percentages of portfolio principal in different asset classes to lower overall risk.

Asset classes Generally speaking, there are three broad asset classes:

stocks, bonds, and cash. Respectively, these classes are characterized by growth, income, and capital preservation.

Averaging down   Adding to a position of a security or asset class after its price has declined. For example, suppose you bought 1,000 shares of XYZ at $50. Two weeks later, when it is trading at $40, you buy another 1,000 shares to bring your average cost basis to $45.

Balanced   A strategy of comprising a portfolio of both stocks and bonds in roughly equal proportions. In terms of expected risk and return, balanced funds fall between bond funds and growth and income funds.

Balanced fund   A mutual fund built on the balanced investment strategy.

Basis point   A measure for quoting yield and other figures expressed in percentages. Equal to one one-hundredth of one percent and used to measure small moves in interest rates. 100 basis points = 1 percent. If a discount rate increases by 50 basis points, it increases by .5 percent.

Benchmark   A standard used to measure performance of a particular fund or portfolio. A benchmark can be an index, another portfolio, or an average of the performance of other managers.

Beta   A measure of risk relative to the stock market. The market has a beta of exactly 1.0. Stocks with more risk have betas higher than 1.0 and those with lower risk have betas lower than 1.0.

Bid   The highest price at which there is a willing buyer of a security or stock. For example, if ABC is quoted at $45^1/4$–$45^3/8$, this means the bid is $45^1/4$ and you may sell at that price.

Blue chip   A large company with a history of success that has become a household name. For example, GE, IBM, AT&T, and Procter & Gamble, to name a few.

Bond   Effectively, an IOU issued by a company or government. Typically represents $1,000 in principal. You lend your capital and in return receive interest on your funds as well as repayment of your principal at the bond's maturity or call. Bonds are also referred to as fixed-income securities, debt instruments, and debentures.

Bottom-up management   An active investment style whereby a manager seeks to choose, security by security, investments believed to be undervalued. This style is based on the belief that the market is inefficient and thus offers bargain investment opportunities.

Buyback   A company strategy of purchasing its own shares on the open market, thus reducing the number of shares outstanding. This typically increases per share earnings and is usually thought to be good for shareholders. However, this may not always be the best use of company capital.

Capitalization The value of a stock based on current market price. For example, if XYZ has 100 million shares outstanding and the price of XYZ is $20 a share, XYZ's capitalization is $2 billion. Also called market cap.

Cap-weighted index Index whose value is impacted more by larger than smaller companies. Examples are the S&P 500 and the Nasdaq composite. Due to the greater weighting of large-cap companies, index returns are heavily influenced by the top holdings. For example, the top ten companies of the S&P 500 account for approximately twenty-three percent of the movement of the entire index, and the top ten of the Nasdaq represent forty-seven percent of the index.

Cash equivalents Liquid, high-quality fixed-income investments with a maturity of less than one year. Examples include U.S. Treasury bills, short-term certificates of deposit, and commercial paper.

Cash flow Cash generated annually by a firm after expenses are paid.

CDSC Contingent deferred sales charge A decreasing back-end load fee applied to shares according to how long they are held.

Closed-end fund A mutual fund with a limited number of outstanding shares. Closed-end funds trade like stock, with bid and ask spreads, and are subject to commission upon purchase or sale. Because of their trading characteristics, closed-end funds can fluctuate above or below their net asset value.

Commercial paper Short-term corporate debt with maturity of 270 days or less. Due to short-term maturity, commercial paper is exempt from SEC securities registration laws. Examples of commercial paper issuers include General Motors Acceptance Corporation and GE Capital. Commercial paper is rated by S&P and Moody's to help investors quantify the relative credit risk of the obligation.

Commingled An asset mix. For example, mutual funds and unit investment trusts are commingled portfolios, with investors holding shares of the mixed portfolio.

Common stock Shares representing ownership in a company.

Conservative A strategy for investors with low risk tolerance. A conservative portfolio is typically allocated toward fixed-income investments and cash equivalents because of their historic lower volatility than stocks. A conservative investor tends to be older with a short time horizon who cannot withstand significant declines in principal value and has greater need for income than growth..

Correlation   A statistical measure of how sensitive the movement of one variable is relative to the movement of another on a scale from +1 to –1. For example, milk and sour cream prices are highly correlated (positive correlation: +1). However, interest rates and financial stocks can be negatively correlated (negative correlation: –1), which means they move in opposite directions.

Cost basis   The amount your shares cost you. If you have accumulated shares of the same security at different times and costs, you have a different cost basis for each set of shares.

Coupon payment   A cash payment made by a bond, usually semiannually. To calculate how much you'll receive, use this formula: [Face Value of Bond] × [Coupon rate of bond] = dividend.

Coupon rate   The stated, fixed rate of interest on a bond, which does not change over the life of the bond.

Covering a position   The act of buying back securities to offset or flatten a short position.

CPI Consumer Price Index   Measures the rate of change in prices for consumer goods.

Corporate bonds   Issued by corporations to raise revenue.

Current yield   Ratio of annual coupon cash flow divided by the current market price of a bond.

Day trade   Trading in and out of a security within the same day's session. Trading of this nature is highly challenging and must overcome commissions, bid-ask spreads, and market impact costs, among other factors, to prove profitable.

Debenture   A debt instrument that has subordinated claims relative to a company's other outstanding debt issues.

Defensive portfolio   One invested in stocks with high dividend yields and/or low P/E ratios. These stocks would be more stable than average and have lower downside risk.

Defined benefit plan   A retirement plan in which an employer contracts to pay a pension to its employees, most often based on a formula relating the amount of the pension to the employee's age at retirement, length of service, and income during a specified period of service. Occasionally, the payment may be fixed in dollar amount or as a percentage of salary.

Defined contribution plan   A retirement plan requiring an employer to make contributions to a segregated fund. Common programs include profit sharing, 401(k)s, money purchase pension plans, and target plans.

Derivatives   Any financial instrument whose value is determined by the value of an underlying asset. Listed futures and options are common forms of derivatives, often used to modify the risk/return characteristics of a given portfolio.

Dilution   The act of diminishing earnings per share by either issuing additional shares or exercising options. Accounting standards call for earnings per share to be stated in two forms: diluted and undiluted.

Discretionary   Client approval for a portfolio manager to transact securities and implement day-to-day decisions within preagreed investment guidelines.

Distribution   Annual mutual fund distribution of investment income and capital gains to shareholders. Capital gains are broken into short-term and long-term distribution components.

Diversification   The method of investing assets in numerous holdings to reduce overall risk and exposure to market volatility. Does not assure against market losses, and there is no guarantee a diversified portfolio will outperform a nondiversified portfolio.

Dividend   A regular cash payment made by a company to shareholders, typically paid quarterly. Dividend payments are criticized by some financial professionals as inefficient due to double taxation. Corporations pay taxes on pretax earnings. As payments are made from a company's net income, investors also pay tax on these dividends.

Dividend yield   Annual stock dividend divided by current market price. Since this is a ratio of two numbers, every change in stock price changes the yield. In other words, think twice before jumping on that stock with a fourteen percent yield. It may be the result of a decline in price, which could imply that the dividend is in jeopardy of being cut or eliminated. Companies may change their dividend policies.

Dollar cost averaging   An investing discipline in which one invests periodically regardless of the levels of the stock market. This results in buying more shares when prices are down and fewer shares when prices are up. A periodic investment plan does not protect from a loss in declining markets, and investors should consider their financial ability to continue purchases through periods of low price levels.

Dollar-weighted rate of return   Calculated on the average dollar balance of a portfolio during a specific period. This method of measuring return incorporates the cash flows into one average dollar balance for the total period, but does not eliminate any beneficial or detrimental effect of a contribution or withdrawal.

Dow Jones Industrial Average   Perhaps the most widely quoted market average, it is a capitalization weighting comprising thirty blue chip companies. Until the recent additions of Microsoft and Intel to the Dow Jones Industrial Average, its components were strictly exchange traded.

Duration   The measure of bond sensitivity to a change in interest rates.

Earnings   A company's net income, usually expressed per share. Recent mandates by the FASB require companies to report earnings per share in two ways: diluted and undiluted. Diluted earnings assumes that options and other instruments convertible to common stock are exercised.

Economic risk   Slower economic growth resulting in investment price declines. Examples include shares of emerging growth companies declining because they typically require a booming economy to sustain robust earnings gains. Cyclical companies, such as automakers and chemical producers, cannot easily cut costs during a recession, so their shares may fall in value. Economic downturns may also undercut junk bonds issued by financially weak firms that might default.

Efficient   A market is efficient if there is rapid dissemination of new information to investors, effective controls and regulation to insure fairness to investors of all sizes, and liquidity. Market efficiency is one of the key assumptions behind the huge growth of index funds.

Equity   In capital markets, equity is the same as stock and the equity market is the stock market. Shareholders own equity in a company.

ERISA   Employee Retirement Insurance and Security Act.

Exercise   Converting a right, warrant, or option into its underlying financial instrument.

Expected return   The rate of return an investor may reasonably anticipate based on long-term historical records.

FASB Financial Accounting Standards Board   This body determines accounting rules, practices, and methods. It is important to note that generally accepted accounting principles (GAAP) change over time as the FASB renders new opinions.

FDIC Federal Deposit Insurance Corporation   An independent federal agency established in 1934. The FDIC insures deposits in banks and savings associations up to $100,000.

Federal funds rate The interest rate charged to banks requiring overnight loans.

Fiduciary Responsibility incurred when an individual (e.g., trustee, foundation director, etc.) manages assets that do not belong to that individual. A fiduciary assumes personal liability.

Fixed income A bond is a fixed-income investment. Bonds typically pay a fixed rate of return until they mature or are called. A bond matures on a specified date. Some bonds may be redeemed (called) by their issuer before their maturity date. If the bond is callable, the date after which it may be called is specified on the bond.

Float The number of shares available for public trading. For example, a company may have 50,000,000 shares outstanding, but a float of 40,000,000 shares because 10,000,000 shares are closely held.

Futures Standardized, exchange-traded contracts enabling investors to commit to delivery or purchase of a specified underlying commodity or financial instrument at a specified price for a specified period.

Fundamental analysis Analysis of company financial statements. This determines the intrinsic value of a stock and factors how the marketplace values that company in relation to intrinsic value. The fundamental investor attempts to avoid buying overvalued securities and seeks to purchase undervalued companies.

Global mutual fund A fund that invests globally, including within the United States. International funds invest strictly outside the United States.

Government bonds Fixed income securities issued by the U.S. government, which are reasonably liquid and free from risk of default. Includes Treasuries, agencies, and mortgage-backed securities.

Growth and income objective Assumes a balance between income and appreciation.

Growth objective Geared specifically toward portfolios seeking appreciation.

Growth stocks Equities of companies with growth characteristics including above average P/E ratio or book value and below average dividend yield.

Growth stock management A bottom-up investment approach attempting to identify companies whose past and projected return on equity, return on capital, or return on assets is growing at a percentage greater than the economy.

Hedge A strategy whereby risk exposure is modified by employing investment instruments with negative correlations.

Hedge fund An unregistered investment pool, typically in the form of a partnership, whereby accredited investors with at least $2,000,000 net worth and $100,000 annual income invest through a fund manager. As the name implies, hedge funds often utilize short selling strategies as well as traditional buying strategies.

High-yield bonds Fixed-income securities issued by corporations, which have speculative grade credit quality ratings. Also known as junk bonds.

The amount of cash a portfolio generates from dividends and interest. Conservative investors tend to require more income relative to aggressive investors who focus more on appreciation.

Income constraint A constraint on a portfolio manager as to a certain level of investment in fixed-income assets determined by the amount of investment income a client requires from the portfolio.

Index A group of securities designed to represent a market or market segment. For example, the Dow Jones Industrial Average comprises thirty stocks designed to represent the overall market, specifically large companies.

Indexing A passive investment strategy designed to replicate the performance of an index.

Industry risk The risk or chance that government regulations or other factors will harm a particular group of companies, such as banks or savings and loan corporations.

Individually managed account (IMA) A portfolio of securities in which the account owner holds direct ownership of each underlying security. An IMA combines the advantages of direct ownership with hiring an experienced investment professional to perform research and make buy/sell decisions in a manner customized to the specific needs and objectives of the investor.

Inflation risk Inflation reduces the purchasing power of an investment. Overcautious investors who hold assets in low yielding investments, such as savings accounts and money funds, may not earn enough to out-pace inflation. In addition, inflation erodes the value of future income on investments with fixed payments, most notably long-term bonds.

Interest rate anticipation The active fixed-income portfolio strategy of lengthening a portfolio's duration when interest rates are expected to decline or shortening duration when rates are expected to rise.

Interest rate risk Rising interest rates typically cause investments to drop in price. For example, higher rates make yields on existing bonds less attractive, so their market values decline. Rising rates also hurt stocks by making their dividend yields and discounted present values less appealing. Individuals who invest borrowed money through margin accounts or have other floating-rate debts increase their interest rate risk by incurring higher borrowing costs.

International bonds Fixed-income securities issued by foreign governments and corporations.

International mutual fund A fund that invests only outside the United States.

International stocks Equities of companies located outside the United States.

Investment guidelines and constraints Factors keeping a portfolio manager within parameters established by a client in pursuit of investment objectives. Specific instructions from a client to a portfolio manager concerning money management.

Investment objectives The numerical standards by which a portfolio manager and a client agree to measure portfolio progress.

Investment policy The fund owner's statement concerning the purpose and tenure, or length of time, money will be committed to that purpose and the strength of that tenure.

Investment process Selecting stock to fit particular risk/reward parameters and weighting these in proportions such that an optimum portfolio is determined. The process is repeated over time to keep the portfolio balanced.

IPO Initial public offering When a company goes public, its shares are available for purchase and sale. The IPO price is determined by investment bankers hired by the company. For hot issues, the first trade on the open market can be and usually is at a significantly higher price than the IPO price. Also known as new issues.

Ladder A bond portfolio established by selecting securities with staggered maturities and coupon payment dates.

Liquidity A relative measurement for converting an investment to cash. For example, a real estate investment is illiquid because it can require a significant period from the time a decision to sell is made until the time the investment is sold. Stocks have a settlement period of three business days and therefore are considered to be liquid investments.

Load A sales charge levied upon purchase of a mutual fund (a front-end load) or upon the sale of a mutual fund (a back-end load). Back-end loads include contingent deferred sales charges (Casks).

Long   If you own 1,000 shares of XYZ, you are long 1,000 XYZ.

Market cycle   A span of time in which the stock market or a subsection of the market had an up-leg (peak) and a down-leg (trough).

Market impact costs   Costs incurred by each trade above and beyond brokerage costs. Growth and momentum investors, with a tendency for high turnover, typically incur greater costs of this type compared with value investors.

Market risk   Includes factors such as political developments and Wall Street fads that can affect investment markets. Tax law changes, trade agreements, program trading and investor psychology all contribute to market risk. These factors account for stock market volatility.

Market timing   The use of volume, price, and other information to forecast market or stock price movement. The basis of market timing is a belief that since the market reflects all investor actions, it also reflects all economic and company information.

Market value   Market or liquidation value of a given security or of an entire pool of assets.

Money market   The market of short-term (maturity of less than one year), high-quality debt instruments and securities. Mutual funds investing solely in this type of security are called money market funds.

MPT Modern portfolio theory   Largely based on the pioneering work of Harry Markowitz in the late 1950s. MPT helps construct an optimal portfolio from a set of portfolios lying on the efficient frontier. These are an optimal set of portfolios with different risk-return relationships.

MSCI EAFE Index   The Morgan Stanley Capital International Europe, Australia, Far East Index measures foreign stock fund performance, calculated on a total-return basis with dividends reinvested. The index is unmanaged and not available for direct investment.

Municipal bond   A debt instrument issued by a state, city, or other municipality to raise capital for a specific civic project. Coupon income from municipal bonds is generally tax exempt at the state and federal levels for investors living in the same state as the issuing municipality.

Mutual fund   Created by the Investment Company Act of 1940, a mutual fund is a professionally managed, pooled investment vehicle. Mutual funds are often called open-end investments because there is no limit on the number of shares a fund can issue. The primary attraction of mutual funds lie in diversification and professional management.

Nasdaq National Association of Securities Dealers Automated Quotation system.

Net asset value (NAV) The market value of one share of a mutual fund. The NAV, which is calculated daily, is determined by summarizing market values of portfolio components, subtracting liabilities, and dividing by the number of shares outstanding.

Option *See* Stock option.

OTC Over-the-counter. Stocks that do not trade on exchanges. This includes some Nasdaq stocks as well as penny stocks.

Overbought Market condition existing when a market has been rising for an extended period. A commonly used overbought-oversold oscillator is the ten-day moving average of the New York Stock Exchange advance-decline ratio.

Oversold The opposite of overbought.

Overweighing Placing a greater amount of weight on an economic sector than the weight given to that sector by a market index such as the S&P 500.

Par value The face value of a bond paid to a bondholder at maturity. For common stock, it is the stated accounting value per share regardless of actual market value per share.

Passive portfolio management Investment process designed to match a benchmark such as a stock market index. Passive investing is based on the assumption that the market is too efficient to permit profiting from either security selection or timing. Passive management styles typically have lower fees and lower turnover than actively managed portfolios.

Penny stocks Equities generally trading below $1 per share. Typically illiquid with little in terms of analyst coverage.

P/E ratio—Price-to-earnings ratio The ratio of how much an investor spends in share price in order to attain $1 in earnings. A means of comparing stocks trading at significantly different share prices. Be careful when comparing P/E ratios of companies of different industries. Not all P/E ratios are calculated in the same manner. The P represents the price of the stock. However, the E can be the trailing fourth quarter's earnings, the last full fiscal year's earnings, or even the consensus forecast of earnings. Compare P/E ratios calculated congruently, and look twice before comparing P/E ratios from different sources.

Portfolio management   The blending of various assets such that they provide investment results meeting the goals of an investor.

PPI—Producer price index.   Measures the rate of change in price of a basket of goods at the producer level.

Preferred stock   Shares with preferential status over common stock in terms of dividend payment and claim to assets should a company go into liquidation.

Prospectus   The legal disclosure document issued by a mutual fund. It contains specific information, including fees and costs, objective, how shares are bought and sold, and the management/ownership of the fund.

Proxy   A document outlining issues to be voted on by shareholders, including matters concerning policy, management, compensation, structure, and so forth.

Prudent man   Investment standard requiring someone operating in an investment decision-making capacity to act with prudence, care, and loyalty in a manner similar to how others with discretion and intelligence would act.

Quarterly portfolio review   Statement sent to a client each quarter recording progress made toward achieving investment objectives.

Real rate of return   Net return after subtracting for the effects of inflation.

Return   Performance achieved over an indicated period, which includes appreciation and income.

Reverse split   A stock split into fewer shares simultaneously causing a corresponding upward adjustment to price. For example, suppose you bought 1,000 shares of ABC at $15. A year later, the stock is trading at $2 per share. The company then authorizes and implements a 1-for-5 reverse split. The stock is then valued at $10 per share, although you own only 200 shares after the split. Often, reverse splits are a tactic used to artificially increase share price.

Rights   A short-term call option granting the holder the right to buy an underlying instrument for a fixed price, typically within a period of twelve months or less.

Risk   The level of variability among quarterly returns of a portfolio or index. Typically represented by standard deviation or beta over time.

Risk-free interest rate   A theoretical rate of interest, which is a foundation of many economic theories. In practice it is the rate of return on Treasury bills.

ROA—Return on assets   Measures ratio of net income to total assets.

Often used to compare the relative level of efficient use of resources by management.

ROE—Return on equity Ratio of net income to common shareholder equity. ROE is frequently used to measure company profitability and show how much additional earnings would be generated per each additional dollar's worth of shareholder equity.

ROI—Return on investment Profitability of a company relative to total debt and equity. Facilitates comparisons of companies with significantly different capital structures and levels of debt.

R-squared Statistical measure of percentage of movement of a particular variable explained by another variable. R-squared is used to evaluate a money manager's change in return that is explained by a change in the market. An R-squared of ninety percent would indicate that ninety percent of the movement of the manager's composite is explained by the market, while the other ten percent is attributable to other factors that are not market specific.

Rule of 72 A means of approximating how many years it takes to double an investment by means of dividing the number 72 by the rate of return in percentage points. For example, if you earn nine percent per year, it should take about eight years to double your investment. If you earn twelve percent, it takes about six years. Or it can be used to determine the approximate rate of return given the time taken to double your investment. If it takes four years to double your investment, you earn approximately eighteen percent annually.

Russell 2000 Index composed of the 2,000 smallest securities in the Russell 3000 Index, representing approximately seven percent of the Russell 3000 total market capitalization. The Russell 3000 is composed of the largest 3,000 U.S. companies by market capitalization.

S&P 500 Standard & Poor's 500 Composite Stock Index is a capitalization-weighted index of 400 industrial, 40 public utility, 40 financial, and 20 transportation equities including dividend reinvestment. It is a widely accepted proxy for the domestic stock market. The S&P 500 can be used as a benchmark for evaluating the performance of equity portfolios. However, since it is a cap-weighted index, the top 10 companies account for about twenty five percent of the entire index with the other 490 companies comprising the remaining seventy-five percent.

SEC Securities and Exchange Commission, created in 1934 to oversee the regulation of financial markets in the United States.

Sector rotation   Strategy of moving investment funds from one economic sector to another, usually through market sector analysis. Followers of a sector rotation style invest only in the most attractive economic sector.

Sector weighting   Weights assigned to each economic sector of a portfolio, either underweighted, overweighed, or market weighted.

Security guidelines   Instructions as to which stocks and bonds may be used and which ones must be avoided in a portfolio.

Settlement date   Date at which money changes hands, typically three business days after a trade is executed.

Sharpe Ratio   A reward-to-variability index developed by William Sharpe, evaluating a portfolio's risk-adjusted rate of return. Higher values are desirable and indicate greater return per unit of risk. The ratio is calculated by dividing the portfolio return premium by the portfolio's standard deviation.

Short sale   The sale of a security one does not own, which must be repurchased, or covered, at a later date. Instead of buying low and selling high, a short seller attempts to sell high then buy back low.

Short squeeze   When a stock runs up dramatically over a short period, it can often be due to a concentration of investors who were previously short the stock and are now buying it back at a loss. The higher the price rises, the more the short sellers cover, causing a squeeze in the stock.

SIPC   Securities Investor Protection Corporation, an investment brokerage industry corporation primarily insuring investors against fraud.

Specific risk   Affecting only a particular company or industry. For example, a developmental drug company may not receive U.S. Food and Drug Administration approval, which could send the stock into a tailspin.

Standard deviation   Measure of the level of variability or volatility of a portfolio or market index return. It is based on quarterly returns, and the higher the value, the greater the volatility, or risk of the portfolio or index.

Stock option   An instrument convertible into an underlying investment at a fixed price for a specified period of time. For example, employees are sometimes granted options to purchase company stock.

Stock split   You give me a $10 bill, I give you back two $5 bills. It's the same thing when a stock splits. Money is neither made nor lost on the split itself. However, investor psychology tends to favor a forward split, which is generally associated with a rapidly growing company.

Style analysis A statistical method used to determine the investment characteristics of a fund. The factors represent the sensitivity of the monthly returns of a fund to the monthly returns of the indices representing a series of global asset classes. For example, if the U.S. large-cap value factor is .80, that should be interpreted to mean the fund performs as if it invests primarily in large stocks with a tilt toward value investing. Factors relative to one another provide an idea of the types of securities in which the fund invests, as based on the analysis of its total returns. Factors are not based on examination of the actual holdings of a fund, but are statistically derived by comparing the fund's performance with the performance of indices, representing different asset classes. Fund factors adding up to more than 1.0 indicate the fund is more aggressive than indices used to compute the factors.

Systematic risk The risk of the economy or the broad market. Also known as market risk, nondiversifiable risk, and beta.

T-bill A short-term (maturity within one year) debt instrument issued by the U.S. Government. One of the most liquid instruments available, it is a cash equivalent. Because of the short term, T-bills are sold at a discount to face value and are worth full face value on the date of maturity. The minimum purchase price for T-bills is $10,000 face value.

T-bond Long-term, coupon-paying bonds issued by the U.S. Government with a maturity of more than ten years. Original issue T-bonds have a thirty-year maturity.

T-note Intermediate-term, coupon-paying bonds issued by the U.S. Government with a maturity of two to ten years.

Taxable equivalent yield Compares taxable and tax-exempt yields based on an investor's marginal income tax bracket. This comparison assumes that all other factors such as maturity and credit quality are identical.

Technical analysis Theory from which investors may draw conclusions based on historical volume and price charts.

Time horizon The length of time an investor has in order to reach a specified goal.

Time-weighted rate of return Rate at which a dollar invested at the beginning of a period would grow if no additional capital were invested and no cash withdrawals were made. It provides an indication of value added by the investment manager and allows comparison of performance to other investment managers and market indices.

Top-down investment management This theory, based on efficient markets, starts with a capital asset allocation decision based on an economic forecast. The market is broken down into economic sectors from which industries and securities are selected. Also referred to as diversified theory.

Total return The sum of investor returns from capital appreciation and investment income.

90-Day T-Bill Index The Salomon Brothers 90-Day T-Bill Index is composed of short-term debt instruments where equal dollar amounts of three-month Treasury bills are purchased at the beginning of each of three consecutive months. As each bill matures, all proceeds are rolled over or reinvested in a new three-month bill. The income used to calculate the monthly return is derived by subtracting the original amount invested from the maturity value. Returns are calculated on a total-return basis with dividends reinvested. The index is unmanaged and not available for direct investment.

Trading costs Fees and costs associated with trading and implementing an investment strategy. These are primarily commissions and the bid-ask spread. Commissions are costs paid to the brokerage firm executing trades. Bid-ask spreads refer to the higher cost of buying a stock than selling it. For example, you may be able to buy a stock at $50 but may only be able to sell it at $49.75. If you were to buy and sell the stock simultaneously, you would lose $0.25 in addition to any commission. The spread can vary between stocks, which means that transaction costs can vary widely.

Turnover Measurement of how long, on average, an investment manager holds a particular position in a security. Typically, the higher the turnover, the more frequently shares are bought and sold. It is also important to note that turnover can be magnified if a fund is experiencing redemptions. High turnover portfolios tend to have larger short-term taxable capital gains distributions paid out to the fund's shareholders, which can significantly inhibit the fund's after-tax performance for investors in high marginal tax brackets.

Underweighting The weighting of an economic sector at a percentage less than that of the economic sector comprising a market index (S&P 500).

Value management A bottom-up investment process, which looks for companies that have the potential of earning more than the market attributes to them.

Value stocks Equities of companies with value characteristics such as below average P/E ratio or book value and above average dividend yield.

Venture capital High-risk/high-profit potential investments aimed at young, start-up companies with innovative technologies, products, or services.

Volatility Measurement of price movement. Wider swings in price means higher relative volatility. Stocks are more volatile than Treasury bills.

Warrant Long-term call option enabling the holder to buy an underlying instrument such as a stock at a fixed rate for a given period. Rights are similar but generally shorter (twelve months or less) in nature, whereas warrants can be in effect for several years.

Yield For common stocks, dividend yield is calculated as the annual cash dividend divided by the current price per share of the stock. In other words, each time the stock price goes up or down, the yield corresponds. Bonds have several measurements of yield, each of which carries noteworthy assumptions. By industry regulations, investors must be quoted the lowest/most conservative measurement of yield.

Yield to maturity The rate of return an investor would earn if a bond were held to maturity. This type of yield assumes that all coupon payments are reinvested at a rate equivalent to the yield to maturity.

Yield to call Measurement of yield used only in cases in which a bond has a call provision and assuming the bond is redeemed by its issuer.

Zero coupon bond A bond with a coupon rate of zero issued at a discount to its face value. The annualized rate of return based on the difference between the face value at maturity and the price paid is the yield on a zero. Because of these characteristics, zero coupon bonds have greater volatility than traditional coupon bonds.

absolute return, 19
account maintenance fee, 37
ADR. *See* American Depository
    Receipts.
Aesop, 118
American Depository Receipts, 204–
    205
asset allocation, 91–100, 110–112,
    123–124, 142–144, 207
    and co-varying relationships, 46, 96
    and equities versus bonds, 124,
        209–219
    for established professionals, 94–
        95, 142–144
    faulty, 110–112
    and holding period, 92
    for older investors, 93–94
    and professional money managers,
        95–100
    for young professionals, 94
assets
    categories of, 92

back-end load fees, 35
Bernstein, Peter L., 75, 85, 102, 105
Bernstein, Richard, 175
beta
    and risk, 84–85, 87, 171–172
blend investment managers, 65, 190–
    202
Bogle, John C., 40
bond analysis, 215–216
bond ratings, 217

bonds, 67–70, 209–219
    high-yield, 217
bottom-up investing, 66, 160–170,
    185, 195, 197–198, 205
Brandes, Charles, 203–205
Brandes Investment Partners, 203–209
Brinson-Beerbower studies, 97, 99, 114
Brown, Melissa, 175
Bursey, Bruce, 223

call option, 89
capital gains taxes
    long-term versus short-term, 25–26
    and mutual funds, 24–27, 140–
        141, 225
certified financial planner
    designation, 129, 233
certified investment management
    analyst designation, 128
Cerulli, Kurt, 225–226
Cerulli Associates, 225, 227
CFA. *See* chartered financial analyst
    designation.
CFP. *See* certified financial planner
    designation.
chartered financial analyst
    designation, 234
chartered financial consultant
    designation, 234
chartists, 66–67
chasing hot stocks, 107, 176
ChFC. *See* chartered financial
    consultant designation.

chutzpah fee, 39
CIMA. *See* certified investment
    management analyst
    designation.
closed-end funds, 55–56
co-varying relationships
    and asset allocation, 46, 96
Cody, Donald E., 141
commodity trading advisors, 70
concentrated investment managers, 65
consulting process, 126
contingent deferred sales charge, 37
core investment managers, 65, 153–
    160, 190–202
corporate bonds, 211–212
Covey, Stephen, 12

DeAngelis, Steve, 130
day-trading, 108
derivatives, 88–90
diversification, 91–100, 142–144, 158
Drexel, Francis, 153
Dunlop, Al, 187

earnings momentum model, 185–186
Eaton Vance, 21
Eddeses, Michael, 226–227
E.F. Hutton & Co., 129, 168, 172, 222
1838 Investment Advisors, 152–160
emerging marked funds, 70
Employee Retirement Insurance and
    Security Act of 1974, 118, 222
equity risk premium, 40
ERISA. *See* Employee Retirement
    Insurance and Security Act of
    1974.
ETF. *See* exchange-traded funds.
exchange fee, 37
exchange-traded funds, 56, 228
expenses
    impact of, 33–42

fees, 33–42, 226–227
    and mutual funds, 33–42, 226–227

Financial Planning Association
    and finding an investment advisor,
        129, 233
financial technology, 230
First Quadrant, 22
fixed-income securities, 67–70
Form ADV, 46
401(k) retirement plans, 19, 43, 137,
    224
    and taxes, 19
FPA. *See* Financial Planning
    Association.
French, Ken, 217
front-end load fees, 35
Froude, 123

Gallagher, Robert, 203–209
GARP investment managers, 192
globalization
    and investments, 166, 203–209
government bonds, 211–212
Graham, Benjamin, 178, 203–204
Granville, Joe, 109
Great Companies, 177–181
Greenspan, Alan, 219
growth investment managers, 63–64,
    160–170, 190–202

Harris, Dave, 161–162
Harris Bretall, Sullivan & Smith,
    160–170
hedge fund partnerships, 70
Hesser, James, 184–190
high-alpha stocks, 171–172
high-net-worth investors
    and mutual funds, 24–25, 139–141
    and newsletters, 147–149
    and self-investing, 144–147
high-yield bond portfolios, 69–70
Horn, Greg, 42
Huguet, Jim, 177–181

IMA. *See* individually managed
    accounts.

IMCA. *See* Investment Management
    Consultants Association.
incentive fees, 37–38
independent turnkey asset
    management providers, 242–
    243
index mutual funds, 51–55, 168–
    169, 171, 175, 200–201
  composition of, 53
  and costs, 55
  and taxes, 54
  and transaction costs, 53–54
individual retirement accounts
  tax efficiency of, 19, 28–31, 224–227
individually managed accounts
  versus buying stocks, 45
  control over, 16
  defined, 13–14
  and lower fees, 17
  major benefits of, 14–16
  monitoring activity of, 16
  and multidisciplinary accounts,
    228–229
  versus mutual funds, 45
  platform providers for, 240–241
  and real life financial stories, 135–
    149
inflation
  compared with investment returns,
    12
investing industry associations, 237–
    238
investment advisors, 123–132
  benefits of, 125, 127
  and CFP designation, 129, 233
  and CIMA designation, 128, 233
  credentials of, 130–131
  and experience, 131
  and financial services firms, 129–130
  finding, 127–131
  and the IMCA, 128
  and professional certified
    designations, 233–235
  referrals for, 130–131

investment advisors. *See also*
    professional money managers.
investment licenses, 239–240
investment management
  business of, 61–73
Investment Management Consultants
    Association, 87, 128
  and finding an investment advisor,
    128
investment management consulting,
    117–132
investment managers
  growth versus value, 64–65
investment newsletters, 147–149
investment opportunities
  in down markets, 106, 112
investment performance, 10, 13
investment philosophies, 123–125,
    151–181
  and newsletters, 148
investment policy statement, 118–
    123, 245–250
  and cash flow requirements, 119
  and communications, 120
  and diversification, 120
  and general administration issues, 121
  and guidelines for manager
    termination, 121
  and IMA manager qualifications,
    119–120
  and investment classes, 119
  and performance measurement,
    120–121
  and performance objectives, 119
  and risk tolerance, 119, 247
  and statement of responsibilities,
    119
  and types of investments, 119
investment products, 11–12
investment styles, 47, 61–73
  for bonds, 67–70, 209–219
  for fixed-income securities, 67–70
  for stocks, 62–67
investment traps, 106–113

investments
  and biotechnology stocks, 141–144
  and bull markets, 145–147
  and demographics, 166
  and dividends, 193, 195
  and fear of the stock market, 138–139
  and finance, 167
  future trends, 166–167
  and globalization, 166, 203–209
  and hot stocks, 107, 176
  and macro philosophy, 165–166
  and market downturns, 112–113
  and market timing, 108–110, 181
  and new economy, 145–146
  and past performance, 12, 46–47, 107
  and pharmaceuticals, 166
  and technology stocks, 145–147, 166–167, 194–195
  and twelve common traits of great companies, 179
investor resources, 243
IPS. *See* investment policy statement.
IRA. *See* individual retirement accounts.

knowing your investments, 7–18
KPMG, 21

large-cap growth stocks, 62–65, 94, 161, 190–191
large-cap value stocks, 62–64, 96, 142
level load fees, 35
load charges, 35–36
Lockwood, Jim, 222–223
Lynch, Peter, 178

MacKillop, Scott, 127
margin trading, 144–147
market capitalization, 187–188
market news, 7–8
market timing, 108–110, 181

McDonnell Investment Management, 209–219
MDA. *See* multidisciplinary accounts.
micro-cap stocks funds, 70
Milken, Michael, 174
modern portfolio theory, 111, 170–171, 174–175, 177
momentum investment managers, 174
Morningstar, 8, 49
MPT Review, 171–172, 174
multidisciplinary accounts, 228–229
municipal bonds, 69, 214–215
mutual funds, 11–12, 20–28, 43–57
  and capital gains taxes, 24–27, 140–141, 225
  and class of shares, 35–36
  closing of, 48
  community pool of, 20, 23–25, 140
  disadvantages of, 20–22
  expense ratio of, 40
  and fees, 33–42, 226–227
  and fund variables, 47–48
  and high-net-worth investors, 24–25, 139–141
  index, 51–55, 168–169, 171, 175
  and lack of disclosure, 44–45
  lack of personal attention, 50–51
  merging of, 48–49
  and SEC mandate, 22–23
  and style criteria, 49
  supermarket, 38–39
  tax adjusted returns on distributions and the sale of shares, 23
  tax-adjusted returns on final distributions, 22–23
  tax efficiency of, 20, 224–227
  and tracking error, 49
  and truth in labeling, 49–50

NASD. *See* National Association of Securities dealers.
National Association of Securities dealers, 17

Navellier, Louis, 170–177
Net asset value, 26
no-load fees, 36–37

opportunity cost, 55
Oscher, Bill, 165–166
Owens, James, 111

passive investors, 51
past performance
  and investment decisions, 12, 107
personal financial specialist
    designation, 234
PFA. *See* personal financial specialist
    designation.
Post, David, 163, 168
price-to-earnings ratio, 186
professional money managers
  and asset allocation, 95–100
  compensation for, 70–72
  and connecting with investors, 79–
    81
  criteria for choosing, 102–106
  duties of, 71–73
  and experience, 104–105
  and judgment, 105–106
  management of, 117–132
  versus other financial
    professionals, 14
  and research, 162–164, 173, 188,
    217–218
  and tax-efficient investing, 30–31,
    151–177
  training of, 102–104
  and turnover, 188, 198–199

quantitative stock analysis, 171–
    177

real life financial stories, 135–149
  divorcee, 137–139
  doctor, 141–144
  gas station chain owner, 135–137
  margin trader, 144–147

mutual fund man, 139–141
newsletter man, 147–149
registered investment advisor
    designation, 234–235
regulating agencies, 238–239
Reinhart, Len, 222–223
relative valuation, 184
research
  and professional money managers,
    162–164, 173, 188, 217–218
RIA. *See* registered investment
    advisor designation.
risk
  and beta, 84–85, 87, 171–172
  measuring, 83–90
  nonspecific, 77
  operational, 81–82
  specific, 77–78
  and time horizons, 80–81
  types of, 77–78
  and variance, 85–86
  and volatility, 83–84, 144, 189
risk management, 75–90, 158, 226–
    227
risk tolerance, 76, 79–80, 92–95, 119
Rittenhouse Nuveen, 190–202
Rorer, Ted, 184–186
Rorer Asset Management, 184–190
Russell 1000 index
  and market declines, 26
  and performance measurement,
    120–121

Santoli, Michael, 27
Scott Paper Company, 187
SEC. *See* Securities and Exchange
    Commission.
Securities and Exchange Commission,
    21–23, 44, 49, 55
  mandates on mutual funds, 22–23,
    44, 49
self-investing, 101–116, 144–147,
    179–180
Sharpe, William F., 87

Sharpe ratio, 87–88, 226
Siegel, Jeremy, 202
small-cap growth stocks, 62–65, 96, 176
Smith, Harry, 161–162, 165
social awareness investing, 65
soft-dollar fees, 39–40
S&P. *See* Standard & Poor's 500 stock index.
Springhouse, John, 28–29
Springrose, John, 152–160
Standard & Poor's 500 stock index
 and holding periods, 113
 and index mutual funds, 52–54
Standard & Poors's 500 stock index, 9–10, 12, 52, 113, 158, 169, 173, 175, 180, 187, 192, 195, 197, 200–201
 annual returns, 12
 and market declines, 26
standard deviation, 86–87, 226
stock analysis, 66–67, 171–177, 188, 196–197, 205–206
stock market
 reasons investors avoided investing in, 115
stocks
 average returns, 9
 high-alpha, 171–172
 and investment styles, 62–67
 large-cap growth, 62–65, 94, 161, 190–191
 large-cap value, 62–64, 96, 142
 small-cap growth, 62–65, 96, 176
Sullivan, Jack, 160–170

TAMPS. *See* independent turnkey asset management providers.
tax-deferred accounts, 19
tax efficiency
 IMAs versus mutual funds, 41, 227–227

tax efficiency ratio, 30, 155
tax-efficient investing, 16–17, 19–31, 151–177
 measuring, 29–30
taxable bond portfolios, 69
taxes, 19–31
 and individual retirement accounts, 19
 and 401(k) plans, 19
 as transaction costs, 29
technical analysts, 66–67
TER. *See* tax efficiency ratio.
time horizon, 80–81, 93–95, 125, 191
 and asset allocation, 93–95
 and bonds, 210–211
top-down investing, 66, 197–198
transaction fee, 37

UBS Paine Webber, 168, 223
U.S. T-bills
 annual returns, 12

valuation
 five methods for, 186
 relative, 184
value investment managers, 63, 184–190, 203–209
Vanguard, 21–22, 40, 51
variable annuities
 tax efficiency of, 27
variance, 85–86
volatility
 and risk, 83–84, 144, 189

Waterman, John, 190–202
Wells Fargo, 171, 174
Witter, Dean, 169
Wlodarski, Steve, 209–219
writing a covered call, 89–90